Fisheries Management

Fisheries Management

Theory and Practice in Queensland

edited by T.J.A. Hundloe

 Griffith University Press

First published 1986 by Griffith University Press
Nathan, Brisbane, Queensland, Australia

Introduction and compilation © T.J.A. Hundloe 1986

Typeset by Dominion Press—Hedges & Bell, Melbourne
Printed in Hong Kong by Silex Enterprise & Printing Co.

Distributed in the UK and Europe by University of Queensland Press
Dunhams Lane, Letchworth, Herts. SG6 1LF England

Distributed in the USA and Canada by University of Queensland Press
250 Commercial Street, Manchester, NH 03101 USA

Cataloguing in Publication Data
National Library of Australia

Fisheries management

    1. Fishery management — Queensland — Addresses,
essays, lectures. 2. Fisheries — Queensland —
    Addresses, essays, lectures. 3. Fish trade —
    Queensland — Addresses, essays, lectures. I.
    Hundloe, T.J. (Torstein John).

639.4'09943

British Library (data available)

Library of Congress

Hundloe, T.J.A.
    Fisheries management

    Proceedings of a conference held August 4–5, 1981 at
Griffith University, Brisbane, Australia.

    1. Fishery management — Australia — Queensland —
Congresses. I. Hundloe, T.J.A. (Torstein John Arneson)

SH318.Q4F57   1986   333.95'6'09943   85 8508

ISBN 0 949725 02 1

*To the commercial and recreational fishermen
of Queensland*

Contents

Foreword

T. White

I believe it is most significant and timely that this is the first conference to be held in Queensland on a topic such as the management of our fisheries. It is indicative of a new status and image for the fishing industry.

For too long, fishing has been a forgotten or "Cinderella" industry with an unfashionable image. This position is now beginning to change. There is a growing awareness and recognition of the fishing industry as a major primary industry in this state.

In 1979–80, the gross value of production of the fishing industry in Queensland was almost $63 million. While the fishing industry ranks behind heavyweight Queensland primary industries such as sugar, beef, grains, wool, and dairying in terms of value of production, it is ahead of other prominent industries such as tobacco, barley, eggs, peanuts, cotton, pigs, and poultry.

Moreover, Queensland is the second largest fish producing state in Australia (ranking behind only Western Australia), and is the largest prawn producing state, with almost 50 per cent of the Australian catch.

However, these basic statistics do not reveal the full value of the contribution both the commercial and the amateur fishing industries make to the Queensland economy. The contribution must be assessed also in terms of the employment and investment opportunities created, particularly in coastal towns; the income generated, including export income; and the secondary benefits derived by support industries. The contribution extends further to a broadening of our very way of life here in Queensland.

Against this background, the government is aware of the need to foster and promote the development of the fishing industry in this state. The committee of inquiry appointed by the government in 1980 produced two comprehensive, wide-ranging reports which provide a basis for the future development of the industry.

The government has already taken a number of initiatives as a result of recommendations contained in those reports. They include:

1. transfer of responsibility for the Queensland Fish Board and the Queensland Fisheries Services to the Department of Primary Industries;

2. changes in composition of the Fish Board to allow fishermen greater involvement in the management and policy decision-making processes of the board;
3. changes in senior management of the Fish Board, including the appointment of a new chief general manager, as well as regional managers for north, central and south Queensland;
4. full recognition for fishermen as primary producers, thereby enabling access to the allowances, concessions and sources of finance available to other primary producers in this state;
5. provision of carry-on finance to fishermen through the Agricultural Bank.

The government is continuing to pursue the issue of debt reconstruction for fishermen, despite the lack of success to date in approaches to the federal government for finance through the rural adjustment scheme.

In addition, the government is planning to replace the Fish Supply Management Act with a new fishing industry organization and marketing act, and amendments to the Fisheries Act are also in the pipeline.

The new fishing industry organization and the Marketing Act will embrace further changes in the role, composition and operation of the Fish Board. The amendments to the Fisheries Act include harsher penalties for illegal fishing of mud crabs, barramundi and other species, especially juvenile or immature product.

Furthermore, implementation of the management plan for the barramundi fishery is under way, although there has not been sufficient time to document the details for discussion at this conference.

All these initiatives are really only the beginning of the road. There are other issues which will require further consultation between industry and government before appropriate action can be taken. Many of these issues will be the subject of intensive and rigorous debate at this conference — issues such as the evaluation and preservation of our fish resources; protection of habitat, breeding and nursery grounds; exploration and development of new fishing grounds; fish marketing, promotion and consumption patterns; the role of amateur or recreational fishermen; and the fisheries research.

I am sure you will all appreciate that there are no clear-cut, quickfire solutions to the problems currently facing the fishing industry. It is natural that fishermen, like other groups in the community, become impatient and expect to see their problems resolved overnight.

Unfortunately, the world is not that simple. The government must seek to strike a balance between the views of independent commercial fishermen, amateur fishermen, processors and other fishing companies, wholesalers, distributors, retailers and consumers. This task becomes even more difficult when the views of fishermen themselves are as many and varied as the species of fish that they catch.

Moreover, the problems of the fishing industry have not appeared overnight. They have built up gradually but inexorably over a number of years. It follows that resolution of the problems will occur only gradually, step by step, over a period of time as the full benefits of government initiatives take effect and as further initiatives are worked out in consultation between industry and government.

At this point, I would like to add a word of caution. The industry should not look to government to solve all its problems. Let me reiterate that the government is committed to fostering the development of the fishing industry.

However, demands for government action can become excessive. There is a limit to the extent to which governments can intervene to solve the problems faced by an industry. Overzealous intervention can result in a plethora of rules and regulations which in the final analysis can be counterproductive.

The relationship between industry and government should be a cooperative one. In particular, governments should seek to provide a stable and conducive environment within which the industry can prosper and advance. Beyond this, governments should be conscious of the need to avoid encroaching on the freedom, the initiative and the enterprise of individuals.

Fishermen, above all others, treasure fiercely their rugged independence and individualism. In a predominantly free enterprise economy, I am sure that fishermen would want to be ultimately responsible for their own destiny.

The industry itself must also take some part of the responsibility for its deterioration in recent years, especially for problems such as overfishing, illegal fishing and black market trading. Likewise, the industry must take some responsibility for improving its own position. It must recognize the changes and the opportunities which are occurring, and how to take advantage of them.

For example, fishermen cannot remain dependent on inshore fisheries indefinitely. They must look at the scope for exploiting new fisheries, especially deepwater fisheries. The best way to combat the threat to these fisheries posed by Japanese, Taiwanese and other foreign vessels is to ensure our own presence in these waters. If our own fishermen are not prepared to develop these fisheries, they can hardly complain that others are grasping the opportunities.

On a different note, the fishing industry has, as its output, products which lend themselves to a wide variety of promotional campaigns, using such characteristics as quality and freshness, high nutritional value and the prestige and exotic nature of many species such as barramundi, coral trout, reef fish, mackerel, crabs, oysters and prawns.

The scope exists to develop a range of images associated with the excitement and adventure of the sea and fishing through to the glamour and delicacy of unusual seafood dishes. I believe that the potential to promote a better image for the industry and its products has been largely untapped, particularly in comparison to the promotional campaigns that have been conducted in recent times for other basic food items such as meat, eggs, fruit and vegetables, butter, cheese, milk and other dairy products.

In opening this conference, I would like to extend a special welcome to Professor James Crutchfield from the University of Washington. It can only enhance the stature and success of the conference that such a world authority on fisheries economics is in attendance and is presenting the keynote address.

Finally, I am particularly encouraged that this conference is being held, because it was the view of the committee of inquiry on which I served that there was an urgent need for greater communication between all sectors of the industry, and between industry, government and other groups in the community. I trust therefore that this conference will herald the beginning of a new era in communication, consultation and cooperation for the fishing industry, and I have much pleasure in declaring the conference open.

Note

At the time the conference was held, in August 1981, the Honourable T. White, MLA, was Queensland Minister for Welfare Services. Before becoming a minister he was a major influence in having the Queensland government undertake a wide-ranging inquiry into the Queensland fishing industry. He served on the committee which undertook the investigations for that inquiry. The then Queensland Minister for Primary Industries, the Honourable M. Ahern, MLA, was the cabinet member responsible for fisheries. As the Primary Industries Minister was unavailable to open the conference, there was no more appropriate substitute than Terry White.

List of Contributors

A.H. ARTHINGTON   is a senior lecturer in the School of Australian Environmental Studies, Griffith University

S.D. BANDARANAIKE   lectures in geography at James Cook University of North Queensland

I.W. BROWN   is a senior biologist with the Fisheries Research Branch, Queensland Department of Primary Industries

D.F. BRYAN   is President of the Queensland Commercial Fishermen's Organization

D. CARTER   is projects manager with KFV Fisheries, Townsville

W. CRAIK   is in charge of research, Great Barrier Reef Marine Park Authority

J. CRUTCHFIELD   is a Professor of Economics at the University of Washington

W. DALL   is Officer-in-Charge of the Division of Fisheries Research, CSIRO Marine Laboratories, Cleveland

M. DREDGE   is a biologist with the Fisheries Research Branch, Queensland Department of Primary Industries

S.M. DRIML   was formerly a Teaching Fellow, School of Australian Environmental Studies, Griffith University

G.B. GOEDEN   is in charge of the Northern Fisheries Research Centre, Queensland Department of Primary Industries

M. GRAY   was formerly a senior economist with the Queensland Department of Primary Industries and is now with the Queensland Treasury

N.M. HAYSOM   is Deputy Director of Fisheries, Division of Dairying and Fisheries, Queensland Department of Primary Industries

B.J. HILL   was formerly in charge of the fisheries research in the Queensland Department of Primary Industries and is now a senior biologist with CSIRO Marine Laboratories, Cleveland

T.J.A. HUNDLOE   is Director of the Institute of Applied Environmental Research, Griffith University

G. KESTEVEN   is a fisheries management consultant

R.J. McKAY   is curator of fish, Queensland Museum

T.F. MEANY   is a senior economist with the Australian Fisheries Service

D.A. MILTON   was formerly a post-graduate student in the School of Australian Environmental Studies, Griffith University

K.E. OWEN   is a senior economist with the Australian Fisheries Service

A.J. PASHEN   is an economist with the Fisheries Research Branch, Queensland Department of Primary Industries

C.T. RUSSELL   was formerly Chairman of the Queensland Amateur Fishing Council

P. SAENGER   is Chairman of the Queensland Amateur Fishing Council and a senior lecturer at the Northern Rivers College of Advanced Education

S. SPENCER   was formerly a senior economist with
                  the Queensland Department of Primary
                  Industries and is now with the
                  Queensland Fish Management
                  Authority

J. STRATTON   is a senior administrator with KFV
                  Fisheries, Townsville

M. WILLIAMS   was formerly a biometrician with the
                  Fisheries Research Branch, Queensland
                  Department of Primary Industries

1

Introduction

T. J. A. Hundloe

This is a book about fisheries management, mainly in Queensland, Australia. Excluding this introduction, Chapter 6, and the foreword, the book comprises revised and in most cases shortened papers of a Conference, which addressed the broad topic of managing Queensland fisheries.[1] Notwithstanding that, the book should be of interest to anyone concerned with fisheries management. Certain chapters of the book address management issues relevant virtually anywhere in the world, the prime example being Professor James Crutchfield's contribution. Also, of general application are the chapters on the biological basis and the economic basis for management. There are further chapters which, though they pertain to specific Queensland fisheries, would be of interest to readers outside the state of Queensland, for example, those on the Great Barrier Reef, often referred to as the "Eighth Wonder of the World" and arguably Australia's best known natural feature, and the marlin game fishery, centred on Cairns in north Queensland, which has gained recognition in far corners of the world. The material presented represents recent research findings on these fisheries.

In fact, each chapter presents some information which should have wide appeal. The problems Queensland fishermen face, whether they be professionals or amateurs, are not dissimilar to those faced in many areas of the world. Professor Crutchfield is writing about one aspect of these problems when he states: "Rest assured the same problem occurs almost everywhere . . . ". The same could be stated about most of the other important management issues considered in this book. The role of processing companies in research and development, the search for efficient marketing mechanisms, the analysis of consumption patterns, and the concerns of government fisheries management agencies are just some of the issues facing most persons involved in fisheries management regardless of where they live.

It is appropriate in introducing the book to say something about the style of writing, the objective, and the format of the book. Taking style first, the obvious feature is that, as with any work which is a collection of essays, this will vary from author to author. Any temptation by the editor to achieve a common style was quickly dismissed. To attempt to seek conformity would be to hinder clarity in exposition by the various authors. The book is written as much for the interested layman as the specialist fisheries manager, so that jargon and complex scientific or mathematical formulae are minimized as much as possible. Each contributor has been conscious of the need to write for a diverse audience. This is a requisite in any discussion of fisheries management, which is a multidisciplinary subject. While that may not have always been the case, it certainly is today. Fisheries biologists need to understand fisheries economists, and vice versa. Both these groups have to work with, understand and be understood by technologists, marketing specialists, sociologists, geographers, lawyers, and others. There are also the politicians and administrators who, respectively, have to make and implement fisheries policies. Of course, the most important group are the fishermen themselves, for without them there would be no fisheries management. Fishermen cannot be lumped together in a discrete group; not only are some professionals and others amateurs, but some harvest crustaceans by nets from modern vessels, others troll for pelagic fish, and yet others handline for demersal fish. These are but a few examples. The species sought differentiate them, as does the method of catching, the means of processing or the markets served. There is no more important need for communication than that between fishermen and the managers and scientists. This has to be a two-way process.

The primary objective of this book, as with the conference which spawned it, is to facilitate further communication between all parties involved with fishing. If it furthers the development of understanding between the fisheries sciences (biology, economics, and others), and between the scientists and the managers, and managers and fishermen, processors and sellers, then it has achieved as much as the editor would wish. If the books happens to do more than this, such as suggest to the reader that, for example, better management regimes and strategies might be fashioned, that particular lines of research might be worth pursuing, then the editor will be more than adequately rewarded.

The format of the book has been arranged so that the major themes cluster into three main groups. First there are what might be termed the theoretical chapters, followed by what might be termed sectoral perspectives. Finally, recent scientific investigations and findings are presented as case studies which were selected on the basis of their direct relevance to present problems and issues. The exception to this general ordering of the contents is the introductory speech by the then Queensland Cabinet Minister, the Honourable Terry White, which has pride of place as a foreword to what follows.

Before introducing the individual contributions, an attempt will be made to put into perspective the present management of

Queensland fisheries. Once more the reader's attention is drawn to the fact that much of what is exercising the minds of fisheries managers in Queensland is doing likewise elsewhere in Australia and other parts of the world. The recent history of fisheries management in Queensland is presented in Chapter 5, so only a few of the issues need be mentioned briefly. First, many discrete fisheries exist in Queensland and different management policies pertain to each. There are other factors which complicate any attempt to define the management regime. For example, one of the major fisheries, the Gulf of Carpentaria prawn fishery, falls within the jurisdiction of other states as well as Queensland. With regard to offshore fisheries and the Great Barrier Reef fisheries, the Commonwealth shares responsibility with Queensland. There is also the fact that management regimes, and particularly policies, are not static, but ever-evolving. The management policies for both the Gulf and the offshore fisheries have been in a state of flux over recent years. There has been a continuous search for appropriate policies and strategies, and solutions to various problems. This search continues, built on past experience, research findings and present needs. One noticeable feature is that the data base on which policies are derived has expanded rapidly in the recent past.

Specific, and new problems have recently confronted Queensland fisheries. In the unregulated fisheries, fishing effort has, in some cases, increased significantly. This phenomenon has raised the questions of overcapitalization, resource depletion and fishermen's incomes. Exogenous factors such as changes in Japanese demand for prawns and fuel price increases have exacerbated the financial difficulties faced by some fishermen and processors.

Another important development relates to marketing. The search for an appropriate structure for marketing fish and seafood has largely dominated both the private and public discussions between fishermen, processors and administrators during the late seventies and early eighties. While a satisfactory solution appears to have been reached, based on the findings of a government enquiry, the situation is not necessarily static.

The recent declaration of the Australian Fishing Zone (the so-called 200 mile limit) has effectively doubled the land and sea area under Australian jurisdiction. Previous policies on foreign participation in fishing have been altered. Controversies have arisen over allocation of foreign rights, and a catalyst for development of new Australian fisheries has resulted.

As mentioned previously, markets have not remained stable. Not only are export prices influencing the livelihood of local fishermen, but so is the import of foreign fish. Fishermen have had to fight to retain their existing market and the fish and seafood consumption behaviour of Queenslanders (and Australians) has become an important consideration. Add to the dynamics of market fluctuations the vagaries of nature, and fisheries management takes on a greater complexity.

The relationship between professional fishermen and amateur fishermen, their sometimes competing demands for resources and their different demands of administrators, have come to be a more important issue than in the past. Complicating this more often perceived than real problem are the operations of the so-called professional-amateurs ("pro-ams").

Yet another relatively new management problem centres on the preservation of marine environments, particularly the breeding, nursery and feeding grounds for commercial and recreational species. The environmental awareness which only started to take hold a decade ago is now a fundamental concern in fisheries management.

There are many other management issues, which have only recently become increasingly important, that could be mentioned here. Most of them, including the ones listed above, are not necessarily unique to Queensland. The various contributions in the book deal with these in their own way.

As with any exercise of this kind, difficulty was faced in making appropriate selections. What topics to address or neglect were decisions made by the editor and his associates at the time of issuing invitations to the conference, the proceedings of which form the basis of this book. In selecting contributions the rule was to include as much theoretical background material as necessary to put recent management and research activities into a framework and give them perspective.

The contributions to this volume will now be introduced briefly. It is not considered necessary to introduce the authors, though some comment is warranted on the keynote contributor, Jim Crutchfield, who is a natural resource economist, specializing in fisheries economics. His chapter on Fisheries Management is by necessity written from the economist's perspective; nevertheless, as with other fisheries economists, he has a knowledge and appreciation of biology, ecology and other relevant disciplines.

His chapter is an eloquent discussion, in language readily understood by the layman, of the problems and possible solutions to fisheries management problems which are virtually universal and thus add greatly to the appeal of the chapter. Whether the reader is a Queenslander, or resident elsewhere, he will readily identify with what is written there. The fisheries economist and many fisheries managers will be familiar with Crutchfield's analysis, either from his other writings or those of other fisheries economists. He starts with the fundamentals of fisheries management, and asks what are the objectives. He stresses that multiple objectives have to be met, and he initially groups these into three broad categories: environmental harmony; economic well-being; and equitable opportunities to participate. To elaborate on his views, Crutchfield wrote: "It is to be hoped that the late 1960s marked the end of the simplistic controversies over the relative merits of maximum sustained physical yield versus maximum net economic yield as the objective of fishery management."[2] In Australia, at least, this controversy can still arise at meetings of fisheries managers, but in general it has been accepted that the conservation of biological resources (through sustained yield policies) is in principle not different from the conservation, or economic efficient use, of inputs such as vesssels, gear and labour—these inputs should not be "overused" in a fishery if they can produce more highly valued goods in some other use. Chapter 5 deals specifically with this issue and hence nothing further need be added here. It is more likely that present-day debates will centre on positions taken with regard to other objectives. Why this is so is explained by Crutchfield as follows:

> . . . we can denote the welfare "output" of a fishery management program as $U = U(Z_1, Z_2 . . . Zn)$ where the Z's are different desirable outcomes: for example, contribution to net economic output, income redistribution, balance of payments equilibrium, reduction in structural unemployment, freedom from arbitrary government action. Maximization of U when all aspects of utility are directly measurable in a common yardstick (dollars for example) is difficult enough on empirical grounds. But when the Z's represent desired outcomes, each of which can be ordinally ranked *but not in terms of single dimension*, then the essential marginal comparisons are even more precarious. We are left with a truly multidimensional set of public interest elements and, thus, with the necessity of making explicit choices among conflicting objectives.[3]

Crutchfield's survey of the various management techniques is comprehensive and does not warrant elaboration. It also covers not only those matters already discussed above, but recreational fishing, marketing and other issues.

Chapters 3 and 4 are confined to narrower subject matter than that of Chapter 2. These chapters address, respectively, the biological and economic bases for management. The reader will note that both the biologist's and economist's perspectives recognize each other's contributions. These two disciplines are very much at the interface of fisheries management.

Chapter 3 highlights biological phenomena relevant in the development of management plans which are to be based on agreed upon objectives, and how biological phenomena can be modelled. The writer stresses the necessity for adequate data: "To understand with any confidence what is going on in a particular fishery, access to reliable catch and effort data is essential". For various reasons discussed in the chapter, this is difficult, sometimes near impossible, to collect. While stressing the importance of sufficient data and refined models, the author describes an approach which is very helpful for the manager having to make immediate decisions. This approach is based on the relationship between the "life strategy" of a species and the characteristics of the stock as a whole. The underlying philosophy is that through natural selection available ecological niches will be filled by species which have evolved in a certain direction. Species can be classified according to where they fit on the so-called "r-K" continuum, and the strength of their "r" or "K" attributes will allow predictions to be made of impacts (for example, fishing effort and environmental degradation) on these species. Chapter 3 provides a particularly useful background and complement to the case studies with a biological emphasis.

Chapter 4 presents an elementary lesson in economics and should assist in explaining various concepts. The explanation is made by using a hypothetical illustration as well as real-world examples drawn from Queensland fisheries. By comparing the "common property" nature of fisheries to the private property nature of another primary industry, agriculture, the writer shows clearly why fisheries management cannot be left to the so-called "free market"; furthermore, it is shown that the causes of overfishing are economic. This chapter also puts into perspective the overriding importance of economic efficiency as a goal to be worked for: by continually increasing the economic efficient (that is, non-wasteful) use of resources standards of living have steadily increased and will increase.

From Chapters 5 to 8 (inclusive) the book takes on a different orientation, providing both a description and analysis of some important elements of Queensland fisheries, and presenting the setting (or environment) for fisheries management in Queensland. Those included are an overview of the Queensland management regime; descriptive statistics on Queensland commercial fisheries; the structure and economics of fish and seafood marketing in Queensland; and consumption.

At least three very important topics have been omitted: descriptive statistics of recreational fishing; the structure, organization and economics of processing; and a discussion of the environmental conditions and coastal management in Queensland. Traditional fishing, that is, fishing by Aboriginals and Torres Strait Islanders, also warranted inclusion. While these subjects are partly dealt with in other sections of the book, they deserve chapters of their own as a background to subsequent discussions. It is valid to ask why these elements were omitted. Descriptive statistics on recreational fishing have yet to be compiled. The contributions on processing and on environmental conditions and coastal management are unfortunately not yet available.

Chapter 5 describes the management regime in Queensland and

explains the factors that have influenced, and are influencing, the regime and fisheries policy. It is essential background material when considering the appropriateness of Crutchfield's various strategies for future management in Queensland. Some readers may wish to re-read Chapter 2 after absorbing Chapter 5. It also includes a summary of the major commercial fisheries. Chapter 6, the only one which did not form part of the conference proceedings, complements the last mentioned section of the previous chapter by presenting descriptive statistics of Queensland commercial fisheries.

Chapter 7 covers the broad topic of the structure and economics of fish and seafood marketing in Queensland. The chapter is partly background, descriptive material and partly an analysis of options for a new marketing structure for Queensland. The authors worked on the Queensland Government inquiry report which addressed marketing options and related matters. Recent changes in this area, and any future changes, will be greatly influenced by the analysis in this chapter. The chapter is divided into sections on the history of fish marketing in Queensland, the then current (mid 1981) structure of fish marketing, the role of government intervention, options for intervention and the role of co-operatives.

One of the fascinating issues raised in Chapter 7 is that of orderly marketing. Reduced to its basics orderly market is government instituted, or at least government sanctioned, control of supply of a product. It is used virtually throughout the world, particularly in agriculture where factors outside the control of the producer (normally the vagaries of nature and/or the fluctuations of overseas demand) can lead to gluts and shortages and thereby unstable incomes for producers. Orderly market runs contrary to the principles of free competition and its critics condemn it as socialism. Consumer associations believe, with some justification, that consumers pay higher prices under orderly marketing schemes than they would under more competitive systems. To some extent, though the issue is far more complex than this, whether orderly marketing is supported or not depends on whose side, that of the consumer or that of the producer, one finds oneself on. As with most other fisheries management issues, conflicting objectives have to be faced and trade-offs made.

Another very interesting factor given some attention in this chapter is the black marketing of fish and seafood. The irony is that black marketing is often resorted to by producers who are required to operate in regulated markets. As a digression, it should be noted that the existence of a substantial black market in Queensland and the associated lack of sales data is the most important factor limiting the formulation of management policies based on fact. To date, too many investigations, the results of which could be of significant assistance to fishermen, have been frustrated, or at least their findings distorted, by the fact that black market (or cash) sales do not appear in the normal recording of transactions. It is not possible to calculate accurately the financial problems of fishermen (for example, whether debt assistance is warranted) or the economic worth of the industry, when one side of the cost-earning's equation is understated.

Chapter 7 offers far more than the two matters singled out here, and as already stated, there exists no better background to the very important marketing and general management decisions presently being taken with regard to Queensland fisheries.

Chapter 8 presents detailed descriptions and analyses of the fish and shellfish consumption behaviour of Queenslanders. It also addresses the question of demand in the future. These subjects have a direct relationship to marketing structures and marketing economics, and the data presented will be of considerable interest to fishermen, processors, wholesalers, retailers and consumers. The most obvious conclusion to be drawn from Chapters 7 and 8 is that a successful management policy has to be based just as much on marketing and consumption variables as on biological and wider economic factors.

After Chapter 8 the book again takes on a different orientation with the next two chapters providing reactions to the existing state of affairs from a different perspective. Chapter 9 presents the view of the independent commercial fishermen and hence is a critical chapter in the book. Chapter 10 gives the view of the amateur recreational fishermen and is an equally important contribution.

Commencing with Chapter 11 the book once again changes its orientation with the presentation of a series of case studies. The principle applied in soliciting these contributions was that they addressed topical matters and presented the results of recent research and investigations. The contributors are mainly either fisheries biologists/ecologists or fisheries economists, and one chapter is in fact jointly authored by a biologist and an economist.

An attempt has been made to arrange the chapters according to broad common interest. For example, there are three contributions pertaining to the prawn fisheries. In as much as a number of the contributions are the only one of a kind it is not possible to group all of them. An alternative method of arranging the chapters, based on the disciplinary perspective from which they were written, was considered and dismissed as inappropriate as most of the contributions do not neatly fit into clear-cut disciplinary categories.

Chapters 11 to 13 address various aspects of prawn fisheries. Chapter 11 commences with a discussion of the principles of management orientated biological research and hence this section of the chapter complements the theoretical discussion in Chapter 3. The remainder of Chapter 11 discusses a biological research programme being undertaken on Penaeid prawns.

Chapter 12 outlines a private enterprise research programme in the Gulf of Carpentaria prawn fishery, the theme of which could be described as industry helping itself with resource and commercial management.

Chapter 13, one of the most detailed case studies presented in the book, discusses the history and future options for the Queensland east coast trawl fishery and, in so doing, refers back to the theories and analysis presented in Chapters 3 and 4. Given the relative importance of this fishery and the urgent need for management policies and strategies, Chapter 13 is essential reading. Other complementary chapters are Chapters 5, 6, and 9.

Chapter 14 logically follows the previous three on prawn fisheries. It addresses the effect of variation in prawn and scallop stocks on the behaviour of a fishing fleet. The prawn and scallop fisheries analysed are those off the central Queensland coast (Tin Can Bay to Yeppoon), where considerably more information has been gathered than for most others in Queensland.

The next two chapters, 15 and 16, present research findings on what we might term Great Barrier Reef fisheries. The emphasis is on recreational fishing and demersal species. Chapter 15 brings together the results of much of the recent research undertaken for management purposes in the Great Barrier Reef, though it does not cover the economic research which has gone hand-in-glove with research reported here. Chapter 16 discusses the results of research into the condition of demersal fish stocks and the effects of fishing on the large-predator community.

Chapter 17 is an economic study of the north Queensland black marlin fishery, which during 1980 was the centre of considerable controversy, when conflict arose between game fishermen, governments and Japanese long-line tuna fishermen. This study attempts to assess the "value" of the game fishery to Australia and to the Cairns region, and the results of this investigation were a crucial factor in the ultimate resolution of the conflict. This chapter also highlights some of the practical difficulties of gathering sufficient data in a short time for management decision making.

Chapter 18 comments on what fisheries economics research has been done, is under way or should be done, in Queensland. This is a relatively simple task, because fisheries economics, as a research activity, is a relative newcomer to Queensland. This chapter makes it clear that, to the present, little more has occurred in economic research than the establishment of baselines (and that work itself is incomplete). Various important management-orientated research topics are suggested, none which could be taken to break Crutchfield's rule that we do not collect too much information.

The last case study, presented in Chapter 19, presents a very detailed description and analysis of ongoing research into the ecology and management of exotic and endemic freshwater fishes in Queensland. When it is realized that 13 million live fish are imported into Australia each year, the significance of this research is obvious. There are potential risks associated with the introduction of diseases, and the impact on native species has to be established before any undesirable effects occur. This case study reports on the main findings to date.

In conclusion, the emerging theme, or consensus in fisheries management is twofold. Firstly, that no single objective will give us the management regime, policies and strategies needed today; and secondly, many concepts and tools, drawn from various disciplines, are required to model the performance of a fishery and subsequently develop management plans.

Some changes in management practice, particularly with regard to commercial fishing in Queensland waters, have occurred since this book was compiled. The most important has been the enactment of new legislation. The *Fishing Industry Organization and Marketing Act* has resulted in the most significant changes in the administrative history of the Queensland fishing industry. It is under this statute that the Queensland Fish Management Authority has been established. Most sectors of the commercial industry are represented by the authority. This Act provides for the licencing of processors and wholesalers who are able to purchase direct from fishermen in competition with the board, though the fisherman's right to consign products to board auctions has been maintained. Retailers also are licensed by the authority. The powers of the Queensland Fish Board have been greatly curtailed with fishermen no longer being forced to deliver to the board.

To date, the new legislation has not had a marked impact on the management of the catching sector, other than the enforcement of strict control on entry and the introduction of seasonal closures for prawn fishing in Queensland waters. These changes, combined with the increased emphasis which both the Queensland and Commonwealth managers are placing on developing new management regimes, would ultimately result in far-reaching alterations to the regulations of the catching sector.

There is increased interest being shown in recreational fishing at both governmental and private interest group levels. The recent formation of the Australian Recreational Fishing Confederation is an example of amateur fishing organizations taking steps to coordinate and represent the interests of amateur fishermen.

Notwithstanding these changes, most of the management principles discussed throughout this collection of essays will serve for a long time as a basis upon which to judge our attempts at management. The descriptive and empirical data could also be considered an historical baseline on which future investigations and research will build, and against which future management policies will be compared.

If only all concerned can maintain the impetus of recent years, it is not too optimistic to believe that acceptable management policies can be formulated and successfully put into practice, dependent upon goodwill and a willingness to exchange ideas and listen to others.

Notes

1. The conference, "Managing Queensland Fisheries", was held at Griffith University Brisbane, during the period 4-5 August 1981. The conference was convened by the editor, in association with the (then) Queensland Fisheries Service, an agency of the Queensland Government.
2. James A. Crutchfield, "Economic and Political Objectives of Fishery Management", in *World Fisheries Policy*, edited by B. J. Rothschild (University of Washington Press, 1972), 75.
3. Ibid., 76.

2
Fishery Management: A Time for Change

J. Crutchfield

In many respects, fishermen undergoing the birth pains of a programme to manage fisheries that are already in deep trouble are like patients in the first stages of a nervous breakdown—both are convinced that their problem is the worst that has ever been seen, and both are sure that no one understands how bad it really is. Let me reassure you on both counts. The tendency for unregulated fisheries to outrun the productive capacity of the resource and, in the process, to mire the industry in low and unstable incomes, regulations that impede efficiency and discourage initiative, and other equally unfortunate symptoms is universal. Rest assured that the same problem occurs almost everywhere, that all sorts of remedies have been tried, and that no one has found a single, painless cure for the ills that develop once a fishery has become seriously overcapitalized.

Let me start, then, by assuring you that I have no magic solutions; that traditional methods of managing a hard pressed fishery are simply a guarantee of different but equally severe problems; and that curing the situation, even partially, involves treading on very sensitive feelings. To put it bluntly, there is no real hope of lasting improvement in a mature, overdeveloped fishery unless we face, head on, the hard problems of restricting new entry and reducing the amount of excess gear in the water. This does not mean creating a privileged class, nor does it deny anyone the right to get into the fishery who is willing to pay for that right. The ability of a fisherman to pass his right to fish on to his sons if he chooses can remain untouched. It does mean that, whether by stick or carrot, a fairly large number of people must be induced to leave the operation over time if the remaining fishermen are to have any hope of stability, decent incomes, and good biological management of the resource.

We start with some fundamentals: what are the objectives of fishery management? What kind of knowledge base is required before management can make any progress towards those objectives? And what kinds of programmes are required to do the job?

I am well aware, as a university professor, of the tendency of my audience to go to sleep promptly when someone mentions the word "objectives". Nevertheless, some discussion is indicated, if for no other reason than the fact that so many fishery management programmes either fail to state clearly what they hope to accomplish; state one thing and actually are doing another; or (in more recent cases) present a shopping list of objectives to be sure of covering all fronts without showing any awareness that some of them are directly contradictory with others.

Perhaps the most sensible approach that I have seen in recent years was presented by Dr Henry Regier in a recent unpublished paper. Stripped down to fundamentals, Regier points out that we are really after three things in managing fisheries: environmental harmony; economic well-being; and equitable opportunities to participate.

Environmental harmony is not just a catch phrase. Restating Regier's more formal language, it could be summarized by saying that we want to manage a fishery in a way that will leave populations, species, and the ecosystems in which they are found in a condition where they can cope with natural environmental variability. Actually, this is not so much an objective as it is a limiting condition within which fishing activities must be confined.

Economic well-being has a number of dimensions, all of which are probably familiar to you. These include: growth in regional economies; increasing returns to those who provide the labour and capital and reasonably fair distribution of the resulting income; and as much economic stability as the inherently risky fishing business will permit.

Finally, under the heading of social opportunity we would include opportunities for recreational fishing and a strong position in the industry for those to whom fishing represents an especially rewarding way of life; and special provisions for native peoples and/or remote communities with limited employment opportunities other than in the fishery; and a maximum amount of personal freedom.

What this requires, in practical terms can be summarized very briefly. Simply trying to preserve the productivity of fish stocks, important as it is, is not enough for good management. If we've learned nothing else from the experience of the last 30 years, we should be aware that neglect of economic effects and economic motives will destroy most of the benefits that an otherwise sound biological conservation programme may bring. Ultimately it may threaten even the ability to protect the stocks concerned. A programme that goes one step further, and looks carefully at the desirablity of maximizing the economic benefits to be obtained from a fishery while achieving, if anything, more effective protection on the biological side is a step in the right direction, but again it is incomplete. There remain vitally important questions: Who gets the benefits? Who is to be allowed to participate in the fishery? How can losers in the game be compensated from the gains of the winners? How can we preserve the stability of fishing communities? All of these additional requirements can make or break even the most sensibly designed bioeconomic management system, since they determine whether or not the programme will be accepted.

The question of a knowledge base is crucial. Without the kind of sensible, reasonably priced stock assessment work that modern fishery science now makes possible, it simply makes no sense to institute any kind of management programme. The possibility of making things worse rather than better is all too real; and, at the very least, the programme is open to legal challenge by anyone dissatisfied with its impact on his own operations. Strange as it may sound, coming from an economist, the scientific underpinnings and the resulting statistical record of any fish stock and the fishery based on it deserve far more funding, attention, and cooperation from the industry and other branches of government than one normally finds.

What kind of information constitutes the essential minimum for good fisheries management? As a nonscientist, I am a little reluctant to step into waters as muddy as these. For what it is worth, however, let me suggest the following. The management authority must have, first, an accurate, up-to-date record of all licensed fishing vessels and their general fishing characteristics; second, an accurate and *timely* set of data indicating catches by species, areas caught and landed, and — most often lacking — fishing effort.

Most of this information is fairly easy to obtain. In many countries the use of the triplicate purchase slip — one to the buyer, one to the fisherman, and one to the fishery authority — provides the basic data on catch, species, and area of landing (which usually can be interpreted fairly accurately as to area of fishing). These can be computerized and recalled easily in any configuration required for analysis. Effort information is much harder to come by, since it normally requires standardized log data from the fisherman and regular reporting of that information. It goes without saying that such information must be absolutely protected, since knowledge of where and when fish are taken is one of the things that mark the difference between the high-liner and the average fisherman. They are most reluctant to divulge such information if there is any possibility that it might leak out to others. Although there may have to be a selling job, it is eminently worthwhile to enlist the cooperation with the industry in providing effort information; without it, it is simply impossible to undertake basic stock assessment and current monitoring of the condition of exploited stocks.

Finally, it is essential that the management authority has the capability of utilizing this data in a timely fashion to provide expert evaluation of the condition of stocks under management. Fishery science has made remarkable strides the last few decades in modelling the dynamics of exploited marine populations and in refining the models to the point where they can be useful with the kinds of partial data that are usually available. At best, stock assessment work is a matter of skilled judgment of fragmentary information rather than a mechanical process of cranking data into a deterministic model. It would be highly desirable to have some knowledge of the requirements of stock assessment work extend down to all levels of the people involved in data collection, assembly, and analysis. Although the field involved is now well defined and there are a number of schools that provide such training, it is surprising how little is spent on this vitally important work by most fishery departments. There is still much to be done to make sure that the progress of fishery science is fully reflected in fishery management.

Having delivered the compliment, let me follow up with the needle. Fishery scientists are no better than economists when it comes to accumulating masses of unutilized information. It is part of normal scientific training to seek all of the information that might possibly be of use in solving the particular problem with which the scientist is concerned. But the crucial question is not how much information could we use some day but rather how *little* information is needed to make good management decisions in timely fashion. It is far better to gather 75 per cent of the benefits of fishery management from an information system that is cheap, reasonably reliable, and fast than to seek 90 per cent with more perfect information that costs far more and generates data two years after the need has passed.

Rational Management Alternatives

We come now to the hard part of the nut: assuming a reasonable set of objectives and a programme that provides the necessary minimum factual base for management, what measures are available that will push us closer to economically, biologically, and socially rational use of our valuable marine resources? Basically, they boil down to three: we can simply let things rip, trusting to the market to determine the rate of fishing exploitation; we can rely on traditional methods of management which relate only to protection of the stocks (i.e., time closures, area closures, quotas, and deliberate gear restrictions to reduce efficiency); or we can try to achieve both biological protection and some economic gain by reducing the level of effort to something approaching the minimum required to harvest what nature makes available.

Traditional Measures

I do not propose to dwell for long on the first two. It is true, of course, that for some fisheries (for example, small fisheries of low value or those only very lightly exploited) management simply is not worth what it costs. The potential gains of more acceptable rates and methods of fishing simply cost more, in terms of data accumulation and the implementation of management programmes, than the resulting benefits are worth. I would only caution that this is a fact to be established, not assumed, and the choice should not be made simply on the basis of administrative convenience.

Where the fishery is valuable and/or heavily exploited, fishing under open access conditions inevitably results in economic trouble, and — all too frequently — in serious biological depletion as well. In the absence of any kind of property right in the fishery, the vital link between the level of today's harvest and the availability of fish in the future is hopelessly ruptured. Even though individual fishermen or groups of fishermen may be well aware that by catching less today catches in the future can be made enough larger to make it worthwhile to "invest in the stock", any curtailment of current catch simply results in an increase for someone else. A long series of industry entry to a marine fishery will always result in excessive quantities of capital and labour, overexploitation of the resource and the possibility of real biological disaster.

In practice, the actual economic performance of a heavily exploited, open access fishery is likely to be much worse. It is far easier for fishermen to get into an expanding operation than it is to get them out when the inevitable downturn in prices, catches, or both occurs. Consequently, every period of flush production or excellent prices leads to an inflow of new vessels and gear which cannot be driven out again when markets or catches fall off. The result is a chronic tendency towards low incomes, underemployment, and a variety of social ills that accompany that combination, particularly in isolated fishing communities. Since fishermen are notably immobile to other occupations, these conditions are not automatically self-correcting, and they can lead to serious regional economic problems. This is not just a theoretical exercise; it is a disturbingly general description of mature commercial fisheries worldwide. Overfishing in the economic sense will always exist in an open fishery even when fishermen's incomes are reasonably good and the resource is in no danger of depletion.

There is little point in dwelling at any greater length on world experience with efforts to control commercial marine fisheries through the traditional methods of limited fishing time, limited fishing areas, the forced use of inefficient gear, or the establishment of overall quotas. Again, theory and long experience demonstrate that the best that can be hoped for with these types of regulation is to do something for the fish; they offer little or nothing in the way of lasting economic benefit for the poor fisherman. Specifically, all of them achieve their effectiveness, directly or indirectly, by making it too expensive to catch too many fish. Since they cannot control fishing effort directly, any improvement in the fishery results in more and more excess capital and labour even though total fishing mortality is controlled. Since there is a built-in incentive to "catch yours before the hoarders do" there is also strong pressure to build excessively large, overpowered, and costly vessels and gear in order to get the largest possible share of a given catch. Since everyone plays the same game, the result is even faster progress toward unnecessary economic waste for any given level of catch.

Equally disturbing, if traditional methods of controlling fishing mortality cannot prevent the accumulation of large amounts of excess fishing capacity, even the biological objectives are threatened. We have had, in North America, some real horror stories in this respect. For example, the valuable Pacific halibut fishery, which is under quota control with no limitation on entry, normally can be exploited over about nine months of the year. But in 1980, thanks to a tremendous increase in prices, the entire quota was taken in ten days in one regulatory area and in 21 in the other! In the case of the even more valuable roe herring fisheries of British Columbia and California, it is not unknown to have the entire season consist of a single day; and on one memorable occasion the season was over in exactly 15 minutes — the time required for the purse seiner to make one set. Admittedly, these are extreme cases, but it may not be entirely inappropriate to compare it to the hundreds of additional vessels that entered the Queensland prawn fisheries with no corresponding increase in output in recent years.

A Bioeconomic Approach to Management

Most fishery economists, then, are looking for methods of management which do as well or better at protecting fishery stocks, but which work through rather than against the market mechanism and which promise some hope of lasting economic benefit. No one has come up with a perfect system, nor are they likely to do so in the future. We are, after all, dealing with highly variable biological systems, harvested by equally variable (and considerably more touchy) industry systems. But it does seem possible to improve the regulatory process by providing the individual fisherman with the incentive to behave in a fashion which seems rational to him and which produces, collectively, a fishing industry that is adequately protected and reasonable efficient.

Essentially, this boils down to three techniques: the use of taxes or fees to make explicit to the individual fisherman the external costs that he imposes on other fishermen by thinning of stocks, or by crowding on favoured fishing grounds; controlling the number of fishing vessels under a limited licensing scheme; or limiting the total catch by quota and subdividing this into individual quotas assigned to individual fishermen and tradeable on the market.

The suitability of these techniques (or of more than one in parallel) must be judged on practical rather than theoretical criteria. Are they technically feasible? Do they provide adequate flexibility to deal with unforeseen changes in the populations exploited? Can they be enforced at reasonable cost and with a minimum of irritation to the fishing industry? Do they induce fishermen to use efficient gear in efficient numbers in their own self interest? Do they provide the incentive for continued research and development which will further improve the economic contribution of the industry?

Taxes or Royalties.   The use of taxes (or royalties) to control the level of fishing effort is designed to equalize private and social costs. Under free access each fisherman inflicts "external costs" on others, since his operations reduce the availability of fish and raise the costs of other fishermen; but such costs do not show up in his accounting. The various types of externalities associated with open access fishing can all be corrected, in theory, by imposing taxes that reflect the full social cost of the operation rather than the direct costs of fishing as seen by the operator himself. The fishery could then be left to the market, without direct intervention by government. The combination of factor costs and taxes would induce each fisherman to adopt the best combination of vessel, equipment, and labour.

Unfortunately, the theoretical neatness of this solution is hopelessly out of line with the realities of practical fishing operations. It rests on the assumption that fisheries operate in a completely static world in which outputs, costs, prices, and fishermen's behaviour are either constant or can be forecast accurately by the fishing enterprise. Nothing could be further from the truth, of course. For most fisheries the "right" level of catch *must* vary from year to year, sometimes over wide ranges. Very few governments will allow an administrative agency the authority to vary taxes over an equally wide range. And even if they did, it is far from certain that taxes could be adjusted to produce the desired level of fishing effort as rapidly as biological circumstances dictate.

The weakness of the tax approach is particularly acute in the case of a fishery that has already become heavily overcapitalized. To reduce the amount of fishing capacity to a level consistent with resource capabilities and efficient use of all vessels and gear would require a tax sufficient to reduce vessel earnings below out-of-pocket costs. The cut would have to be even deeper than in most industries, since the payments to labour are normally paid on a share basis in a fishing enterprise. To achieve any real reduction in excess capacity would require a tax heavy enough to put every fisherman in a loss position. The job of standing before a group of fishermen and explaining how such a programme will solve their problems is not attractive!

This does not mean that taxes should not be used to shape

incentives in ways that supplement other programmes to reduce or prevent overinvestment in fisheries. In particular, a tax on landings could be used effectively to cover the cost of research and management programmes, and to capture some of the benefits of those programmes for the general public. But taxes simply cannot be used as a short run adjustment mechanism whenever fluctuations in natural abundance dictate a change in allowable catch. These must be handled by other fast-response measures that can be used to close down or curtail fishing whenever unexpected developments pose serious resource problems.

Controlling Inputs: Limited Entry Programmes. A more realistic approach to more efficient management, now coming into fairly common usage, is to control inputs to the fishery by limiting the number of fishing units. This could be done by controlling licensing either of fishermen or fishing vessels, but in practice it has proved more effective to license vessels—the primary unit of the fishing enterprise. For any desired level of catch, it appears relatively simple to determine the number of optimal vessels, of proper size and properly equipped, required to take that catch during an average year.

In practice, limited entry programmes are much more complicated in operation. Normally the pressure to adopt such a programme comes only when the industry is already heavily overcapitalized, and discussion of the intention to establish a limited entry programme always leads to a rush of new entrants to establish a position in the industry before the number of licences is frozen. Thus, there is invariably a great deal of excess capacity to deal with from the outset.

This can be minimized in several ways. One is to establish criteria for eligibility for the limited licences that exclude many of the inactive units and late entrants. For example, the cutoff date for active vessels to establish eligibility could be set back far enough to eliminate many of the last minute entrants, and minimum landing requirements could serve to weed out inactive licensees. The importance of cutting back excess capacity as far as possible at the outset of the programme cannot be overemphasized. Unless this is done, every licensed unit, no matter how small its contribution to the fishery, has the potential to become an active, well-equipped, modern fishing unit. Even if the number of licensees is held constant, the actual fishing power of the fleet could continue to increase substantially as less productive vessels are upgraded.

A second and tougher approach to the problem of cutting back the number of licensed units in a limited entry programme would be to auction the initial number of licences desired. While it presents obvious political difficulties, particularly if the number of unsuccessful bidders will be large, the idea of auctioning to deal with the initial distribution of rights has much to recommend it. In the first place, it has a selective tendency toward efficiency. The highest bids are likely to come from the most skilled and best equipped fishermen. Second, it bypasses the difficult distributional problem of bestowing upon people who happen to be in the right place at the right time valuable property rights in a publicly owned resource. Finally, it gives fishery management more latitude in the use of other regulatory techniques if the threat of excess capacity in the fishery is minimized at the outset. Opposition to this "brute force" approach to reduction of excess capacity could be reduced by compensating unsuccessful bidders who had a record of active participation in the fishery from the proceeds of the auction. (They would still be able to participate in the fishery, of course, by buying a licence from a successful bidder.)

Once established in the possession of fishermen, limited licences become a fairly conventional type of property, the value of which would depend on the extent to which the number of fishing vessels in the operation had been reduced, and the resulting increase in expected future incomes of the remaining licence holders. Although some programmes of licence limitation have specified that the licences be nontransferable, presumably to prevent speculative gains to the initial holders, there are stronger arguments for making them freely transferable. The most significant advantage would be the flexibility that would be achieved in permitting exit from or entry to the industry and the freedom of individual licence holders to dispose of their right as they see fit (i.e., by sale, lease, bequest to children, etc.). The prices of the licences would provide a highly useful barometer of the economic health of the fishery. And, perhaps most important, since the going price of a licence would represent the opportunity cost of the right to go fishing, there would be *continuing* pressure for the licences to go to the most efficient operators.

It is difficult to conceive of any government administered programme that could handle the allocation of fishing rights as efficiently as an organized market in licences. Experience in Australia, Canada, and the United States confirms the expectation that an active market for fishing licences will develop quickly, and that attempts to restrict transferability of licences are usually ineffective, since there are innumerable ways of getting around such limitations.

If it seems too difficult, for political or social reasons, to reduce the number of active licences at the beginning of a limited entry programme, the full economic benefits of licence limitation can be realized only by some type of "buy-back programme," under which government purchases and retires licences (and perhaps vessels as well). Theoretically, there is no reason why a buy-back programme could not be made self-financing, with taxes on the remaining licensees (who gain from each reduction in active vessels) providing the funds for repurchase of licences.

Experience in other countries reveals some difficulties with this approach, however. Unless reduction in the number of licences is accompanied by increasing taxes on those remaining, the capitalized value of the remaining licences will increase, and prices asked for them will quickly exhaust the resources of the buy-back programme. But unless it was announced at the beginning of the programme that progressive tax increases would be levied, the holders of licences are likely to argue vigorously (with some justification) that they have been expropriated in part. Their investments in licences and vessels, undertaken in good faith, could be expected to yield only a competitive rate of return. If a tax is now levied on licence holders to finance a buy-back programme, existing licence holders will find their property rights sharply reduced in value and current earnings will fall below the rate of return anticipated when the licence was purchased. It is not surprising, then, that buy-back programmes in most countries have always come to an abrupt halt before they had achieved any significant results.

In short, buy-back programmes can be used to reduce the number of licences to any desired level in a limited entry programme, but it is nearly impossible to do so without specifying in advance the level of taxation on remaining licencees that will be required to service the programme. It is unlikely, and, in general principle, undesirable, that a buy-back programme be financed out of general tax revenues. It would therefore be most desirable to reduce unnecessary capacity as much as possible at the outset of a limited entry programme, either by auctioning licences initially or by establishing restrictive criteria on eligibility. It must also be specified *in advance* that the holders of valuable rights to use the public domain will be expected to pay for that privilege.

It goes without saying that if a buy-back programme is utilized to reduce the number of licences and vessels participating in the fishery, the redundant capacity must not be permitted to enter other fisheries that require management.

Another major problem with a limited entry programme is the difficulty in preventing increases in fishing power and/or increases in unnecessary capital investment on individual fishing vessels. In theory, with an active market for licences, one would expect the average vessel to earn an average competitive rate of return, with the capitalized value of the licence representing the cost that must be incurred in order to enjoy a portion of the economic rent that the fishery can generate. If all fishermen could foresee all consequences of their actions, it would also follow that each would adopt the best size, equipment, and seasonal and area deployment of the vessel.

Unfortunately, the apparent self-interest of the individual fisherman is likely to lead him in other directions. In the simplest case, this simply means upgrading less productive licensed units. To the extent that upgrading brings the vessel and gear closer to optimal configuration in terms of today's technology, the efficiency of the individual unit might well improve, but the total level of effort would again be excessive. This could be controlled only by undertaking further reduction in the number of licences.

More serious is the perceived opportunity for an individual fisherman to expand his share of the catch by increasing the fishing power of his vessel in a variety of ways (for example, increased engine capacity, more electronic equipment to permit fishing in rougher weather, increased number of crewmen in order to handle gear faster). As long as the value of the expected increment to catch exceeded the additional cost of the added equipment, the individual fisherman would regard himself as better off even though the resulting combination of inputs produced higher average costs of production.

But this process would obviously be self-defeating for the fleet as a whole. Everyone will obviously play the same game – indeed, each fisherman may be forced to do so in order to "protect" his share of the catch. The end result is again excessive fishing power, higher costs of operation for each individual vessel, and a reduction in aggregate fleet efficiency.

How important this effect may be is an empirical matter. It certainly has been a problem in prawn, rock lobster, and North American salmon fisheries. In other cases, the technological nature of the harvesting operation may dictate a fixed combination of inputs, and any attempt to alter this would result in very rapid increases in costs. Trying to "catch yours before the hoarders do" simply would not pay. Any thorough effort to control the process of upgrading would run the risk of freezing the fishery to a given technology, which would certainly tend to discourage technical development and innovation.

A bit of caution must be noted in interpreting the data on "excessive" investment in the individual vessel under limited entry programmes. For example, analysis of the British Columbia salmon fishery indicated that a major part of the "wasteful" investment was in electronic equipment which is standard aboard fishing vessels of many developed countries, and which reflects a justifiable concern by the fisherman with his own safety at sea. Similarly, many fishermen live aboard their vessels (or at least spend a great deal of time aboard them), and some of the additional expenditures reflect the desire for a more comfortable life aboard – something that would not have been possible until the limited entry programme improved incomes to the point where the fishermen had access to the capital market through normal channels.

Finally, it should be emphasized that a limited entry programme, even under ideal circumstances, can only provide the correct number of vessels for an *average* situation. It is not a flexible weapon for dealing with short run fluctuations in abundance and availability of fish, and would have to be supplemented by direct controls over fishing to meet emergencies.

With that kind of support, a limited entry programme, coupled with a stable or gradually increasing landings tax, could do much to move any marine fishery in the direction of more rational exploitation, though it would still fall short of ideal performance in economic terms. It does, of course, enjoy the great advantage of being a relatively simple and straightforward technique which could be instituted with a minimum of disturbance to the industry.

Controlling Output: Individual Fish Quotas.   Another alternative would be to attack the open access problem by controlling the individual fishermen's output rather than inputs. This would involve the creation of individual rights to a given quantity of fish (individual fish quotas), tied to an overall quota, rather than a property right to go fishing, with the quantity unspecified. In practice, of course, it would probably be necessary to define the individual fish quota in terms of a percentage of the overall quota rather than an absolute number, since total catch quotas for most fisheries would be changed from season to season.

Although the attractiveness of the proposal may stem from the fact that it has never been tried in practice and therefore is free of the "bugs" already known to plague limited entry and tax programmes, it does have some intriguing advantages. Not the least of these is the certainty of its control over each season's catch. Once the overall quota is determined, the sum of the individual fish quotas is also determined, and the possibility of wide variations from expected catches can be minimized.

The most important advantage of this approach is the freedom it allows the fisherman to make his own choice of vessel, gear, area and time of fishing. There is no reason why more than minimal government interference would be required if the overall quota is properly chosen and if the individual quotas are tightly enforced. Since each operator would have a firm entitlement to a given amount of fish each year, depending on the number of quotas he had been issued initially or had acquired, the decision to pursue a single fishery or equip his vessel for multifishery operation could be left to the individual's own choice. Unlike other management systems, control over individual fishing quotas would encourage the development of better gear and techniques, since they would add to the individual fisherman's earnings without increasing pressure on the resource.

Initial allocation of individual quotas would present no more difficulty than initial allocation of fishing licences, and—like licences – the quotas, once issued, could become permanent, freely transferable rights. There seems little doubt that an active market for these rights would arise quickly, although some government assistance in "making the market" might be required initially. If quotas are freely transferable the programme would avoid the serious drawbacks to fixed catch limits for each vessel: the inherent penalty to more energetic and skilled fishermen, and the restriction on incentives for innovation.

It is difficult to find serious disadvantages with the proposal, at least on the theoretical level. In practice, of course, there are bound to be some bugs. Perhaps the most important relates to enforcement. Experience everywhere with landings taxes demonstrates the ease with which underreporting can develop. Since both buyer and seller may also have incentives for underreporting under a fish quota system, the problem of maintaining control over quota catches and the integrity of the basic data system on which fishery management rests might be compromised.

No less important, in many respects, is the attitude of fishermen themselves. Fishermen tend to be conservative by nature, and it is unlikely that they would look on an entirely different system of fishery management with any great enthusiasm. A system of individual fish quotas, which would involve a complete change in the way fishermen plan their initial investments and their year-to-year changes in vessels, gear, and fishing strategies, is likely to be viewed with more than usual suspicion. Obviously, these difficulties are not insuperable. They simply suggest that a major effort would have to be made to meet with fishermen throughout the areas affected and explain, carefully and in as much detail as possible, the meaning of the new programme and its effect on individual operators.

Common sense would also suggest that the initial fishery picked to test the programme should be relatively simple in structure, carried on by well-organized, businesslike operators, and not subject to excessive economic or biological stress. It would be far easier to extend the scheme to more difficult fisheries with a success story in hand.

The individual quota system may soon meet the hard test of reality. Chile is seriously considering such a programme, and the Economic Council of Canada has recently received a report strongly recommending the idea for a number of important Canadian fisheries.

Some Problems and Nonproblems

We now turn to a number of problems (and nonproblems) that would arise under any management scheme aimed at economic rationalization of heavily exploited fisheries.

Income Distribution Effects

The first concerns distribution effects. I find it difficult to generate much concern about adverse distribution effects of a properly designed limited entry or individual fish quota programme. The changes induced in regional income distribution by limited changes in a small part of the total labour force are not likely to bulk large as public issues. In fact, the most serious distribution conflicts are likely to come from disagreements over shares of the catch by groups of fishermen from different areas or using different types of gear.

If a restricted entry or individual quota system were accompanied by appropriate tax measures, it seems most unlikely that large differentials in income between those remaining in the fishery and other sectors of the fishing industry would arise. It is even less likely that economically rational fishery management would create unacceptably large windfalls to fishermen. Indeed, one of the objectives of a fishery management programme should be to bring fishermen's incomes back to a parity with those of other groups. As indicated earlier, one of the sad commentaries on the existing state of fishery management is the general tendency for fishermen's incomes to lag behind the rest of the economy, even when biologically effective controls have been instituted.

Creation of Monopoly

Various methods of restricting inputs by creating property rights in fisheries have often been criticized as monopolistic in effect. Usually this reflects simple ignorance of the mechanics of such programmes. To the extent that licences or fish quotas are freely transferable and available to anyone, fisheries are no more closed to new entry than agriculture, forestry, or any other industry in which one must acquire a right to use a natural resource before one can participate.

Company Fishing

The problem of company fishing presents some difficulties, since no single answer covers all possible situations. In North America, for example, experience has been mixed. Canadians argue that company control of fishing operations on the east coast of Canada has resulted in serious disadvantages to independent fishermen. On the west coast of Canada, on the other hand, company fishing has been reasonably successful and has coexisted with independent fishermen for many decades. Company fishing has been the rule rather than the exception in the extreme northwestern parts of the Alaska fisheries, primarily, as in the Canadian case, because of the remoteness of the fishing grounds and the necessity of providing virtually all living requirements in advance of the season.

The two countries have taken rather different approaches to distributing fishing rights under limited entry programmes where company fishing is involved. Alaska took an extreme position, requiring that all limited entry permits be utilized by an individual fisherman, and expressly forbidding corporations or other processing enterprises to own licences in their own name. In British Columbia, limited entry salmon licences were retained by the company-owned vessels, but no additional licences could be acquired by the companies, and in the event of any enforced reduction the companies would have to take a pro rata reduction in their licences.

Ultimately, the issue seems to boil down to economic necessity and industry and government preference. There are cases where the necessity for long-term heavy capital investment in remote facilities makes company fishing virtually inevitable. On the other hand, there are other areas where the independent fisherman, independent processor/marketer arrangement is technically feasible and economically efficient. In the latter case, it becomes a matter of choice as to whether limited entry permits should be made available to companies or not. Frankly, the overall impact, in a purely economic sense, does not seem particularly important whichever choice is made. What may be important, however, is that independent fishermen be able to pursue their livelihood on equal terms; and since the hope is that a properly regulated fishery will generate larger and larger economic benefits for those who participate after the rationalization process is complete, there would appear to be less and less reason for company participation in the fishing process as a matter of economic necessity.

I will admit that my own position is somewhat biased by what seems to me a general tendency for company fishing operations to be less efficient over time than independent, properly equipped fishermen, dealing with equally well-structured waterfront buyers. Experience in North America and in many of the developing countries where I worked suggests strongly that it is very difficult to get an employed skipper or crew to fish with the same intensity and effectiveness as a team fishing on its own, even where compensation is on a share basis.

All of this assumes, of course, that there is no danger of monopolistic practices in the fishery. If there is, the development of excessively large controlling units on the processing side or the fishing side can be detrimental to the welfare of both fishermen and consumers. In general, this is a rather uncommon phenomenon; fishermen and fishing companies appear to be among the worlds' worst conspirators where price fixing is involved, and the necessary degree of concentration and control over new entry is very difficult to achieve in most marine fisheries.

Effects on Small Scale and Part-Time Fishermen

A more serious set of problems arises from the social impact of limited entry programmes on small, part-time fishermen, particularly those living in isolated areas where alternative employment opportunities are severely limited. It is certainly possible that either limited licences or limited numbers of fish quotas would be bid up to levels that would exclude many of these fishermen — not necessarily on the basis of economic efficiency, but rather on the basis of better access to capital, better business organization, and the ability to operate in more than one fishery. To the extent that the problem is simply one of providing better financial services, it could be dealt with in conventional fashion — through government loan assistance or the formation of vigorous cooperative organizations. But where efficiency in the fishery calls for a significant reduction in the number of fishermen and there are, literally, no alternative jobs to which they can turn, social considerations may dictate modification of economic objectives. It may be possible to achieve social goals for coastal communities more efficiently by utilizing more people in the fishery than are required than through any other type of programme. But it must be stressed that this argument has often been misused to dodge the difficult problems of regional development. It is easier to hide unemployment in isolated fishing communities by sloppy administration of fishery programmes than to undertake more difficult regional economic programmes to increase mobility and employment opportunities.

A related but separable problem concerns part-time fishermen. There are many parts of the world in which part-time fishing is undertaken as a logical complementary activity to seasonal farming, logging, or other occupations. It is quite possible that a limited licence programme, for example, might impose a serious barrier to this type of operation. The part-time operator could not afford to bid as high as an operator engaged full-time or nearly full-time in a single fishery. A programme of individual fish quotas would be much more flexible in this respect.

There may be a hue and cry about reducing employment in boat-building and other service industries related to the fishery if the amount of excess gear in the water is reduced. But surely secondary as well as primary activities associated with excessively large capital investment in the fishery are equally wasteful. To the extent that service activites simply support idle capacity, reducing them is clearly in the national interest. No one in his right mind would argue that these adjustments can be achieved overnight, in the service sector any more than in the fishery itself; but neither can it be argued that the nation benefits by perpetuating unnecessary capacity indefinitely. One of the sad facts of life in the world of fisheries is the nearly universal tendency to dump the trouble of inefficient boatbuilding industries on the backs of fishermen by preventing them from buying vessels from the best market.

The Way of Life

Even less convincing is the argument that insistence on economic efficiency as an objective of fishery management is invalid because it does not take into consideration the nonmonetary satisfactions derived from the lifestyle associated with commercial fishing. It is true that fishing tends to attract highly individualistic people who derive a great deal of satisfaction from association with the sea, but precisely the same argument could be made with respect to a host of other occupations. Teaching, farming, professional and managerial work, and the entertainment world come to mind as examples. One of the most undesirable aspects of an open access fishery is that casual participants make it difficult or impossible for a dedicated and truly professional fisherman to make a decent living. There is no particular reason why those to whom fishing is a particularly appealing way of life should not also eat regularly and live in comfort.

Recreational Fishing

One of the most perplexing problems in fishery management is the allocation of a scarce fishery resource between competing recreational and commercial fishermen. The word "allocate" always has unpleasant connotations, and there is a strong tendency for everyone concerned to avoid using it wherever possible. But the hard fact is that if there are not enough of a particular fish population for all competing users, allocation is implicit in any kind of management programme—even if it is done by default. It makes sense then, to handle a problem on a basis of some kind of reasoned criteria with respect to efficiency and fairness to all concerned rather than to let the process of sharing be done blindly.

If it were possible to develop figures on the economic contribution of amateur fishing that could be compared directly to those derived from using the same fish commercially, the problem would be easy. The fish could be divided on a basis such that the marginal unit, used in either fishery, would provide approximately the same value contribution. Unfortunately, the world is never that simple. Thus far, a great deal of fairly sophisticated economic analysis has gone into the problem of valuing recreational fisheries, and the nature of the problem has been isolated; but usable numbers in which one can place great confidence are still remarkably limited. I speak with feeling, since I have been responsible for developing several sets of dubious values for sport fishing, all of which have come back to haunt me at one time or another.

The reasons for the difficulty are inherent, not a matter of bad practice. The first, and probably the most difficult to overcome, is that the "products" of commercial and recreational fishing are different things. Commercial fishing produces a tangible physical product, sold in a recognized market, and carrying prices determined by demand and supply. In recreational fishing, on the other hand, the product is not fish but fishing — that is, the pleasure derived from a day's fishing is the end purpose of the activity, and fish catches enter into it only in the sense that we would normally expect people to derive more satisfaction from angling if more fish are taken per day's effort. Thus we have two difficult functional relations to establish in estimating values for amateur-caught fish: first, an estimate of what people would be willing to pay for a service which normally is available to them free or at a nominal price; and second, a measure of how that willingness to pay would be altered by a higher (or lower) average catch.

With respect to the first measure, the obvious and sensible way to find out what people are willing to pay is to charge a fee for sport fishing involving populations that have a value in other uses. Unfortunately, this still raises the hackles of most amateur fishermen throughout the world, despite the fact that some of the most highly priced fisheries — Atlantic salmon, for example — have long been regarded as private property and subject to private property rights, with angler days selling for as much as $200. Even if anglers are willing to sit still for a nominal licence, there is a strong tendency to restrict the fee to an amount which would barely cover the cost of administering the programme — a figure which bears no remote resemblance to the real economic value of the right to use the resource conferred on the angler.

There are two legitimate or analytically legitimate ways of approximating willingness to pay. One is to derive, from careful surveys, the areas from which anglers come to enjoy the sport at a particular site. It is then possible to estimate from travel costs borne by the more distant visitors what those closer in would have been willing to pay rather than do without the sport. The second method is to survey willingness to pay directly, by asking a series of related questions bearing on the amounts people would be willing to give up rather than do without their sport.

Neither technique, though analytically correct, produces numbers that are more than marginally useful. (For example, my last study produced a value for a day's salmon fishing ranging from $17 to $47 per day. Even for economists that range is a bit wide for comfort!) Both measures also involve technical difficulties that need not be discussed in detail in this paper. They may be useful in some cases where the lowest possible estimate of sport fishing value is higher than the corresponding commercial value (or vice versa). In intermediate cases a great deal of judgment still has to be exercised in using such data.

Most resource economists have come, reluctantly, to the conclusion that we will need to set prices on angling in cases where there is really severe competition among commercial users. Not only can we allocate the limited resource more efficiently with that knowledge in hand, but there is an inherent justice in asking recreational fishermen to pay at least the value of what their catch would have produced for other competing users. (Before the anglers jump down my throat, I hasten to add that exactly the same recommendation would apply to commercial fisherman as well. There is no logical reason why they should graze on the public pasture at sea for little or no charge when a valuable product is being generated.)

With respect to the details of management of sport fishing there are a number of conclusions from experience elsewhere that might be of interest to a Queensland audience. First, there is much to be said for rigorous control of what we call, in the United States and Canada, "com-sports". These are, as the name implies, either commercial fishermen who are using a sport licence to avoid other limitations or sport fishermen who wish to avoid bag limits by holding a commercial licence. The use of angling equipment to produce what are obviously commercial catches is extremely difficult to control and leads inevitably to bad feelings with true commercial and true amateur fishermen.

Bag limits are obviously one way of dealing with the problem. Our own experience suggests that a bag limit — three salmon per day in Washington, for example — affects less than 5 per cent of the fishermen who take out licences. For the rest the bag limit is a more or less unattainable goal which keeps the game more interesting than it might be otherwise! Another tougher alternative is to prevent or to prohibit possession of angling gear aboard a commercially licensed vessel and vice versa. Provided the fishing area and the port receiving facilities concentrate landing sufficiently, such regulations can be enforced without too much difficulty, and they do serve to separate true sport fishing and commercial fishing segments.

One of the most frustrating aspects of a frustrating regulatory problem involving recreational fishing is the absence of usable data. At the very least, the number of participants, the number of angler days, and the catch are absolutely essential for any sensible management of sport fishing. Yet these data are rarely available on a consistent basis, even in areas where there is direct competition between commercial and sport fishing and therefore a need for data to back up whatever allocation decisions are to be made. After some initial resistance, the states of Washington and Oregon have had a great deal of success with a sportsmen's punch card for salmon. There is no limit on the number of fish that can be taken, but the card must be punched out and the date, statistical area, and species must be noted each time a fish is taken. Moderately severe penalties are imposed for failure to punch out the card on the same day the fish was taken. In recent years, a daily bag limit of two or three fish has been imposed though no seasonal limit is in force. Two years ago a modest fee of $3 was imposed for a salmon stamp to be placed on the punch card. Apart from the salutory idea of having sportsmen feel that they are contributing to the cost of management, the salmon stamp has the very practical advantage of making it a bit more expensive to take out more than one punch card if one happens to forget the card on a fishing trip.

The cards are supposed to be returned to the Department of Fisheries, and the actual return rate is quite high at present. The department regularly conducts carefully planned small surveys of those who do not return their punch cards in order to determine the amount of non response bias. Punch card data are then adjusted, blown up to represent the full angling population that has purchased punch cards, and the resulting computation is a surprisingly accurate record of how many fish were taken, where they were taken, and the number of angler days. While this will not guarantee good management of the fishery, it certainly represents a long step forward.

In summary, it is easy to understand the reluctance of sport fishermen anywhere in the world to submit to regulation. The idea of recreational fishing as a God-given right in an open country lies very deep in sparsely populated areas. But the time has come when many, if not most, of the world's game fish are subject to such pressure that conscious management is essential if the opportunities for this exciting recreation are to be preserved for the future. Given the right kind of educational campaign, it has been possible in many parts of the world to enlist the support of organized angler groups, and to obtain their participation in getting the kind of information required to make management effective. Perhaps a better way to put it is that no fishing regulations can ever be enforced successfully on a reluctant group—what is needed is compliance based on the knowledge that everybody benefits.

Of all the mythology that pervades the fishing industry, none is more deeply established than the idea that middlemen are always crooks whose primary job is to exploit fishermen and whose secondary purpose is to exploit the consumer. While there may be more than a grain of truth in this allegation from time to time and from place to place, the fact remains that marketing of fish products is an extraordinarily difficult physical and economic task. Since the product does not improve with age, and since freezing cannot keep it from becoming any less dead, speed is of the essence. Fish marketeers are called on to transport fish in marketable condition over long distances; to store them over varying periods of time; and to adjust supply to demand in the face of unpredictable and sometimes wide fluctuations in the supply of raw material and the demand for finished products. Risk always carries a price, and since fish processing and marketing are about as risky an enterprise as one could find, it is inevitable that the margin between the price paid to fishermen and the price received for processed products is typically quite wide. Again, I am not arguing that abuse of the often dominant position of the fish buyer is unknown; rather that high margins frequently reflect the fact that fish marketing is expensive, not necessarily monopolistic.

Where fishermen are scattered out over wide areas of a coast in relatively remote locations, the problem of noncompetitive buying does become severe in many cases. There simply is not room in the market for more than one or a handful of buyers, and, inevitably, the evils associated with noncompetitive practices are likely to appear.

There are three possible remedies. First, if the number of buyers is limited because of arbitrary restrictions on new entry, imposed by existing members of the industry, appropriate action to open up the primary market to prospective buyers can do the job. Secondly, the use of the cooperative organization as a means of consolidating fishing and marketing activities can be effective, particularly if marketing activities are accompanied by integrated buying and supply functions on behalf of fishermen. Finally, government can intervene directly in the price setting process by establishing prices or by actually becoming a marketing agent itself.

At the risk of stepping on tender toes unknown to me as a stranger, I would argue that world experience with state fish marketing corporations and fish marketing boards has been generally bad. There are several good reasons for this. Fish products are completely different in physical characteristics than most agricultural products, since they must be sold fresh very quickly, or, if frozen, can be stored only at relatively high cost and with almost inevitable deterioration in quality. The buffering action desired of most marketing board arrangements, under which carryovers are used to stabilize prices, simply will not operate effectively under these circumstances; or, what amounts to the same thing, will stabilize prices but only at a cost which is often far greater than the benefit achieved.

Most government intervention with the pricing mechanism is aimed at providing better and more stable incomes for primary producers. While this is certainly a desirable objective, it may be extremely difficult to achieve if the market for the final products is competitive, and fluctuates widely in response to regional, national, or international supply and demand conditions. Under these circumstances, the government inevitably becomes the residual buyer of products that the market will not take at the set price, and the general public bears the burden. In addition, there seems to be an inevitable tendency, worldwide, for price stability to become associated with higher prices. A mechanism for stabilization is also a highly convenient mechanism for pushing prices higher. While this may seem to be a temporary advantage of fishermen or farmers, over time there is a very real danger of pricing themselves out of promising markets.

In short, the pricing mechanism has a job to do in adjusting uncontrollable and frequently unpredictable instability in both physical supply and market demand. While the resulting unstable incomes are undesirable from the standpoint of the fishermen, attempts to provide greater stability almost always introduce inefficiency in the market mechanism, rigidity in prices that is harmful to the growth and expansion of markets, and an equally general tendency towards ratcheting upward adjustments. Experience with marketing boards in everything from milk to fish in various parts of the world has convinced me that the answer to every problem faced by a marketing board is to raise prices — and that way, disaster lies.

There are a number of ways which unstable income to fishermen can be alleviated without mucking around with the price system in ways which impose longer term costs. It might also be worthwhile to point out that a commercial fishery operating under an efficient limited entry or individual quota system has the margin with which to provide that kind of buffering action. That is, royalties or taxes imposed on those who participate in restricted entry fisheries could be adjusted upward or downward to take account of fluctuations in catch and/or market conditions. Without such margin, the entire fishery is usually on the ragged edge of disaster, and any unfavourable development results in unnecessarily severe hardship.

Conclusion

I must end this paper on a disquieting note. We are not making anything approaching full use of the increased insight that fishery scientists and resource economists have made available, regardless of the objectives chosen for fishery management. And the objectives chosen are, all too frequently, narrowly biological or so general as to have no content. Both reflect the universal tendency for struggles among user groups to pervert both the goals and the practice of management — to the ultimate detriment of everyone.

I suspect that future generations will not be kind to us if they inherit abused and depleted marine resources, not because we did not know what to do but because we lacked the will and the political courage to get on with the job.

3

Managing the Resource: Biological Factors

I. W. Brown

The objectives of fisheries management may vary, depending on the type of economy involved and upon socioeconomic factors within the community. The primary objective may be to maximize the catch, to conserve the stock, to maximize the financial return to the individual, or to provide optimum benefit to the industry as a whole. Some of these management objectives are in conflict with others, and unfortunately there is no simple formula for determining which objective is preferable for any given fishery.

The life of a fishery can be divided into three phases: development, growth and maintenance. The development phase consists of the identification and assessment of the resource, development of appropriate gear and associated technology, and the establishment of markets. During the growth phase commercial operators enter the fishery, fishing and processing techniques are refined, and markets are expanded. The maintenance phase is primarily concerned with the "fine tuning" of the system by the development of management strategies and the enforcement of appropriate legislation. Ideally, management plans should be developed concurrently with the developing fishery, but in most practical situations management does not appear until the end of the growth phase.

When a small number of fishermen are operating (growth phase) the demand for their produce is high in relation to supply and the consequent high prices obtained for their catch tend to attract others into the fishery. This is essentially a free market situation: industry does not want any interference from the authorities, and government is too often content to let the situation develop until a crisis occurs. Unfortunately this optimism sooner or later turns sour. Catches decline because of overexploitation, middlemen refuse or are unable to pay realistic prices to the producer because of their own profit margin expectations, or soaring operating costs and interest rates impose unforeseen financial burdens.

Suddenly the free enterprise supply and demand system does not seem so good after all. The government is under pressure to provide subsidies, low interest rate loans, tariff barriers and import restrictions to save the industry from disastrous collapse, and to implement the management controls which should have been operating years before. The time is ripe for corporate takeovers, anathema to most independent fishermen, and we hear cries of "licence limitation", "restricted entry" and "area zoning". The fact is that there are just too many fishermen, each justifiably demanding an economic slice of the finite resource cake.

Assuming that a broad overall management objective *has* been decided upon as a matter of policy, precisely how do the fisheries managers formulate a plan to meet this objective? All too often the process is entirely a conceptual one, based on very few hard facts, and carried out in isolation from the community groups most closely involved with the problems. The so-called management plan is often a hotch-potch collection of regulations introduced in response to individual pressure groups (sometimes at odds with one another) from various sectors of the industry.

Ideally, the fisheries manager should have all the necessary information at hand to allow him to translate his conceptual model of the fishery into a useful mathematical model. He could then determine how the system would react to changes in those input parameters over which he has some legislative control.

Fisheries management historically has been concerned primarily with the dynamics of fish populations: the incorporation of economic and social considerations has been a relatively recent development, about which we will hear more from other speakers at this conference.

The types of information needed by the manager to allow him to make an informed decision fall into three categories: (a) biological, (b) population dynamics, and (c) socioeconomic.

Population dynamics is the study of processes which affect the stability and size of the stock as a whole. Perhaps a useful means of identifying these processes is to construct a conceptual model of the stock, which we can compare with a water tank with various inlets and outlets (figure 1).

The maintenance of a steady state depends on a balance between input (increase in biomass due to reproduction and growth) and output (decrease in biomass due to deaths). When considering a typical fishery the "stock" tank is effectively divided into two parts — those animals which are of a size sufficient to be legally, economically or practically captured, and those which are not. Thus we can separate the stock into a prerecruit and postrecruit component (figure 2).

The pipe between the two represents recruitment (i.e., attainment of "fishable" size) and is controlled by a valve which regulates the rate of flow, or recruitment rate. The relative size of these two tanks is basically determined by the minimum legal (or sometimes practical) size of fish available for capture.

Reproduction and growth are characteristics which, at an

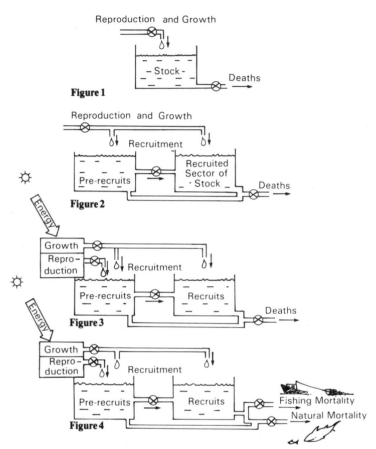

Figures 1-4 Development of a simple conceptual model of the main processes affecting a fish stock.

individual level, are under genetic control, and at the stock level are influenced by the availability of food and ultimately dependent on radiant energy from the sun. By cleverly manufacturing water from solar energy we can rearrange our hydraulic model again (figure 3).

Furthermore, we can partition the "deaths" output into deaths resulting from natural causes such as parasitization, predation and disease, and those resulting purely from fishing activities (figure 4).

This is obviously a very simplistic model of the stock system, but it does identify the major dynamic processes as being growth, reproduction, recruitment, natural mortality and fishing mortality. The model shows us *how* the system works, but to be able to use it constructively we need to know something about the *rates* at which the various processes occur. In terms of our model we need to know what the valve settings are.

Some of the processes are purely biological, and gaining an understanding of growth, reproduction and natural mortality is clearly the job of the fisheries biologist. Often, however, the biologist is also a part-time population dynamicist and finds himself involved in less scientifically clear-cut areas such as the estimation of fishing rates, analysis of catch-per-unit-effort, and assessment of the effects of changing gear efficiency and minimum legal sizes. The acquisition of information necessary to make such assessments is often beyond the direct control of the scientist. He has to rely, to a large extent, on data supplied by commercial fishermen and, as we know, the average fisherman is notoriously reticent about divulging any information on his catches (and, by extension, his income) which could conceivably be of some interest to the taxation authorities. However, in order to understand with any confidence what is going on in a particular fishery, access to reliable catch and effort data is essential.

Returning to the biological factors, we can see that the fundamental process tending to increase the size of a stock is growth. How does the biologist measure and describe the growth process? As you would expect, growth is defined as the time rate of change in size. Instantaneous size can easily be measured, but the rate of change is rather more difficult to determine. Various techniques may be used, depending on circumstances. Fish can be kept in aquaria and measured repeatedly over a long period of time, tagged fish released in the ocean can be remeasured upon recapture, and age can be determined directly in many species whose bony parts (scales, fin, spines, vertebrae) exhibit annual growth rings.

In the majority of species growth conforms to the general shape of the curve shown in figure 5. The mathematical description of this curve is known as the von Bertalanffy growth formula:

$$L_t = L\alpha \, (1 - e^{-K(t - t_0)})$$

in which three parameters (L_α, K and t_0), which can be estimated in various ways from the length/age data, define the individual

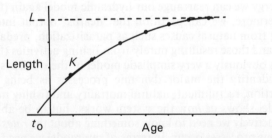

Figure 5 Typical growth curve of the majority of species.

growth pattern of the species. Often, however, the fisheries manager would prefer to talk about weights than about lengths. Construction of a weight-length "key" or graph (figure 6a) is relatively straightforward. However, the derivation of a formula to convert lengths to weights is not quite so simple, as the relationship between weight and length is nonlinear.

By converting weight and length measurements to logarithms and replotting, we discover a straight line (figure 6b) whose position on the graph is determined by two parameters — the intercept (a), and the slope (b). The weight-length relationship is described by the formula

$$\log W = \log a + b \log L \text{ (or } W = aL^b\text{)}$$

where the exponent (b) is usually in the vicinity of 3.0. The equation basically says that the weight of a fish varies proportionately with approximately the cube of its length.

The numbers of fish in a given year-class or cohort will decrease over a period of time as a result of disease, predation and fishing. Let us assume that these mortality factors reduce the size of a year-

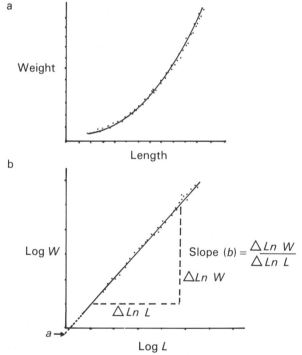

Figure 6 (a) Typical relationship between length and weight, (b) between log-transformed length and weight.

class by 50 per cent each year, and that the initial numerical strength of the group was 1,000 at t_0. At the end of the first year there will be 500 survivors, at the end of the second year 250, at the end of the third year 125, and so on. The change in numbers can be plotted (see figure 7a) as a "survivorship" curve.

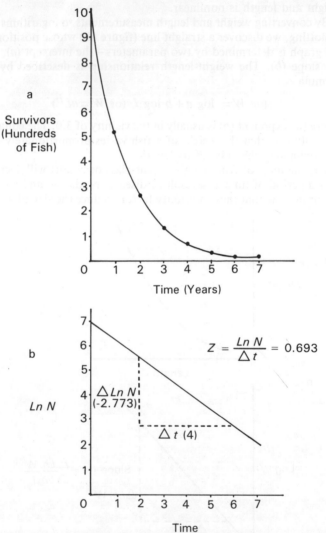

Figure 7 Graphical derivation of instantaneous rate of total mortality (Z). Survivorship curve for a hypothetical year-class with constant annual survival rate of 50 per cent is shown in (a). The lower figure (b) uses the same data as (a), but with numbers of survivors transformed to natural logarithms. The value of Z corresponding to 50 per cent annual survival is 0.693.

By converting the "numbers" axis to logarithms (figure 7b), we once again come up with a straight line, whose slope is a convenient measure of the instantaneous rate of total mortality, usually referred to as Z. For the example above, Z is calculated to be 0.693.

Partitioning the instantaneous rate of total mortality into its "natural" (M) and "fishing" (F) mortality components can be achieved in various ways, most of which require that age can be determined and that estimates of catch and fishing effort are reasonably reliable. One way is to compare Z and relative fishing effort in two equal time periods when the levels of effort (f) are unequal. Assuming natural mortality is constant, F_1 and F_2 can be calculated by solving the following simple equations:

$$F_1 + M = Z_1$$

$$\text{and } \frac{F_1}{F_2} = \frac{f_1}{f_2}$$

$$F_2 + M = Z_2$$

By rearranging these equations we find that

$$F_2 = (Z_1 - Z_2) \;/\; ([f_1 - f_2] - 1)$$

which then allows us to find solutions for F_1 and M.

From a combination of direct biological research and analysis of catch and effort data, we have been able to estimate the parameters of growth (L_α, K, and t_o), the relationship between weight and length (a and b), and instantaneous mortality rates (M, F, and Z). How can we put these figures together to produce a useful working model of the fish stock that we are interested in? Once such model has been constructed by two British fishery scientists (Beverton and Holt) in the late 1950s:

$$Y = F\, N_o e^{-Mr} W_\alpha \left(\frac{1 - e^{-Z\lambda}}{Z} - \frac{3e^{-Kr}(1 - e^{-(Z+K)\lambda})}{Z+K} \right.$$

$$\left. + \frac{3e^{-2Kr}(1 - e^{-(Z+2K)\lambda})}{Z+2K} - \frac{e^{-3Kr}(1 - e^{-(Z+3K)\lambda})}{Z+3K} \right)$$

The derivation of this rather daunting string of terms involves a profound understanding of basic life processes as well as a fair bit of mathematical handwaving. It contains the previously mentioned parameters of growth and mortality, plus a couple of others (r and λ) which are a function of t_R, the average age of recruitment or, if you like, the age corresponding to the minimum legal size of the species in question.

The formula produces an estimate of Y, which is the yield of fish that would be expected in an equilibrium situation under conditions dictated by the various input parameters. If we are fortunate enough to have an estimate of N_0 (the initial numerical strength of the stock), Y gives us an absolute yield figure. Usually, however, N_0 is virtually impossible to estimate with any accuracy, and the equation is normally used to determine the *relative* yield, or "yield per recruit". The variables that interest the fisheries manager are by and large those over which there is some human control — F (fishing mortality, affected by the minimum legal size regulations) and t_R (recruitment age, affected by minimum legal size regulations). By manipulating the values of F and t_R and calculating Y, we can get some idea of how the stock would react to changes in fishing pressure and minimum size restrictions.

This then is one possible approach that the fisheries manager might take in order to gain a better understanding of the processes that influence the size and stability of a particular fish stock. However, despite its mathematical elegance, the Beverton-type yield equation is not always particularly useful, since it contains various assumptions that can often not be satisfied. Other models have been developed which are based on different sets of assumptions.

In circumstances where the manager is required to make a decision on the basis of "gut feeling" rather than sound scientific evidence, it is surprising how much help can be gained from a knowledge of the particular animal's obvious biological characteristics. Situations like this can arise when catch and effort data are lacking or research staff are unavailable to carry out an intensive study of the stock.

Some biologists in recent years have turned their attention to the relationship between the "life strategy" of a species and the character-istics of the stock as a whole. This type of approach is based on what is known as the "logistic" growth model which, in effect, says that the rate of population growth is a function of its intrinsic growth potential (r), and the carrying capacity of the environemnt (K). It is basically a question of the allocation of limited energy resources between two conflicting options. Animals adapted to unstable, unpredictable environments tend to channel a large part of their energy into the production of offspring. By maturing early and producing large numbers of eggs, they ensure that (provided environ-mental conditions are favourable) reproductive success is maximized and the population is maintained at a high level.

These animals are environmental opportunists, often subject to "boom or bust" fluctuations in stock size, and are said to be "r-selected". They are characterized by high fecundity, lack of parental care for eggs and larval stages, early maturity, rapid growth, short life span, small body size, and poorly developed behavioural, physiological and physical defence mechanisms. Their populations exhibit considerable biomass fluctuation from year to year, an ability to recover rapidly from depredations caused by environmental instability, and a high instantaneous rate of natural mortality.

At the other end of the $r - K$ spectrum we find animals that concentrate their energy resources into survival processes rather than high reproductive effort. These "K-selected" types have evolved a species conservation strategy which depends on producing numerous small batches of offspring rather than a few large batches. K-strategists are typified by low fecundity, some degree of parental care for eggs, late maturity, slow growth rate, long life span, large body size, and well developed defence and competitive mechanisms. The population tends to be relatively stable from one year to the next, unable to recover rapidly from the effects of perturbations to its usually stable environment, and has a low instantaneous rate of natural mortality. In reality, of course, most species exhibit a mixture of "r" and "K" characteristics, and would thus be placed somewhere in between the two extremes. Moreover, this sort of classification is a comparative exercise—to choose a species in isolation and say that it is "highly K-selected" doesn't make much biological sense.

As an example of how such life-history information could possibly be used in the local management context, let us look at a typical prawn and a typical shark and see how they fit into the scheme. Since stocks of these animals are both subject to fishing pressure, it might be interesting to hypothesize from the biological evidence what factors should be taken into account by people concerned with managing the respective fisheries.

According to the criteria mentioned previously, the prawn is clearly r-selected with respect to the shark. We should then expect that the prawn stock might vary a good deal in size from one year to the next, as a result of environmental "ups and downs" (for example, changes in rainfall patterns affecting stream flushing, salinity, etc.). The shark's offshore marine environment does not vary too much, and so we would expect the shark stock to remain fairly constant in size.

On the other hand, with regard to possible exploitation rates, we woud be advised to take a very close look at the dynamics of the shark stock. Because of the K-strategist's poorer ability to recover from stress, these types are far more susceptible to overexploitation than are their r-selected counterparts. In other words, fishing effort would require much finer tuning in the shark fishery than it would in the prawn fishery, at least in terms of stock conservation. It may well be that in the prawning industry economic considerations are of more practical importance than stock dynamics considerations. In fact it is tempting to hypothesize that the relative importance of economic versus population dynamics data in fisheries management is a function of where the target species is situated on the r-K continuum. This sort of life strategy information, often obtained from casual observation, should be used cautiously as a basis for management decisions. However if the only alternative is to make decisions based on no biological information at all, such criteria can be extremely useful.

There are, of course, many other biological phenomena which can have a profound effect on the way a fish stock should be managed. A very important one concerns the actual delineation of the stock. Migratory species such as tunas and billfishes can be a real headache, since effective management can depend on international diplomacy and foreign policy as well as the usual stock dynamics considerations.

The question of sex reversal is an interesting one, and could have significant management implications in some instances. A surprisingly large number of tropical and subtropical fish species are capable of undergoing a change in sex. Sometimes this is "standard procedure", with fish perhaps spending their first few years of life as males, then becoming females. Others apparently change in response to environmental stimuli.

The effective management of a single species fishery is difficult enough, but when the fishery is aimed at two or more target species, the problems are magnified.

The maintenance of a viable fishing industry depends to a large extent upon conservation of the resource at a viable and productive level. The processes which regulate living natural resources are fundamentally biological in nature. I would be among the first to admit that we will never hope to know all there is to be known about these processes, but I am equally convinced that that is not a valid argument against trying.

4

The Role of the Economist in Fisheries Management: The Concept of Economic Rent

T. F. Meany

Most people readily recognize the biological problems which necessitate the management of fisheries resources. Put quite simply, if you catch fish faster than they can be replaced by nature, you have an overfishing problem. Steps must then be taken to restrict fishing effort so that the resource has a chance of recovery, or at least so that the overfishing problem is not allowed to become any worse.

As overfishing is a biological problem then it would appear that purely biological solutions should be used, for example, minimum size limits, closed season, gear restrictions, and so forth. A lot of fishermen would argue that since it is a biological problem, biological solutions are sufficient and that economics and economists should have no part to play in fisheries management, and that the free market system should be left to determine the allocation of resources in the fishing industry as it does elsewhere in the economy.

It is the aim of this article to show that while the observed results of overfishing may be biological, the causes are economic; and that the operation of the free market system in the fishing industry leads not to the rational allocation of resources but to their wasteful usage.

The Economic Causes of Overfishing

If two Queensland fisheries, mullet and barramundi, are considered we find that the mullet fishery is in no biological danger while the barramundi are exploited to the extent that in some areas their very survival is considered to be under threat. Admittedly there are differences in the behaviour of these two species that may make barramundi more vulnerable to overfishing. The real reasons for the greater fishing effort expended on the barramundi fishery are however economic.

Any fisherman who has marketed mullet knows only too well that while the price received on the market may be reasonable when catches are low, moderate to heavy landings result in a drastic fall in prices—sometimes to the extent that the price received does not even cover the costs of catching and marketing the fish. Under these circumstances there is no incentive to increase the catch of mullet. This lack of market demand is itself sufficient to restrict the catch to a level below that which would pose any biological danger to the species. In other words there is a naturally existing economic protection system.

On the other hand, with barramundi the price received by fishermen is high relative to the cost of fishing; it is therefore profitable to fish even at relatively low catch rates. This results in the fishing effort on barramundi being high relative to the stocks available, so high in fact that overfishing has resulted. If barramundi sold for the same price as mullet it would be most unlikely that overfishing would be a problem.

The Prawn Fishery

The effect of the rise of fish prices relative to cost is well illustrated with respect to the Queensland prawn fishery. The graphs in figure 1 have been prepared by Dr Burke Hill of the Queensland Fisheries Service. Figure 1B indicates that between 1975-76 and 1979-80 the number of boats in this fishery more than doubled from under 700 to 1,400. What this graph does not indicate is that there was also a substantial increase in the average size of boats in this period and in the sophistication of the equipment carried. One would expect that this very great increase in fishing capacity would result in a substantial increase in total catch.

Figure 1A, however, indicates that this did not in fact occur. The three year moving average for catch from the fishery showed an increase from about 7,000 tonnes in 1975-76 to about 9,000 tonnes in 1979-80. Figure 1D indicates that despite the increase in size and sophistication of fishing boats the average annual catch per boat actually dropped from about 10 tonnes in 1975-76 to about 8 tonnes in 1979-80.

The other measure shown on these graphs is the value of the catch, which rose from a total of about $10 million in the 1975-76 to about $50 million in 1979-80, while the average value per boat rose from about $15,000 to about $42,000 over the same period. It is clearly the increased unit price of prawns relative to fishing costs which has been responsible for the increase in boat numbers in the fishery.

Increased Economic Efficiency

The questions that must now be answered are: whether the developments observed in the prawn fishery are those that would normally be expected in other industries, and if not why do they occur in the fishing industry?

The economic system which has developed in the Western world

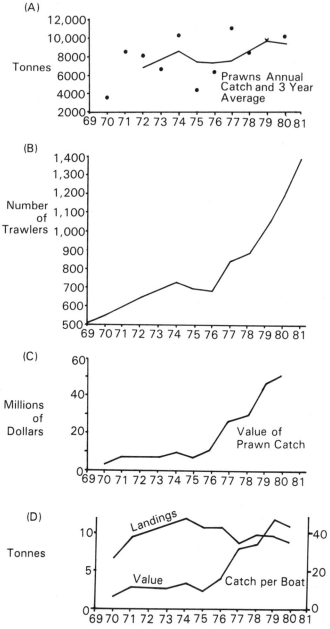

Figure 1 Actual trends in the Queensland prawn fishery, with slightly rising production, rising prices and improved technology.

since the industrial revolution has provided a steadily increasing standard of living for an increasing population. This has been achieved by continually increasing the economic efficiency with which the basic building blocks of our economic system, labour, capital, natural resources and technology are combined.

Increasing economic efficiency is measured by the relative cost of performing a particular task. If, for example, a technological innovation allows a certain task to be done more cheaply by replacing labour with machinery then it will be adopted, hopefully freeing the labour for some other task. Again if a more efficient steam turbine is developed that enables the same amount of electricity to be generated at the same cost but using less coal or oil, it will gradually replace the less energy efficient technology.

It is the increasing efficiency in the use of scarce resources (including labour and capital) which enables us to enjoy an increased standard of living. For example technological innovation coupled with the use of machines (capital equipment) has in most areas of industry enabled one man to produce what would have required several men in times past.

The features of this development have therefore been an increasing output per unit of labour or per dollar invested. This is well illustrated in the case of agriculture where there has been a long-term downward trend in total employment, an increase in the average size of farms and a substantial increase in the total volume and value of production as well as the volume and value of production of the average farm.

Figure 2 shows the trends that would be expected in agriculture on the same basis as those shown in figure 1 for the Queensland

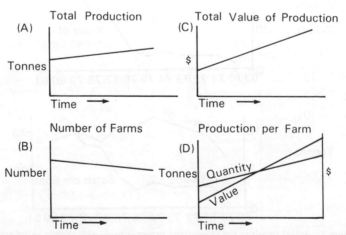

Figure 2 Expected trends in agriculture, assuming slightly rising production, rising prices and improved technology.

prawn fishery. Figure 2 assumes a steady increase in total production similar to the increase in total prawn catch.

The main difference between the two relates to the number of producing units. Whereas the number of trawlers has increased substantially there has been a decrease in the number of farms. This decrease in farm numbers would be explained by farm amalgamations, with more successful farmers taking advantage of new technology which enabled them to work increasing areas and less successful operators being forced off their holdings by cost/price pressures. In other words with farming, a balance is maintained between technological capacity and the number of farms. As machinery was developed which enabled farmers to work larger areas the size of farms and the amount produced on each farm increased, and as there is a finite amount of suitable land available this resulted in a decrease in the total number of farms.

Why then in the prawn fishery did not the same sequence of events occur? There has undoubtedly been an increase in the size and technical efficiency of Queensland prawn trawlers, certainly at least matching the increase in total catch in the period under consideration. Why then did the total number of boats fishing increase rather than decrease, even though this resulted in a decreased average catch per boat (which in turn contributed to the severity of the problems experienced in the fishery in 1980 when the effects of a poor catching year were compounded by a sharp drop in prices).

Property Rights

The real difference between agriculture and fishing is in the nature of the property rights available. The farmer owns his farm, and this gives him control over what happens with respect to its exploitation. He can match his technical capacity to the size of the resource (land) available to him.

The fisherman by contrast owns only his boat, which is comparable to the farmers' machinery rather than the farm. He has no exclusive property rights with respect to the fishing grounds; these he shares in common with all other fishermen exploiting the resource. Even though the resource may be fully exploited there is nothing to prevent additional boats entering the fishery or existing fishermen changing to bigger boats even though this results in a decrease in the catch of other fishermen. In fact the competition for the unowned stock of fish will always lead to increased effort and costs in the fishery with no real benefits to fishermen in the longer term.

In the case of farming we therefore find the resource to be in private ownership (private property) while in fisheries it is in common ownership (common property). This difference is fundamental and has extremely important implications on the results flowing from the operation of the free market system in each case.

The Concept of Resource Rent

To understand why common property presents special economic problems it is necessary to consider some basic economic theory. Early theorists recognized three basic components in the creation of wealth: land (or as it will be called in this paper natural resources), labour and capital.

Each of these was seen as generating a different type of wealth, or profit: that generated by capital was called interest, that generated by labour was called wages, and that generated by natural resources was called rent.

The term "rent" as used in this context can be somewhat confusing, it is a term often encountered in fisheries literature but differs somewhat from its everyday usage such as the rent paid for a house.

To explain the concept of rent a little better we will consider three blocks of land each of equal size; the first block is rich river flats, the second is medium grade land while the third is poor ground. Each of these blocks is used to raise a crop. In each case the labour and machinery required to plant and harvest the crop is hired. The hire of the machinery in each case costs $100,000. In addition wages paid for labour is $50,000 in each case. Total cost of planting and harvesting the crop is therefore $150,000.

The quantity and value of the crop produced from each block is as follows:

River flats	420 tonnes valued at	$210,000
Medium land	300 tonnes valued at	$150,000
Poor land	200 tonnes valued at	$100,000

Cultivation of the river flats therefore yields a profit of $60,000, the medium land has just covered costs while a $50,000 loss is sustained in the cultivation of the poor land. The variation in these returns is quite clearly due to the different productivity of each block of land, the land in this case being the natural resource.

The first block therefore returns an economic rent of $60,000 and was quite clearly worth cultivating. The second block made neither a profit nor a loss and was therefore marginal and may or may not be cultivated in future. The poor block with its $50,000 loss was submarginal and under the existing cost/price structure would not be used again.

The cost/price structure is not of course fixed. Were for example the cost of capital or labour to increase and the value of production remain unchanged, the medium grade block would become submarginal. A drop in the cost of production, either through a fall in the cost of capital or labour or an increase in the price received for the crop, would on the other hand result in the medium block returning a profit, or more correctly a resource rent.

If we look at the total result of cultivation of only the best block, the two best blocks and all three blocks we get the following results:

	River flats only	River flats and medium land	All three blocks
Total production (tonnes)	420	720	920
Total value of production	$210,000	$360,000	$460,000
Total cost of production	$150,000	$300,000	$450,000
Net income (resource rent)	$ 60,000	$60,000	$10,000

Each level of production results in an overall profit. This does not however mean that the farmer will use all three blocks; he will for example certainly not use the poor land as its cultivation increases his total cost by $150,000 but reduces his net income by $50,000. To farm this block would be a waste of capital and labour as it would not result in his maximizing his profit. The rational farmer would cultivate only the river flats or at most only the two best blocks.

In doing this he is quite clearly not maximizing total production from his land; this is done when 920 tonnes are produced from all three blocks. This is, in terms more familiar to fishermen, the maximum sustainable yield from his land.

Attaining maximum sustainable yield is often seen as a most desirable objective in fisheries, yet in the example shown above it is clearly economically irrational. From an economic point of view it is often just as irrational in fisheries.

The above exercise has attempted to show what the concept of economic rent means. Because a farmer has property rights he can organize his operations so as to maximize the amount of economic rent accruing to him; this he does by ceasing to invest at the point where marginal[1] cost equals marginal revenue.

Each farmer will have this same objective of maximizing net income, and as the activities of each farmer are carried out virtually independently, the result of each maximizing his own profit will be that total profits are maximized.

The Fisheries Situation

The biological yield curve for a fishery shows the total catch for a fishery increasing as fishing effort increases up to the point of maximum sustainable yield. If effort is increased still further overfishing will occur and total catch will decline, theoretically at least to the point where the species becomes extinct.

By multiplying the various levels of catch shown on the yield curve by the average price received for the fish, the yield curve can be converted to show the value rather than the quantity of catch with the point of maximum sustainable yield becoming the point of maximum sustainable value of catch.

If it is assumed that the cost of each unit of fishing effort is the same, then as the amount of effort increases so will total costs. Both the yield curve (in dollar value) and the cost curve can then be plotted on a graph (figure 3).

The cost curve OX cuts the yield curve at Y. This is in fact the break-even point for the fishery where total costs equal total income. It is a point where only "normal" profits are being made. (All the potential resource rent is being dissipated.)

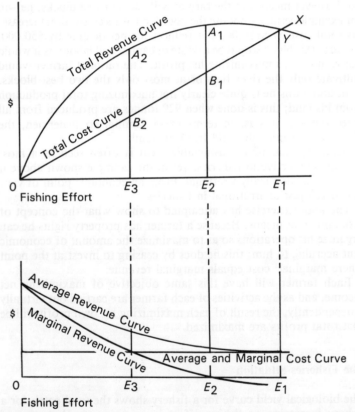

Figure 3 Economic model of fisheries yield curve, showing marginal and average cost and revenue curves.

If we move back along the yield curve to the point of maximum sustainable value of catch it can be seen that this level of catch can be taken with a fishing effort OE_2. The fishing cost associated with this level of fishing effort is E_2B_1. As the total value of catch is E_2A_1, the value exceeds the costs by A_1B_1, this represents the return to the resource or a resource rent.

A_1B_1 is not however the maximum profit the fishery can yield. The maximum value of the resource rent can be plotted by drawing a line parallel to the cost curve OX so that it just touches the yield curve. This occurs at A_2 and the amount A_2B_2 represents the maximum resource rent the fishery can yield.

In our farming example it was pointed out that profits are maximized at the point where marginal cost equals marginal revenue, and that any rational investor would not wish to increase his investment beyond this point.

The average and marginal cost and revenue curves are shown on the bottom part of figure 3. Because it has been assumed that the cost of a unit of fishing effort (this could be boat days, hours trawled, etc.) will be the same, regardless of the level of total fishing effort, the cost of a marginal unit of fishing effort will equal the average cost; as a result they will both be on the same straight line. The average revenue curve can be plotted by dividing the total value of catch taken at each level of fishing effort by the number of units of effort used. This average revenue curve will cross the average (and marginal) revenue curve at a level of effort OE_1 or where the total revenue curve cuts the total cost curve. The marginal revenue curve would be plotted by calculating the change in the total value of catch resulting from each additional unit of fishing effort. Marginal revenue equals marginal cost at a level of fishing effort OE_3. This, as already explained, is the level of effort where the total value of catch exceeds the cost of fishing by the greatest amount (A_2B_2), or the point where the economic rent from the fishery is maximized. The cost of each additional unit of effort that goes into the fishery with levels of effort greater than OE_3 will exceed the increase in total revenue it generates, or in other words total economic rent will be reduced.

At the level of effort OE_2 where the maximum sustainable value of catch is taken, marginal revenue will equal zero, or in other words no additional increase to total revenue will result from another unit of effort. If fishing effort increases beyond OE_2 marginal revenue becomes negative.

Where property rights exist as with our farming example, it was pointed out why further investment ceases when marginal cost exceeds marginal revenue. If this occurred in the fishing industry, investment and further increase in fishing effort could be expected to cease at OE_3. As the catch taken at this level of effort must be less than the maximum sustainable catch this could present no threat to the resource. If this was in fact what happened no fishery would ever be threatened with overfishing and regulation by governments to protect fishery resources would be completely unnecessary.

The example of cultivated land has been used to show how combinations of inputs of labour, capital and natural resources (land) would be used so as to maximize profit. Each individual farmer would aim to do the same, and because apart from the vagaries of the weather, each farmer has complete control of his crop, from planting to harvesting, the system allows each to achieve his objective.

Each farmer would for example know that his own production would be too small to affect the world market price. He would from past experience have an idea what combination of natural resources (land), capital and labour would give him the maximum difference between his costs and expected earnings. He would know that expanding the acreage planted would result in the utilization of less and less productive land; what levels of application he would require to get the best returns from fertilizer used; at what levels of production he would have to acquire additional units of equipment, labour, etc. Most farmers would not of course sit down and work these things out on paper but rely very much on past experience to determine the combination of inputs that will maximize their profits.

Because they have individual property rights each farmer can make his decisions and carry on his operation without interfering in any way with the results obtained by neighbours. Each farmer will seek to maximize his profits and in so doing the end result will be the maximization of total profits to the industry. In other words by maximizing their individual profits the farmers quite unintentionally maximize total industry profit. The free enterprise system can be seen to be working and the end result is not only in the best interests of each individual but also the nation as a whole.

In fisheries however the absence of individual property rights leads the free market systems to result not in the rational utilization of resources but to extreme inefficiency. As in the case of the Queensland prawn fishery the fact that individuals cannot claim exclusive rights to a certain part of the resource leads to wasteful use of all the resources involved; the prawn stocks themselves, capital, labour, fuel, etc.

There can be no doubt that in the last few years at least a considerable amount of potential resource rent from this fishery has been dissipated.

If we make some very simple assumptions with respect to the prawn fishery as shown in figure 1, we can plot the yield curve as shown in figure 4.

The catch in 1979-80 is assumed to be near the maximum sustainable yield; it is also assumed that the fleet broke even at that

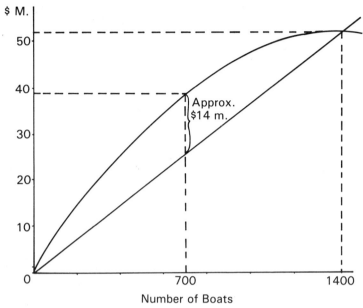

Figure 4   Yield curve, showing possible economic rent from the Queensland prawn fishery.

point, or in other words that the total running cost of the fleet of 1,400 boats equalled the total value of catch (about $52 million).

The 1975-76 catch (about 7,000 tonnes) is valued at 1979-80 prices and is assumed to be taken by the 700 boats which took this level of catch in 1975-76. On this basis the fishery would in 1979-80 have generated a resource rent of some $14 million or an average of $20,000 per boat.

Conclusion

There are several points which I will make by way of conclusion.

Firstly, the concern of the economist with respect to fisheries, as elsewhere, is with efficient allocation of what he defines as scarce resources. The very nature of fisheries is such that a considerable wastage of resources tends to occur; the economist would wish to design systems to prevent this.

Secondly, it is not, as is often assumed, the objective of economists involved in fisheries to develop systems which guarantee some minimum income to fishermen. Economically rational exploitation of fisheries would however effectively raise fishermen's incomes.

Thirdly, the taking of maximum sustainable yield as an objective of fisheries management is seen by the economists as having no greater validity than the idea of maximizing say, wheat production, without regard to the level of costs or profits involved.

Finally, the concept of a resource rent should not be confused with the notion of a resource tax. In talking of a resource rent the economist is merely drawing attention to its existence and the economic advantages to be attained in preventing its dissipation. The question of whether or not fishermen should be allowed to retain all of this superprofit (i.e., the concept of a resources tax) is a matter not for economists but for politicians and governments.

This article has attempted only to explain why economists feel they have something to contribute to the concept of fisheries management, in the hope that others involved with fisheries, be they fishermen or administrators, will be better able to understand what it is that economists are trying to achieve and to recognize that they are not simply trying to interfere with the free market system but to develop fisheries management strategies which will permit the free market system to fulfil its role in the efficient allocation of resources in fisheries as it does in other areas of the economy.

Notes

1. The term "marginal" as used here refers to an additional unit of investment (marginal cost) or unit of income (marginal revenue). This could be $1 or $10,000. If at any level of investment the question was asked "what additional income would another unit of investment generate?" then that additional unit of investment and income are the marginal cost and marginal revenue at that point. If the results of asking that question at each level of investment were joined together as a graph it would represent the marginal cost and marginal revenue curves.

5

The Management Regime in Queensland: An Overview

N. M. Haysom

This paper presents a general outline of the background against which the specific fisheries management problems exist or have developed in Queensland. Various issues are discussed, including government and industry organization, the geographical and historical background of Queensland fisheries, and recent developments which will affect fisheries management in that state in the future.

Government and Industry Organization

Firstly I would like to discuss the organization of government control over fisheries generally, and the organization of the industry to facilitate interaction with government. At present, state governments exercise control over fisheries out to the outer limit of the territorial sea (that is, three nautical miles from low water mark or designated baselines) and the commonwealth government exercises control beyond this limit.

Fisheries which lie wholly within the state's internal or territorial waters are, of course, dealt with unilaterally by the state authority, but the management of others may require coordination by the Australian Fisheries Council, a group of the various cabinet ministers holding fisheries portfolios in the commonwealth and state governments. The council carries out its business through its standing committee (the chief public service fisheries advisers to the ministers) and a number of regional and technical advisory committees.

There is another aspect which has considerable impact on the management of Australian fisheries and particularly on those where a limited licence regime is envisaged. I refer to Section 117 of the Australian constitution which states: "A subject of the Queen, resident in any State, shall not be subject in any other State to any disability or discrimination which would not be equally applicable to him if he were a subject of the Queen resident in such other State".

This means, in effect, that we cannot legally limit participation in a fishery, say to Queensland residents only, which has been the expressed wish of local fishermen's groups in the past and still crops up as a hardy annual resolution at many meetings. On the other hand, a previous history of involvement in a fishery may well be acceptable as a criterion for entitlement of participation in a limited licence fishery, even though in practice the chances of qualifying under such a criterion must be heavily loaded in favour of the local resident.

Industry organization in Queensland has also been fragmented, which does not assist when we are seeking industry input in formulating management plans. When the Queensland Commercial Fishermen's State Council was formed some years ago, there were high hopes that here at last was a body which would speak for the fishermen "with one voice". The state council has been racked with internal dissent which very nearly culminated in its complete disintegration last year (1980).

I am pleased to say that it now appears to be reorganized on a much more professional basis, in a way which recognizes that perhaps it is unrealistic to expect fishermen to speak with a single voice, but that they should at least speak firmly, articulately and with a sensibly balanced view.

Much the same sort of high expectations were held out for the Australian Fishing Industry Council (AFIC), which was supposed to be the united voice for the industry as a whole (covering both primary and secondary sectors). Although AFIC has performed this role very well in some states, it has had a chequered career in Queensland. This has undoubtedly caused difficulties in getting a Queensland industry view put forward to the commonwealth government on many issues of federal significance.

Geographical and Historical Background to the Development and Management of Queensland Fisheries

Queensland's commercial production of fish (or that of Australia as a whole for that matter) is not large by world standards. The state's annual catch is of the order of 5,000 tonnes of finned fish and 13,000 tonnes of shellfish. Australia ranks about fifty-fifth or thereabouts amongst the seafood producing nations, but probably lies within the top ten or so in the ranks of fish exporters, mainly because of its high quality rock lobster, prawn, scallop and abalone fisheries. Queensland is responsible for a large segment of the nation's prawn and scallop production.

As in most tropical areas, Queensland's fisheries are characterized more by variety than by quantity. Moreover, the length of the coastline (over 2,000 nautical miles), its major orientation in a north/south direction (covering some 19 degrees of latitude), the presence of the Great Barrier Reef, and the variety of coastal habitat types, gives Queensland a highly varied marine fauna, a wide range of different types of fisheries, and hence scope for a multitude and diversity of management problems.

Until the 1950s, Queensland fisheries consisted almost exclusively of small-time independent fishing units, very much localized in their area of operation. Queensland at that time was a state whose economy in coastal areas was very largely dependent on seasonal primary industries — in particular the sugar and meat industries. Politicians of the day saw commercial fishing as a very useful alternative occupation for the canecutters and meatworkers in the off-seasons of their particular industries, and anybody could acquire a commercial fisherman's licence on payment of a nominal fee.

Queensland's mild climate and the comparatively sheltered waters along our coastline have, over the years, facilitated continued participation in our fisheries by part-time operators and those with a low level of professional expertise.

The community attitudes engendered by these factors, and the historical development of Queensland's fisheries have made it very difficult to introduce changes in the industry aimed at restricting participation to genuine professionals, or even to upgrade the professionalism of those who are full-time operators, despite the fact that both the department and industry leaders are convinced of the desirability of such changes. I believe, however, that we have made in the last few years considerable strides in the direction of these objectives, though perhaps not as fast as you in industry or I would like to see. The current climate of unemployment, of course, has not helped in the introduction of moves to curtail severely outside entry into the primary sector of the industry. Moreover, many genuine fishermen have been forced by conditions in the industry to seek supplementary income from outside fishing, which has further complicated matters.

Within the industry itself, we have reached the point where, after a long period of underexploitation and slow development, a number of fisheries are now overexploited or rapidly approaching that condition. Moreover, some of the inshore operations are, rightly or wrongly, seen to be in conflict with other users of the maritime resources. The employment of limited licensing as a management tool to deal with such situations as an alternative to the classic approach of "management by legislated inefficiency", is a comparatively new concept in Queensland, and like many new concepts, is battling for acceptance.

I believe that opposition to the concept is largely based on ignorance of the principles behind what Garrett Hardin has called the "tragedy of the commons", and that this opposition has been reinforced by some practical mistakes in implementation associated with the first attempts at limited licensing here — mistakes such as giving Gulf of Carpentaria licensing entitlements to any operator who had fished the gulf previously, irrespective of the extent of his past participation or future intentions. This led to the formation of a large pool of unused fishing power which could be bought for a price and injected into the fishery, and thus create the very condition which the limited licence regime was trying to avoid.

Furthermore we in Queensland are in the unfortunate position that because we are one of the last states to limit licences, we tend to be saddled to a great extent with the additional problems associated with forcing people out of a fishery in which they are already engaged, rather than merely restricting further entry by outsiders; moreover, we have run out of alternate fisheries of similar type in which ejected units can be placed.

I do not believe that limited licensing is the "be all and end all" of fisheries management. It does create in some cases severe problems of practical implementation, and by creating a privileged group in the persons of the licence holders themselves, it raises some interesting questions of social ethics, for example, why would some participants at no cost to themselves be presented with a saleable commodity of considerable value? Should they pay for the original privilege and for the continuance thereof? Frank Meaney's discussion of the concept of economic rent may help in the resolution of these questions.

Summary of the Major Fisheries

The main Queensland fisheries may be summarized as follows:
(a) An intensive multispecies prawn fishery in the Gulf of Carpentaria, limited for a number of years past to a fleet of less than 300 vessels, which are nearly all large freezer craft over 17 metres in length. Operational strategy is being orientated more and more towards fleet operations dictated by the various processing companies who provide infrastructure and backup facilities in what is a harsh environment remote from normal urban communities.
(b) An east coast multispecies prawn fishery carried out by a heterogeneous offshore fleet of some 1,200 otter trawlers of varying sizes as well as a river fleet of several hundred small beam trawlers. The fishing pressure on the east coast has been greatly accelerated by vessels displaced from the closed gulf fishery under the terms of the vessel replacement policy governing that fishery.
(c) A set gill-net fishery which in the gulf rivers is orientated almost exclusively towards catching barramundi, and on the east coast towards catching a variety of estuarine fishes. Barramundi is a high-priced commercial commodity which is also of high significance to the sports-fishermen.
(d) River, estuary and beach fisheries using a variety of types of working nets. These fisheries are generally carried out by local

fishermen, are long established and stable, and because the target species are comparatively low-priced products, are not likely to pose management porblems of a type associated with an excessive influx of operators. However, some of them are at risk because of increasing loss or alienation of habitat through alternative use, or pollution, and some of them are in either real or imagined conflict with recreational fishing.

(e) Line fishing for pelagic and demersal "reef" fishes. Again the main management problem is the conflict situation between the professionals and an increasingly mobile recreational and quasi-commercial fishery.

The above is by no means an exhaustive list of our fisheries, but an important note is that most of them are tropical or subtropical multispecies fisheries for which the classical population dynamics models developed in the northern hemisphere appear to have little relevance.

Other Regimes Affecting Fisheries

Finally, I would like to mention two fairly recent developments which will affect fisheries management in Queensland waters to a greater and greater extent in the future. The first is the increasing involvement in fisheries management of the Great Barrier Reef Marine Park Authority, a regional planning body set up by the commonwealth government to ensure the wise use of the many and varied resources of the Barrier Reef region and the preservation of its unique features for the enjoyment of future generations.

The second is the special arrangements which will need to be made to ensure that fisheries management measures within Queensland territorial waters of the Torres Strait are complementary to and compatible with commonwealth arrangements to implement the recently signed Torres Strait Treaty between Australia and Papua New Guinea. The provisions of this treaty are complicated and probably unique in formal international agreements. They involve a sharing of the catch within an area called the "protected zone" in accordance with a rather complicated proportional formula which will be very difficult to apply except in very broad-brush terms. The paucity of past research effort, the lack of statistical data, and the difficulties of enforcement in such a remote and sparsely settled area, will undoubtedly make this regime a fisheries manager's nightmare.

6

Descriptive Statistics on Queensland Commercial Fisheries[1]

M. Williams

A Queensland survey of licensed master fishermen has revealed some interesting trends in the industry.

These trends, identified this year (1980) in the third annual survey of master fishermen[2] by the Queensland Fisheries Services, include increases in the number of trawl fishermen and scallop fishermen, and significant falls in the number of mud crab fishermen and reef fishermen (see table 1).

The survey referred to fishermen's operations during the 1980 calendar year. It showed that:

1. the number of otter trawl fishermen increased from 1,345 in 1979 to 1,459 in 1980;
2. scallop fishermen (also otter trawlermen) increased from 30 to 66;
3. mud crab fishermen dropped from 107 to 80; and reef fishermen dropped from 156 to 112.

Involvement in all other types of fishing was about the same, except for net fishing. (Types of netting operations were redefined slightly in the latest survey form.)

The combined total of beach seine, and set and drift netting categories had an overall decrease of 100 fishermen between 1979

Table 1 Estimated total numbers of primary fishermen in each fishery. Percentage of total number of master fishermen is given in brackets.

Type of fishing	1979		1980	
Otter trawling: prawns	1 345	(51.0)	1 459	(55.2)
Otter trawling: scallops	30	(1.1)	66	(2.5)
Beam trawling: prawns	102	(3.9)	103	(3.9)
Sand crabbing	63	(2.4)	65	(2.5)
Mud crabbing	107	(4.1)	80	(3.0)
Spanner crabbing	–	–	3	(0.1)
Reef fishing: mackerel	100	(3.8)	103	(3.9)
Reef fishing	156	(5.9)	112	(4.2)
Beach seining	315	(11.9)	129	(4.9)
Tunnel netting	39	(1.5)	36	(1.4)
Set or drift netting	337	(12.8)	429	(16.2)
Other types	41	(1.6)	57	(2.2)
Total	2 639		2 642	

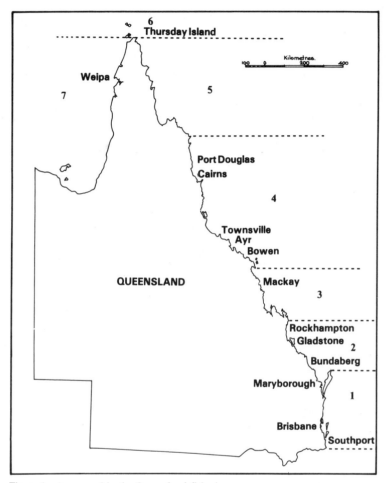

Figure 1   Areas used in the Queensland fisheries survey.

and 1980. This decrease in net fishermen may be related to the introduction of limited licensing in the net fisheries north of about Bundaberg (areas 2 to 7 — see figure 1) and/or a poor season in 1980.

Details of major changes in some fisheries are given below.

Otter Trawling

There has been a virtual explosion in the numbers of otter trawlers licensed to fish in waters around Queensland in the last few years.

About 700 trawlers were registered in 1975; currently some 1,400 trawlers are registered.

The increase in numbers of trawlers is naturally reflected in the increased numbers of master fishermen involved in trawling. In our first survey of fishing activities in 1978 some 42 per cent of fishermen were primarily engaged in otter trawling; in 1979 the figure was 51 per cent; and in 1980 it rose to 55 per cent.

The increase in boat numbers has led to greater competition for a limited resource – the prawn and otter trawl species stocks. This competition is seen in the greater use made of available time for trawling, in the greater use made of alternative fisheries, and in developments in gear technology.

In 1979 each trawlerman trawled, on average, for 8.6 months (± 3.5 months standard deviation) of the year, whereas in 1980 the average was 9.4 months (± 3.0 months standard deviation).

Unfortunately we do not have estimates of the actual hours or days trawled but the above averages indicate an increase of at least 9.3 per cent in the time spent trawling. If, as supposed, fishermen also trawl for longer hours each day than previously, this percentage increase is indeed an underestimate.

A greater percentage of trawlermen were working in each month of 1980 compared to the corresponding month of 1979, thus indicating that this greater fishing effort was spread over the whole year (figure 2).

More trawlermen are now making use of other fisheries than in previous years. In 1979 only 34.4 per cent of otter trawlermen were engaged in other types of fishing but in 1980 48.1 per cent did so. This increase was mainly due to more fishermen fishing for scallops as well as prawns.

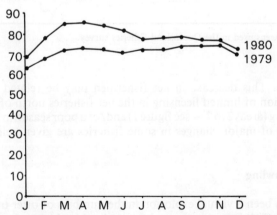

Figure 2   Percentage of total number of otter trawlermen working in each month.

In 1980 otter trawlermen also showed more interest in beam trawling and mackerel fishing than in previous years.

Although otter trawling for scallops in central Queensland is usually only a secondary fishery for prawn trawlermen, the number of fishermen who consider scallops their main target species is increasing. In 1979 the figure was only 30 but has jumped to 66. This is further evidence of a diversification of interests within the otter trawling fleet.

In the case of gear changes, the 1980 results indicate a trend towards towing more than two nets (table 2). The numbers of nets towed by trawlers follow regional patterns which have emerged strongly in the last few years. Triple gear is most commonly used in the relatively deep water prawn fisheries offshore from the Gold Coast and Mooloolaba (table 3). Four-net rigs are usually used in the Gulf of Carpentaria and to a lesser extent on the northeastern coast (Bowen to Cape York). In central Queensland, twin gear is the most common type.

Table 2 Numbers of nets towed by otter trawlers

No. of nets	% of sample in 1979	% of sample in 1980
1	10	5
2	59	46
3	24	37
4	7	12
5	1	0

Table 3 Numbers of nets usually towed according to port or region

| Port/Region | Percentage of trawlermen in each region | | | |
	1 net	2 nets	3 nets	4 nets
Gold Coast	13	8	79	0
Brisbane	3	61	33	3
North Coast	7	6	84	3
Tin Can Bay	0	59	41	0
Bundaberg to Rockhampton	11	62	26	1
Mackay	19	76	5	0
Bowen to Innisfail	3	53	27	9
Cairns to Cape York	0	63	12	25
Gulf of Carpentaria	0	16	0	84

Spanner Crabbing

This type of fishing was included for the first time in the 1980 survey, having begun only recently in southeastern Queensland from about Cape Moreton to Double Island Point.

Only 3 fishermen called this type of fishing their primary activity but about 50 master fishermen have engaged in this type of fishing to some extent.

Mud Crabbing

The numbers of fishermen primarily engaged in mud crabbing fell from 107 in 1979 to 80 in 1980. The major crabbing areas of Maryborough and Gladstone both lost fishermen — Maryborough fell from 20 to 9 and Gladstone from 38 to 22.

Also the numbers of fishermen of other types who were secondarily involved in mud crabbing — especially sand crabbers, reef fishermen and net fishermen — fell slightly in 1980. There appears to be a trend away from mud crabbing in the traditional major areas.

Reef Fishing

Whereas numbers of mackerel fishermen were unchanged in 1980, the numbers of reef fishermen dropped from 156 in 1979 to 112 in 1980.

The greatest changes were in area 1 (from 65 to 42), area 2 (26 to 13) and area 3 (31 to 22). The number of reef fishermen in area 4 remained unchanged at 34.

Other Fishing

Table 4 lists the types of fishing given under the heading "other". Shark fishing and fishing for rock lobsters (crayfish) were dominant among these categories.

Other Comments

In general the geographic distribution of fishing operations, the interdependence of certain types of fishing, and the mobility of fishermen in different fisheries had changed little since the previous surveys.

A summary of the distribution of fishermen of different types by area is given in table 5.

Table 4 Other types of fishing.

Type	No. of fishermen (primary, secondary, etc.)
Eels	1
Tuna	1
Trochus & pearl	1
Bugs	8
Bait	8
Shell dredging	1
Prawn stripe net	5
Oysters	2
Crayfish	22
Aquarium fish	6
Fish traps	4
Shark fishing	18
Sand worming	2
Marlin fishing	1
Fish trawling	2
Line fishing	1
Spear fishing	1

Table 5 Estimated numbers of primary fishermen by area of home port.

Type of Fishing	Otter trawling: prawns	Otter trawling: scallops	Beam trawling: prawns	Sand crabbing	Mud crabbing	Spanner crabbing	Reef fishing: mackerel	Reef fishing	Beach seining	Tunnel netting	Set & drift netting	Other	Total
Area 1	609	5	67	58	15	3	8	41	69	26	58	8	967
Area 2	149	61	25	6	45	0	12	13	16	8	61	10	406
Area 3	25	0	2	0	9	0	4	22	14	0	27	1	104
Area 4	535	0	9	0	11	0	72	34	25	2	147	16	851
Area 5	0	0	0	0	0	0	0	0	0	0	4	0	4
Area 6	4	0	0	0	0	0	4	2	2	0	0	22	34
Area 7	33	0	0	0	0	0	0	0	3	0	132	0	168
Interstate	104	0	0	1	0	0	3	0	0	0	0	0	108
Total	1 459	66	103	65	80	3	103	112	129	36	429	46	2642

Notes

1. Originally published in *Australian Fisheries* 40, 12, (Dec. 1981) under the title "Queensland Fisheries Survey Reveals Interesting Trends".
2. Although the term "fishermen" is generally used, there is an increasing number of women joining the fishing industry. At last count there were at least 23 women among the 2,642 licensed master fishermen in Queensland.

7

The Structure and Economics of Fish and Seafood Marketing in Queensland

M. Gray and S. Spencer

Marketing involves a wide variety of activities designed to move a commodity from producers to final consumers, and it can be considered from several different viewpoints. From the businessman's viewpoint, marketing involves the creative aspects of selling, promotion and other distributive functions. In contrast, the economist is more concerned about the manner in which marketing is organized, and the implications for its behaviour and performance.

Fish marketing in Queensland is a highly complex and competitive operation.[1] It encompasses a range of activities, including supply, handling, transport, storage, wholesaling, processing, distributing, importing, retailing and promotion. In a dynamic sense, these marketing functions cannot be divorced from interdependent factors such as fisheries research, the evaluation and management of fish resources, biological and ecological considerations, and the development of harvesting techniques and associated equipment.

However, this article has more limited horizons, and abstracts from these broader industry issues. It focuses attention purely on the structure and economics of fish marketing. What this entails is an examination of the development of the marketing structure, the supply of product, the participants, the institutions affecting the market and the exchange or price-making functions of the market. Here our concern is primarily with the marketing of fresh fish, although observations are made about the processing sector in view of its significance in the industry and its impact on the overall structure of fish marketing.

Current Structure of Fish Marketing in Queensland

The current (1981) structure of fish marketing in Queensland was reviewed in the two reports of the Committee of Inquiry,[2] and is summarized in figure 1.

At the heart of the current structure of fish marketing is the concept of "orderly marketing". Since 1936, orderly marketing has been pursued through the operations of the Queensland Fish Board, a statutory marketing authority which is currently constituted under the provisions of the "Fish Supply Management Act 1972-1976".

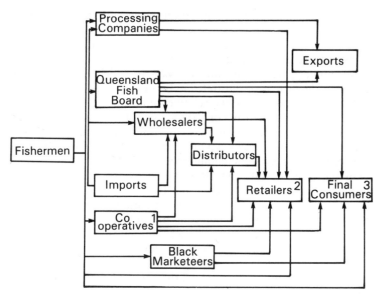

Figure 1 Structure of fish marketing in Queensland
1 Mooloolaba and Sandgate cooperatives.
2 Includes fish shops, fish vendors, supermarkets, hotels, clubs, restaurants, etc.
3 Local and interstate.

Under this Act, the Fish Board is responsible for the management and control of the supply and marketing of fish through the state. Marine produce landed and intended for sale in an area nominated as a fish supply district must be delivered to the Fish Board for inspection and sale, unless exemption from these compulsory marketing provisions is granted by the board. Generally, exemption is not granted for the sale of edible fish in areas adjacent to a board market or depot.

The Fish Board has had a virtual monopoly position in the marketing of fish in Queensland for many years. However, in recent years, the board's compulsory marketing powers have been eroded in a number of ways:
1. the board's powers relate only to fish harvested and sold in Queensland. The board does not have control over Queensland product destined for sale on interstate or export markets. This has enabled a number of companies to establish operations in Queensland, especially companies processing prawns for the export market and wholesalers buying product for interstate trade. Similarly, the board has no control over interstate or overseas product intended for sale in Queensland;
2. the board has granted permits of exemption in certain cases. For example, the Sandgate and Mooloolaba cooperatives hold

permits of exemption to sell certain species of fish through retail premises;
3. a large and lucrative black market has emerged to bypass the board's receival and handling procedures.

In summary, there is a range of ways in which fishermen may dispose of their catch, as illustrated in figure 1. It is difficult to obtain an accurate assessment of the relative importance of each of these marketing avenues. Statistics on the total size of the Queensland catch tend to be unreliable, because they do not include the substantial quantities of fish taken by amateur or recreational fishermen and unrecorded sales by some commercial fishermen.

On the basis of information supplied by the Fish Board, the Committee of Inquiry estimated that the board receives almost 70 per cent of the total commercial catch of fresh fish (finned fish and fish fillets) and about 20 per cent of the total prawn catch in Queensland. These figures represent the most reliable official information, although private sources claim that they overstate the board's market shares. For example, it is claimed that the board receives only about 50 per cent of the catch of fresh fish.

Queensland Fish Board

The powers and functions of the Fish Board are defined by the Fish Supply Management Act. Its powers are divided into three broad categories: general powers relating to the actual business operations of the board; financial and borrowing powers; and regulatory powers relating to the supply and marketing of fish (including such matters as licences, buying and selling, health and its inspectorial role).

As stated earlier, the provisions of the Fish Supply Management Act require all product caught and intended for sale in Queensland to be delivered to the board. The board then has the power to direct the manner of sale. It is not compelled to accept (purchase) all product. It can instruct that product be sold on consignment at a board-operated auction or can issue a permit of exemption for product to be sold privately. In this sense, the board's powers differ slightly from other Queensland marketing boards constituted under the Primary Producers' Organisation and Marketing Act which have powers of compulsory acquisition and are required to accept all product delivered to them.

The board can also exercise some indirect influence over the supply of product. For example, it can set lower prices for lower quality product and it can conduct education programmes to encourage fishermen to improve the quality of their product through better handling and storage practices. It can also actively discourage the taking of small fish and crustaceans, for example by refusing to purchase such product. The Committee of Inquiry recommended that there be prohibitions on the marketing of juvenile or immature product such as prawns and scallops.

Apart from product purchased for processing, the board disposes of product either through the auction system or by trading, that is, purchasing product from fishermen at a firm net price and then reselling at either the wholesale or retail level. The board has estimated that about 70 per cent of its intake of wet fish and cooked prawns is now marketing on a trading basis.

All persons buying fish at an auction conducted by the board must be the holder of a buyer's licence issued by the board. At present, there are about 1,200 buyers licensed to operate at the board's (1981) markets, including 431 for the metropolitan market at Colmslie. However, in practice the number of buyers who regularly attend auctions are considerably smaller.

Three main buyer groups operate at the Colmslie auction — wholesalers, vendors (or hawkers) and retail shopkeepers and restauranteurs. While there are no accurate figures available, the board estimates that the wholesalers and retailers each take about 40 per cent of the product from the auction floor, and the vendors take the other 20 per cent. Fish vendors have represented a declining share of the marketing chain in recent years, particularly with the growth of supermarkets. However, somewhat of a resurgence in the number of vendors, and in their activities, has been in evidence on the auction floor at Colmslie in the last 12 to 18 months.

The board has some general powers with respect to pricing and establishes buying prices for product based on its perceptions of market conditions. It also has scope to implement particular schemes to support prices. For example, it has operated a price stabilization scheme for mackerel in north Queensland. It also has provision to operate minimum price schemes on the auction floor at Colmslie for the principal species of finned fish, i.e., mullet and tailor. In addition, there is a market support scheme which can operate on a day-to-day basis for prawns and fish not covered by predetermined minimum price schemes.

In its trading operations, the board has a direct involvement in determining both buying and selling prices. By paying fishermen a firm net price and removing the uncertainty of auctions, trading allows the board far more flexibility in its approach to marketing and increases its ability to monitor and control the market by adjusting the volumes supplied at various times and places.

The board's entry into retailing in 1973-74 is an extension of its trading operations. The board now (1981) operates retail outlets at 15 of its depots along the coast. However, there has been opposition from some private retailers who claim that the board represents "unfair competition" because it is not applying full retail margins.

With respect to processed product, the board is largely a price taker. The relationships between buying prices and selling prices is complex, and selling prices are largely outside the control of the board and other processors. They are determined in export markets such as Japan, and are influenced by economic conditions in those markets as well as international factors such as exchange rate fluctuations. In setting its buying prices for raw product, the board takes into account these export market prospects as well as the costs of processing, recovery rates and overheads.

Private Processors

Private processing companies were established originally to take advantage of the opportunities to export frozen prawns to Japan. However, there is now a trend towards greater product and market diversification in an attempt to spread the risks otherwise associated with the collapse of a critical market. In addition, some companies are developing new product lines based on the processing of supplies which are surplus to the requirements of the fresh fish market, for example, vacuum packed whole fish or fillets of mullet, tailor, mackerel, barramundi, reef fish, and so forth.

A survey conducted by the Commonwealth Department of Primary Industry in 1980 identified 16 land-based processing plants in Queensland, of which 5 were based in metropolitan areas and 11 in nonmetropolitan areas. (This includes the Fish Board's plants at Colmslie and Townsville.) There are few barriers to entry and exit from the processing sector, and there has been considerable turnover in the number, ownership and type of private processing facilities in the last 10 years.

The Committee of Inquiry experienced considerable difficulty in assessing the relative shares of fish supplies handled by private processors, the Fish Board and nonprocessing wholesalers and distributors. Private processors hold the vast majority of licences to fish in the Gulf of Carpentaria, which is the largest single source of prawns in Australia. The board's share of the intake in the gulf is considerably less than 1 per cent. It is estimated that private processors received in the vicinity of 60 per cent of the total Queensland prawn catch and a minor but increasing percentage of the fish catch.

Private companies have generally outperformed the board in processing operations, because their access to a more regular supply of quality dry product from their own catcher-freezer vessels has enabled them to exert greater control over recovery rates and processing costs. However, it was not only the board which was adversely affected by the collapse of demand and prices in the Japanese market at the end of 1979. Certain private processors suffered serious financial setbacks, and in some cases their longer term viability remains in doubt. In addition to the inherent uncertainty and instability of export markets, the high level of investment required for fleet operations and the high operating costs mean that there are significant risks involved in private processing operations.

Wholesalers

Wholesalers are a diverse group of operators, and they are very difficult to identify. There are no current official statistics on their activities, as the last census of wholesale establishments was conducted by the Australian Bureau of Statistics in 1968-69. The three main groups of wholesalers are interstate traders, secondary wholesalers (that is, wholesalers who hold licences to purchase product from the Fish Board's auctions), and black market operators.

According to Fish Board estimates provided for the Committee of Inquiry, wholesalers obtain about 25 per cent of the wet fish intake, and about 15 per cent of the prawn intake in Queensland. Other sources in the fishing industry suggest that the leakage of product to wholesalers is much higher than is claimed by the board, and that in general, wholesalers receive about the same volume of product (both wet fish and prawns) as the board. (These estimates include the activities of black market operators who will be considered further in the next subsection.)

The cooperatives at Sandgate and Mooloolaba are involved in interstate trading, and they also supply product to processors. In addition, they are permitted by the Fish Board to conduct retail sales from their premises. The cooperatives were established largely as a result of dissatisfaction with existing marketing arrangements provided by the board and a desire by fishermen to find alternative avenues for marketing their product.

Estimates from the board suggest that the cooperatives receive respectively about 60 per cent of the product at Sandgate and about 25 per cent of the product at Mooloolaba where there is a very large fleet. Since those estimates were compiled, the market shares of the cooperatives have been increasing.

The Black Market

In the black market goods are bought and/or sold illegally by operators who violate an established set of regulations or restrictions, such as the Fish Supply Management Act. The emergence of an extensive black market for fish in Queensland reflects widespread dissatisfaction with the Fish Board's marketing performance and a desire by fishermen to obtain a better price for their product.

In fact, fishermen are often offered less than the ruling market price by black market operators, yet receive a better return, because they do not have to pay the board's commission for handling and storage. The other attraction of the black market is that most transactions are for cash. This enables fishermen to meet immediate commitments such as wages for crew and also offers scope to evade tax liabilities if the transaction is not declared as taxable income.

As illustrated diagrammatically in figure 1, the black market operates in a number of ways:

1. by fishermen selling direct to the general public, usually from their boats;
2. by fishermen supplying retailers such as hotels, sporting clubs and restaurants in their local areas;
3. by hawkers who purchase product direct from fishermen and supply catering and retail outlets, or sell direct to consumers from their vans;
4. by traders who purchase product ostensibly for interstate sale but who in fact channel the product to outlets in Queensland.

The black market is now firmly established in most fishing ports, but is particularly prevalent at places such as Cairns, Townsville, Rockhampton, Bundaberg, Scarborough and the Gold Coast. The extent of the black market is difficult to gauge, but is estimated to represent as much as 80 per cent of the prawn catch at Southport and as much as 50 per cent of the total Queensland catch of fish and prawns.

It is argued that action should be taken to combat the black market by employing more inspectors, strict enforcement of the legislation, convictions for breaches of the Act, and heavier penalties. There may be some deterrent value in such action. However, apart from being costly and cumbersome, it is unlikely to be very effective while disenchantment with existing marketing channels persists. This suggests that there is a need for the Fish Board to provide a better marketing service to fishermen, and for fishermen to be offered a choice of "legal" marketing alternatives, or both. This issue will be explored further in later sections of the paper.

Distributors

Several major fish distributing companies operate in Queensland, and supply a wide range of products for subsequent retail sale or for use in catering-type operations. Unlike the wholesalers of local fish, these companies rely mainly on imported product and in effect act as import agents as well as distributors.

Distributors generally have only limited contact with the Fish Board. There are occasions when they purchase local frozen fish fillets from the board to supplement imported supplies. In most cases, they rely on established outlets for the distribution of their product to supermarkets, takeaway food stores and restaurants. Apart from fish products, they also handle a wide range of other precooked frozen foods.

There is a lack of concrete evidence on the relative importance of imports in the marketing of fish in Queensland. However, some broad indications can be obtained from an assessment of the Australian situation contained in a report on the "Fisheries and Fish Processing Industry" by the Industries Assistance Commission.[3]

The report estimated that imports accounted for about 55 per cent of total Australian market supplies of fresh and frozen fish in 1976-77. The report observed that the domestic industry supplied the bulk of fresh fish consumed but that the bulk of retail sales of prepackaged fish fillets and fish fingers was met from imports. In the case of canned or preserved fish, it was estimated that some 75 per cent of total Australian market supplies was met by imports in 1976-77. However, imports of crustaceans and molluscs accounted for only a very small proportion of Australian consumption.

Distributing companies have played an important role in the market in that they have filled a void by supplying the type of product required by supermarkets, fast food outlets and the catering trade. In so doing, they not only meet consumer demands but also ensure continuity of supply, and in these respects have undoubtedly contributed to a greater consumer awareness of fish as a convenience food.

It is anticipated that the recent tendency for increasing amounts of fish to be sold through supermarkets will continue. In these circumstances, imports remain a challenge to Queensland fishermen and to marketeers of Queensland fish to become more active and competitive in this segment of the market.

Retailers

The retailing sector of fish marketing is also diverse and fragmented, embracing private individuals, small businesses and large companies as well as the Fish Board. It includes the traditional "fish and chip" shop, specialist fish outlets, fish vendors, supermarkets, hotels, clubs and restaurants. As with wholesalers, there are no current official statistics on the activities of retailers. The last census of retail establishments was conducted by the Australian Bureau of Statistics in 1973-74.

In the past, local "fish and chip" shops handled a large percentage of the retail sales of fish. More recently, there has been a tendency for fresh fish to be sold through specialist fish outlets. Whereas many of the more traditional fish retailers also conducted mixed businesses, the specialist shops concentrate totally on fish products. They rely heavily on obtaining fresh supplies on a daily basis, in contrast to the traditional retailer who also sold a range of frozen imported fish.

As shown in figure 1, retailers may obtain their supplies from a wide variety of sources. The source will generally vary according to the type of retailer. For example, restaurants and retailers who sell fresh fish generally obtain their supplies from wholesalers or distributors, or they may hold buyer's licences to purchase directly at Fish Board auctions. It is understood that at least some restaurants and many hotels and clubs buy heavily on the black market. In general, frozen fish and tinned and canned seafood tends to be retailed through supermarkets and supplied by processing companies or, in the case of imported product, by import agents (that is, distributors).

The Role of Government Intervention

Against the background of the current marketing structure and the problems faced by the Fish Board, the remainder of this paper evaluates the role of government intervention in the marketing of fish in Queensland.

The cornerstone of the current structure of fish marketing is the concept of "orderly marketing". Orderly marketing has the connotation of being inherently "good" because it implies the elimination of any instability or disorganization in the system. However, this is a rather naive interpretation. In its broadest sense, orderly marketing can be interpreted as any interventionist policy for the pricing and marketing of a product.

With respect to agricultural products in Queensland and in other states, orderly marketing has generally been used to describe the creation of producer-controlled or producer-dominated marketing boards, or statutory marketing authorities, with monopoly powers to regulate and perform marketing and pricing functions. A statutory marketing authority has been defined as a "statutory body with producer representation whose purposive intent of regulating the marketing of the primary product for which the body is constituted is backed by legal powers of compulsion".[4]

As at June 1979, there were 69 marketing boards in Australia. Descriptive studies of Australian statutory marketing authorities have concentrated on institutional features such as: identification of the statutory basis of the authority; composition, method of appointment and tenure of the authority's governing body; management and staff; method of operation; general powers; marketing powers; licensing powers; financial aspects; and the autonomy from and extent of state responsibility as evidenced by the role of the minister and the governor-general or governor in council. The focus of this article is the structural and economic implications of the marketing and pricing powers of these statutory authorities.

The monopoly position enjoyed by the Fish Board has been gradually eroded over time, undermining the effectiveness of the orderly marketing of fish in Queensland. The Committee of Inquiry's recommendations are directed towards strengthening the marketing performance and commercial viability of the board within the existing marketing structure. This highlights a dilemma for the board. In essence, it is caught in a no-win situation.

On one hand, the board has been criticized and berated by fishermen and by the Committee of Inquiry for being backward, negative and passive in its marketing policies. It has been used as a dumping ground for poor quality product which could not be sold elsewhere, and has been regarded as a welfare agency which should pay fishermen the price they expect for their product irrespective of quality or prevailing market conditions.

On the other hand, the board is seen by private companies as "unfair competition" because it is a government agency with "special privileges". It is tolerated by companies so long as it remains passive and does not disturb their market shares or opportunities. There are loud protests if it shows signs of becoming positive, aggressive or innovative because it then poses a threat to their trading operations.

The Fish Board is at the crossroads in attempting to resolve this dilemma, to achieve commercial viability, and to justify its role within the industry structure. A number of fundamental questions remain unanswered. Should marketing legislation be strengthened to enable a tightly regulated system of orderly marketing to be restored? Or should there be a greater degree of flexibility and competition in the marketing structure, by recognizing the existence and importance of private traders?

At a more basic level, what role should the government play in shaping the structure of fish marketing in Queensland? Should there be direct intervention in the form of a central marketing authority which trades on behalf of fishermen, or should the government limit its involvement to providing a stable environment (for example, health, hygiene, handling regulations) within which private enterprise is responsible for the actual marketing functions?

Government intervention through the establishment of marketing boards has generally been justified on the basis of factors such as the need to prevent profiteering by middlemen and to provide a countervailing power to protect individual producers from the bargaining strength of a small group of large buyers. With respect to agricultural marketing, it is also argued that competition as a mechanism works unevenly in matching demand and supply at a reasonable stable price level and that a marketing board is necessary to overcome this imbalance. Given these motivations, the primary objectives of marketing boards appear to have been to stabilize and increase returns to producers.

However, the ability of a board to stabilize and improve the returns to producers depends to a large extent on the nature of the product and its market, for example, the price elasticity of demand, competition on the local market (from interstate or imported goods), competition in export markets and competition from substitute products. Moreover, the establishment of a board to pursue such objectives may not produce an efficient marketing system, in terms of either resource use or effects on consumers.

Accordingly, the following presents a range of four alternative structures which could be adopted for fish marketing in Queensland, and assesses the advantages and disadvantages of each option. The marketing structures reflect varying degrees of government intervention and are defined and discussed in terms of four basic characteristics, namely, control over supply of product; trading powers; pricing powers; and other regulatory powers.

Options for Intervention

Central Marketing Authority, with Sole Trading Powers

For some agricultural products, orderly marketing has become synonymous with "demand-supply management". Demand-supply management is orderly marketing in its most rigid and regulated form and is generally achieved through a central marketing authority with sole trading powers. In reality, demand-supply management is a misnomer because no industry, board or government can control demand. Demand is a phenomenon which is ultimately in the hands of consumers although of course producers and producer organizations may seek to influence—with varying degrees of success—the nature and level of demand.

Demand-supply management should be renamed supply-price management because it is these two factors which are generally subject to control by marketing authorities. Supply is subject to control through powers of compulsory acquisition of the output of an industry and this provides the key to control over the price of that output. In effect, the concept of orderly marketing is translated into the legislative backing for marketing authorities to act as monopsonists and monopolists.

In its purest form, demand-supply management implies sole control over supply, trading and pricing of a product, coupled with other regulatory powers and the legal sanctions to enforce its powers. These powers are most readily executed for a product which is largely homogeneous and is not subject to large unanticipated fluctuations in production, for example due to seasonal factors. One of the closest examples of this form of demand-supply management would be the Egg Marketing Board which broadly has these sole powers with respect to the marketing of eggs within its defined region of southeast Queensland.

The pressures for the introduction of demand-supply management schemes generally occur in circumstances where production is in excess of demand requirements at reasonable prices to the producer. It follows that the formulation of a demand-supply management scheme involves consideration of the need to limit supply, both in regard to total production and the output of individual producers, rather than simply regulate the supply of product to the market. Direct control of production can be exerted through licensing, zoning or quota measures which physically define the quantity to be produced or sold.

The major advantages advanced for such controls are the maintenance of a relatively stable supply within the limits of normal seasonal fluctuations, a reasonably stable price to consumers, and a higher and more stable income for producers. In addition, there may be an improvement in product quality where quotas are fixed in terms of the quantity which may be produced or marketed.

On the other hand, there are a number of disadvantages associated with these controls. Firstly, difficulties can arise in determining individual production levels for producers and in restricting the entry of new producers. Secondly, there can be a tendency to maintain less efficient producers in an industry. Thirdly, rigidities can develop in the industry with a consequent failure to adapt to changing needs and circumstances. Fourthly, quotas or licences tend to acquire a scarcity value which accrues to producers in the form of an economic rent. Finally, there is a problem in striking a balance between producer and consumer welfare.

In the fishing industry, the range of species, the spread of fishing grounds and the wide variability in seasonal catches all militate against the efficacy of production controls. There are a number of traditional forms of fisheries management which provide partial control on production, for example closed seasons, restrictions on the types and sizes of fish which may be caught, bag limits, boat length restrictions and gear restrictions. However, these measures have been directed primarily towards the biological objective of conserving fish stocks.

More recently, resource management has been concerned with not only the biological objective but also economic objectives such as ensuring the maximum economic return is obtained from a fishery and providing a more equitable distribution of income among fishermen. As a result, measures such as limited entry licence schemes have been introduced for some fisheries, for example in the Gulf of Carpentaria.

There are many aspects to fisheries management and they will all be discussed extensively at this conference. From a marketing viewpoint, measures such as limited entry schemes, zoning and quotas would provide only a partial and piecemeal element of any demand-supply management scheme because the characteristics of the fishing industry limit their applicability. Moreover, from a broader economic viewpoint, strict controls over production are of questionable long-term benefit and could result in a complex, inflexible and overbearing regime of rules and regulations which stifle enterprise in the industry.

Price control by a cental marketing authority may take a number of forms: for example, price support schemes, equalization schemes, stabilization schemes or direct price fixing. Price fixing represents one of the most serious intrusions into the operations of the market as prices are determined by administration rather than by the interaction of demand and supply forces. However, it is often seen by producers as the most effective way of ensuring a "fair" return for their product, that is, a return which will meet their average costs of production. It is also seen as a way to overcome the inability of the market to match demand and supply at a reasonably stable price level.

Prices may be fixed in terms of a minimum price, a maximum price, a combination of both, or an absolute price. There are difficulties in determining the level at which an administered price should be set. A popular method is to use a costs of production formula. However, there are many conceptual and practical problems which limit the relevance and applicability of this method. Moreover, the demand elasticities for some products are such that price increases based on a costs of production formula can reduce total returns to an industry. In other words, the decline in consumption due to the higher price outweighs the increase in unit profit of the product.

At a broader level, administered prices can distort the signals occurring in the market place. The role of a price is to equate demand and supply conditions in the market. If the price is set too low, shortages can occur because production is discouraged while demand is encouraged. Conversely, if the price is set too high, overproduction can occur because additional production is encouraged while demand is discouraged. In the longer term, this can have serious repercussions for the nature and pattern of production and resource use in an industry, and for the price which consumers are forced to pay.

Preliminary results of a study of fish prices at the Colmslie auction confirm the intuitive feeling that price elasticities of demand for most fish species are relatively high. Price elasticities of demand for six selected species — mullet, whiting, mackerel, snapper, sand crabs and mud crabs — ranged from about 3 to 7 in negative terms, indicating the extent to which quantity demanded (at a wholesale level) responds inversely to small changes in fish prices.[5]

Other studies of fish consumption have shown that consumers tend to be price conscious, particularly with respect to fresh fish.[6] The highly competitive nature of the market is reinforced by the range of species and the range of alternative and substitute products available. In these circumstances, price fixing to cover costs of production and increase returns to producers could be counterproductive by encouraging consumers to switch to alternative species, to product imported from interstate or overseas, or to substitute products such as meat and poultry.

Price support schemes allow greater flexibility than direct price fixing, and can be effected in several ways. For example, the marketing authority may actively operate in the market place when prices fall below a predetermined level. Alternatively, the marketing authority may simply undertake to receive from producers all of their output which is not sold at a specified minimum price or range of grade prices.

One of the major problems with price support schemes is that there is a tendency for large unsold stocks to accumulate in the hands of the marketing authority. Frequently these stocks consists of lower quality product and their mere existence can place downward pressure on the market. The accumulation of large stocks can also place considerable financial strain on the authority. For this reason, price support schemes should be financed separately, and should not be a liability on the normal commercial activities of the authority.

The ultimate disposal of stocks presents additional problems, since their release on to the market at any time can depress prices. Furthermore, trends in demand are notoriously difficult to predict. For example, if a downward trend in demand is misinterpreted as a short-term fluctuation, the disposal of stocks can be made more difficult at a later date as the market continues to fall.

Price support schemes of the type employed by the Fish Board can work effectively, provided they are used merely to iron out short-term fluctuations and unduly large stocks are not allowed to build up. Under such circumstances, stocks should be well spread over the quality range and should not be allowed to reach a level higher than is necessary to cope with normal seasonal fluctuations in supply. In its pricing policies, the Fish Board must ultimately have regard to the extent of product competition and substitution in the market.

In a demand-supply management scheme, the role of the central marketing authority is to provide the mechanism for relating production and price to the demand for the product. This role usually extends to sole responsibility for physical handling and trading the product through powers of compulsory acquisition. However, there are cases where this does not happen, for example, the Queensland

Milk Board regulates the supply and price of market milk in southeast Queensland but does not actually perform any trading functions.

Sole trading powers prohibit the existence of private traders, and therefore restrict the choices available to producers in selling their product and consumers in buying the product. Moreover, there is an absence of competitive pressures to ensure that excessive marketing costs are not imposed. Where there are limitations to economic freedom and initiative, black markets can arise to circumvent sole trading powers. The extent of the black market in the fishing industry in Queensland illustrates this point.

In conjunction with their powers with respect to production, pricing and trading, marketing authorities also perform a general regulatory role embracing matters such as health and hygiene standards, packing and grading standards, registration obligations, licensing requirements and delivery requirements to name but a few. All the coercive powers of marketing authorities are established and enforced by legislation which includes inspectorial or policing functions and other legal sanctions (for example, to combat black market trading). There are numerous cases where marketing authorities have taken legal actions against "renegade" producers who have attempted to by-pass restrictive or oppressive marketing requirements.[7] Indeed, a board can sometimes become more concerned about its regulatory powers than its marketing functions. This criticism was levelled at the Fish Board by the Committee of Inquiry.

Central Marketing Authority with Cooperatives

An alternative approach to the concept of orderly marketing is to retain a statutory authority with centralized marketing powers but to decentralize the marketing functions through a network of local cooperatives. The primary example of this type of marketing structure is the New South Wales Fish Marketing Authority (FMA).

The FMA has overall responsibility for the conduct and management of fish marketing in New South Wales. The formal structure of fish marketing is shown in figure 2. Under legislation passed in 1963, the FMA is empowered to establish and maintain markets for the sale of fish and to arrange for the sale of fish on behalf of the fishermen or other persons. While the FMA administers the regulations relating to the marketing of all fish in New South Wales, its direct involvement in the market is limited primarily to the operation of the auction at the Sydney fish markets.

In New South Wales, only licensed professional fishermen may catch fish intended for sale. With few exceptions, this product must be sold through registered markets — either the Sydney fish market operated by the FMA or a fishermen's cooperative. Where there is

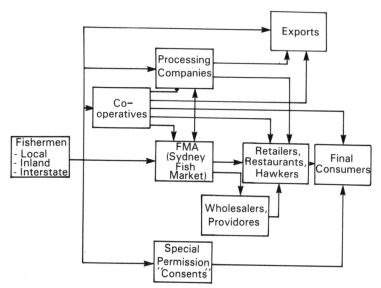

Figure 2   The formal marketing structure for fish in New South Wales.

no local cooperative, fishermen may apply for a consent to sell directly to the public.[8] Fishermen may also deliver product to private companies for canning, processing, and so forth.

In practice, the FMA has taken a low-key approach to its regulatory powers, and there has been a de facto devolution of these powers to the cooperatives which in turn have not been concerned to enforce provisions relating to the delivery of fish. As a consequence, there is considerable "black market" trading outside the formal marketing structure at local ports.

Twenty of the 34 registered fishermen's cooperatives in Australia are located in New South Wales, ranging along the coast from Bermagui to Brunswick Heads. Some cooperatives are merely small packing houses catering for a few fishermen, while others are large modern factories with processing facilities and serve a large number of members. About 60 to 70 per cent of the wholesale value of fish handled by cooperatives is sent to the FMA for sale at the Sydney fish market.[9] The remainder is disposed of in the local area, interstate or overseas. For example, some cooperatives operate their own retail outlets, provide local traders with fish products and process products such as frozen fillets.

All fish that cooperatives send into the County of Cumberland (Sydney metropolitan area) must be sold through the Sydney fish market. This is designed to prevent private sales by some cooperatives undermining the auction system and effectively precludes private trading outside the formal marketing chain established by the FMA. However, certain exemptions are granted for processed fish products (for example, packets of frozen fillets) which can be sold by cooperatives directly to Sydney wholesalers without substantially affecting fresh fish prices at auction.

The Sydney fish market handles approximately 65 per cent of all fish caught by New South Wales fishermen. Of this amount, about 85 per cent is received from the various cooperatives. A further 10 per cent is received directly from individual fishermen, including those in the Sydney Harbour fleet. In addition, the market receives supplies from interstate sellers.[10]

The FMA operates as a trading organization deriving its revenue from commissions on the sale of fish at the Sydney fish market complex and from rents. About 90 per cent of the fish delivered to the FMA is sold at auction, the remainder being sold on consignment or by private treaty. There are about 600 registered buyers for the auction, including wholesalers, providores (supplying supermarkets), retail shopkeepers, hawkers, restauranteurs and even individuals who wish to purchase a full container of fish at a wholesale price. It is estimated that about 60 per cent of the buyers are retailers purchasing product on their own behalf. However, the largest volume of product is handled by wholesalers, some of whom have their own retail outlets.[11]

The commission charged by the FMA varies according to the species of fish. In 1977-78, the average rate of commission was 9.6 per cent. Cooperatives also deduct handling, storage and cartage charges before the net return to fishermen is determined.

Unlike the Fish Board, the FMA is not involved in processing operations. Fish processing in New South Wales is totally in the hands of private enterprise and has a much broader base in terms of the species which are used for processing; for example, there is greater processing of molluscs (mainly oysters) and finfish, as well as processing of crustaceans.

The FMA has no pricing powers, and prices are determined largely by the interaction of supply and demand on the auction floor. The auction system is a traditional form of fish marketing throughout the world. An auction serves as a barometer of current marketing conditions. It provides a central location where information on demand and supply can be brought together and a price-making mechanism which permits the rapid and equitable transfer of product. It is also a highly efficient form of market for a product which is perishable, heterogeneous, and highly variable in terms of both quantity and quality. This is because it enables product to be displayed for inspection and selection by potential buyers and facilitates the formation of price differentials based on quality, species, quantity and size.

Criticism of auction systems such as those operated at both the Sydney and Brisbane fish markets invariably relates to allegations of collusion between buyers, and fluctuations in prices, especially during glut periods, leading to instability in the incomes of fishermen. Other criticisms generally cover procedural matters such as the handling and storage of product and the manner in which the auction is conducted.

In economic theory, a competitive market is one where neither the individual buyer nor seller can influence the price of the product. This theoretical norm is seldom encountered in reality, and is rarer yet in markets for perishable products. Because he has to sell his product as soon as possible, the owner of a perishable product is at a disadvantage relative to the potential buyer.

Collusion between buyers tends to occur in all auction markets, but it is more likely to occur where there is a small number of large buyers who are able to keep the price down or force the price up when they wish to limit competition. It is always difficult to substantiate allegations of collusion and even more difficult to apply preventive measures.

However, the existence of alternative markets for the products usually implies relatively more bargaining power for the sellers and thus the impact of any collusion on the part of the buyers can be lessened. It is not necessary that all fish should pass through the auction. It is only necessary that a sufficient quantity of fish flows through the auction to provide a guide to ruling market conditions and prices. The problems encountered with the auction system are among the reasons the Fish Board is moving more towards a system of direct purchasing and trading in fish at a firm net price. Nevertheless, an auction remains one of the most efficient methods of marketing fish, and it is envisaged that the Colmslie auction will continue.

Fluctuation in prices and incomes are an inherent feature in an industry where there are large seasonal variations in supply. However, the effects are not always deleterious. While fishermen may be disadvantaged by low prices during gluts, they may benefit handsomely from high prices during shortages.

As noted already, various support schemes can be employed to dampen fluctuations in prices. The FMA does not intervene in price-setting procedures (although it may authorize sales of fish to acceptable buyers at agreed prices). In such circumstances, the problems associated with gluts and depressed prices can be reduced by measures such as the redirection of surplus stocks for use as frozen or smoked fillets. In times of heavy supply, the FMA (in liaison with suppliers) has directed supplies of fish away from the Sydney fish market to processing factories to avoid wasteful gluts. In times of short supply, the FMA may also liaise with processors to obtain stocks of processed fish to ease the shortage.

The FMA has tended to place emphasis on its marketing functions rather than its regulatory powers. It performs a vital role in matching buyers and sellers and is heavily involved in promotion and coordination within the industry. For example, it has a market development and sales promotion division which is responsible for finding new markets, conducting advertising and sales promotion campaigns for the industry, and producing posters, booklets and recipe cards. The FMA also provides retail facilities at the Sydney fish market which are leased to private operators.

Central Marketing Authority, with Competition

The basis of this option is the retention of a central marketing authority, but in a more flexible and less regulated environment, in which competition from private traders is permitted. Within this framework, the marketing authority would have little, if any, control over supply, but would have certain powers with respect to pricing and trading and would be vested with overall responsibility for industry coordination and regulation.

The best example in Queensland of a central marketing authority with competition is the Committee of Direction of Fruit Marketing (COD), established under the Fruit Marketing Organization Acts 1923 to 1964. In fact, the COD provides a highly relevant model worthy of closer scrutiny because of the strong similarities between the characteristics of the fruit and vegetable industry and the fishing industry—in both cases, the output is perishable, with a large number of varieties or species, large seasonal fluctuations in supply, volatile prices and the scope for processing surplus supplies.

The COD is cooperative in principle and in its mode of operation, although it is not registered under legislation as a cooperative business. Its activities include grower representation and trading activities. Grower representation embraces liaison with government, promotion, education, research and any other matters of general relevance to the industry, and is financed by a levy on all growers. Trading activities are financed on a "user pays" basis, and include wholesale and retail trade, processing, exporting, transport services, packing and prepacking, cool storage, container exchange, merchandise sales, country order sales and road distribution service.

The structure of the COD consists of local associations of fruit and vegetable growers, six sectional group committees and an executive committee. The sectional group committees represent the growers of bananas, pineapples, citrus, deciduous fruits, other fruits, and vegetables.[12] These committees have full policy-forming powers for their respective commodity or commodities, but no administrative authority. The executive committee is responsible for implementing the policies formulated by the sectional group committees, and administering the grower representation and trading activities of the COD.

The COD does not normally have any powers of compulsory acquisition. In most circumstances, growers are free to choose whether they send their product to the COD or to other agents (for sale on consignment) or merchants (who purchase product at a firm net price for resale). Prices realized for fruit and vegetables are determined by their quality and the demand on the market to which they are consigned. Realizations are not pooled as is the practice adopted by many marketing boards.

However, there are isolated cases where fruit and vegetables are subject to certain Directions. A direction is a piece of marketing legislation prepared by the COD in accordance with policy determined by one or more of the sectional group committees. By means of a direction, the COD may exercise statutory control over a particular fruit or vegetable with the object of having the whole of that fruit or vegetable which growers voluntarily offer for sale, for processing or on the fresh market in Queensland, handled and dealt with only under the instructions and with the authority of the COD.[13]

There is considerable flexibility in the nature and scope of a direction. It can cover all or part of a product, all or part of Queensland, the complete marketing of a product or only certain functions of such marketing (for example, processing) and it can incorporate provisions with respect to price (for example, a minimum or reserve price).

There are three types of directions:
1. factory directions, where fruit and/or vegetables for processing must be sold through COD;
2. fresh fruit directions, which regulate the flow of fruit and vegetables onto the fresh fruit market;
3. contract directions, concerning direct grower-processor contracts where the COD approves of the form of contract, including the price to be paid to growers.

The first type of direction relates to the directing of surplus supplies of product to factories, and has been rarely used in recent years. The second type of direction is designed to regulate heavily supplied markets by prohibiting the marketing of certain unpopular sizes and/or grades for short periods. There has been some reluctance to use this type of direction, because it is difficult to enforce and because any stability achieved by the direction can be undermined by supplies from interstate. At present, the only direction applying on the fresh market relates to Wilson plums.

The third type of direction is favoured by growers. It enables processors to enter into contracts with individual growers for their commodities and to pay their contracted growers direct. The relevant sectional group committee meets with processors concerning the form of contract and the price to be paid. Prices are determined by negotiation, not by decree. At present, there are directions relating to peas, beans, cauliflowers, carrots, tomatoes, beetroot, passionfruit and papaws grown for processing.

The COD is no longer directly involved in processing, although the Golden Circle cannery at Northgate was founded by COD in 1947. The cannery is now a separate legal entity, but COD is still represented on the cannery board through its executive committee, its pineapple sectional group committee and its general manager. The COD involvement in processing was caused by dissatisfaction among growers with the service provided by private canners.

The COD's regulatory powers relate to matters such as conduct of elections (for example, for sectional group committees), rates of commission to be charged, levies and penalities for breaches of the Act. Matters relating to the regulation and administration of the Brisbane fruit and vegetable markets at Rocklea are the responsibility of a separate body, the Brisbane markets trust. The markets trust is required to establish and maintain a public market for the sale and storage of fruit and vegetables, and provides facilities such as sheds, cold rooms, holding areas, and so forth.

The COD is the central point of a marketing structure which has been designed to take into account the special characteristics of the industry, especially the perishable nature of the output. It is a highly flexible structure which leaves growers free to make their own choices regarding the marketing of their product. There is minimum interference in prices and market forces, and there is a minimum degree of regulation. The COD does not have a monopoly in any branch of wholesaling. Rather, the existence of private agents and merchants ensures healthy competition in the market, and enables retailers and consumers to choose from a range of traders, prices and quality of product and service.

At the same time, the COD represents a form of orderly marketing and exists to serve the interests of growers to the maximum extent possible. To this end, it offers a highly competitive service, its presence in a wholesale market ensures that growers have a stabilizing influence at their disposal, and it provides growers with market power in the form of a large organization which has numerous outlets throughout Australia. In addition, its performance has been reinforced by the quality of its management.

Open Trading

This option represents a departure from the concept of orderly marketing. It does not involve any central authority with statutory control over the supply, marketing or pricing of fish. Fishermen are free to sell their catches where they choose. A number of alternative marketing channels may be available, including fishermen's cooperatives. The only regulation of the industry would relate to matters such as the protection of undersized fish for biological reasons, and public health and hygiene considerations.

Open or unrestricted marketing of fish occurs in all Australian states and territories except Queensland and New South Wales. In South Australia, the South Australian Fishermen's Cooperative (SAFCOL) sell fish by auction in Adelaide. Other fish is marketed through agents and private companies. Agents operate an auction market in Perth, although much of the fish in Western Australia is sold direct to wholesalers. There are no fish auctions in Tasmania, the Northern Territory or the ACT. Fish is distributed either direct to consumers or through wholesalers and cooperatives to consumer outlets and to interstate markets. In all states, fresh and frozen fish is generally imported either through an importing agent or a wholesaler.

More than half of the edible fish landed in Victoria is auctioned through the Melbourne fish market and the rest is sold interstate or through wholesalers, retailers, cooperatives, canners and processors. The Melbourne fish market is controlled through by-laws administered by the abattoirs and market committee of the Melbourne City Council. Revenue is derived from commissions on the sale of fish and from rents on the use of facilities (for example, filleting rooms, cold storage facilities). Conditions governing the sale of fish by auction are designed to ensure that the prices received by the fishermen are determined through genuine competition between buyers and sellers.

In 1979-80, auction sales at the Melbourne fish markets amounted to $10 million, a 12 per cent increase on the previous year. Throughput at the market has remained relatively static over the past decade, with average annual sales of about 5,000−6,000 tonnes.[14] The fish market added a processing plant to its facilities during 1979-80.

A further example of large unrestricted marketing of fish occurs in Japan which is the world's leading fishing nation with an annual production of between 10 and 11 million tonnes. The major form of marketing is the auction system. About 1,000 of Japan's 2,800 fishing ports have central wholesale markets. Fish is sold to wholesalers by auction. Wholesalers then sell to secondary wholesalers (middlemen) for local distribution through retailers and other outlets. At smaller ports, wholesalers also send product to the larger cities for processing and freezing.

The Tsukiji fish market in Tokyo forms part of the city's huge central wholesale market which handles vegetables, fish, meat and poultry. The central market is operated by the Tokyo Metropolitan Government on a landlord basis and wholesalers operating at the market are licensed by the Ministry of Agriculture, Forestry and Fisheries. Fish is consigned to wholesalers by producers or is bought by wholesalers on their own account from producers. These primary wholesalers sell to middlemen, or direct to retailers, food processors, large consumers or other wholesalers catering to private markets.[15]

Open marketing implies a minimum degree of government intervention in the nature, structure and economics of fish marketing. In particular, there is no statutory authority to regulate the disposal of product, to provide fishermen with bargaining power in the market, or to stabilize prices and incomes for fishermen. Organization of the marketing system is left to private enterprise and the interaction of market forces.

The case for open marketing is based on the principle that an environment which leaves individual decisions to the market as far as practicable is generally to be preferred to administrative fiat. In other words, the more market forces are allowed to operate, the more likely is the development of an effective and efficient marketing structure.

This does not require that the assumptions of pure competition prescribed by economic theory should be fulfilled. There will always be imperfections in the market. However, these imperfections can often be overcome adequately by private enterprise without the need for government intervention. For example, the existence of extensive black markets in the two states where statutory controls apply indicates that private marketing channels are available to dispose of fish supplies in the absence of a central regulatory authority.

Similarly, the existence of market power among buyers can be combated by means other than a compulsory marketing authority. Voluntary cooperatives at the local, regional or central level provide the opportunity for small, individual producers to group together to exercise market power and maximize their returns without resort to the compulsion or legal sanctions associated with statutory marketing arrangements. In these circumstances, fishermen would be free to take advantage of the bargaining power which a cooperative can offer, or to choose alternative avenues for disposing of their product. This would preserve the economic freedom of producers and consumers, as both groups are able to choose from competing marketing channels and to find the most attractive arrangements for selling or buying product.

Conclusion

The purpose of this article has been twofold: firstly, to describe the development and nature of the current structure (1981) of fish marketing in Queensland; and secondly, to consider examples of alternative structures which may be of relevance. The evolution of fish marketing arrangements in Queensland over the last fifty years has been wedded to the concept of orderly marketing through a statutory authority. However, the recent marketing and financial problems experienced by the Queensland Fish Board have raised serious doubts about the effectiveness and future of the current system.

We have examined the strengths and weaknesses of the current system and have outlined four alternative marketing structures drawn from the experiences of other industries and the fishing industries in other states. The options embrace a broad spectrum in terms of the degree of government intervention and are illustrative of the large number of combinations of supply, pricing, trading and regulatory arrangements which could be conceived.

This article was not intended to prescribe or to recommend the type of structure which may be most appropriate for the fishing industry in Queensland. Rather, it was intended simply to present an evaluation of the advantages and disadvantages of alternative structures as a basis for further consideration (at an industry and government level) of the role of the Queensland Fish Board and the structure of fish marketing in Queensland.

Notes

1. Throughout the paper, the term "fish" should be taken to include both fish and seafood unless otherwise stated.
2. Hereinafter, "Committee of Inquiry" refers to the Committee to Enquire into Matters Relating to Fish Marketing and the Future of Operations of the Fish Board, appointed 25 March 1980. The Committee issued an interim report in May 1980 and a final report in January 1981.
3. "Fisheries and Fish Processing Industry", report by the Industries Assistance Commission, No. 182 (AGPS, Canberra, 20 September 1978).
4. "Statutory Agricultural Marketing Authorities of Australia – A Compendium", A Report for the Economics and Marketing Committee of Standing Committee on Agriculture (Canberra, 1980).
5. The study of prices and sales volumes at the Colmslie auction in 1980 was supervised by Dr S. Strong, University of Queensland. Further work is planned to refine and expand the analysis of fish pricing.
6. "Fish and Seafood Consumption in Australia – A Consumer Survey 1976-77", PA Consulting Services and Fisheries Division, Commonwealth Department of Primary Industry (AGPS, Canberra, March 1978).
7. Some examples are included in K. O. Campbell, "Are Producer-Controlled Marketing Boards Necessary?", *Farm Policy* 17, 2 (September 1977).
8. In 1977, there were 291 consents, the principal locations being Tweed Heads, the Gosford-Newcastle region and Bateman's Bay. See *Australian Fisheries*,

Fisheries Division, Commonwealth Department of Primary Industry, 38, 7 (July 1979).

9. Ibid.

10. Report from the Select Committee of the Legislative Assembly Upon the Fishing Industry, Parliament of N.S.W., 18 February, 1976.

11. Figures obtained from the Fisheries Division, Commonwealth Department of Primary Industry.

12. Prior to 1980, potatoes, onions, pumpkins and sweet turnips were excluded from the provisions of the Fruit Marketing Organization Act. The amendment which included these items in the Act also incorporated provisions for the marketing of flowers, flowering and other plants and shrubs and horticultural and nursery products.

13. The Fruit Marketing Organization Act sets out a standard procedure to be followed whenever it is proposed by COD to exercise its statutory powers through a Direction. Growers likely to be affected by a direction are given full opportunity to support or oppose each such proposal.

14. *Australian Fisheries* 39, 9 (September 1980).

15. This description of fish marketing in Japan is extracted from reports of the Australian Fishing Industry Mission to Japan (1978), contained in *Australian Fisheries* 37, 9 (September 1978).

8

Present Fish and Shellfish Consumption in Queensland and Future Demand

S. D. Bandaranaike

The geographical location of Australia, surrounded in all directions by water and its extensive latitudinal spread from temperate to tropical waters should theoretically facilitate a high rate of seafood[1] consumption. Yet owing to a number of reasons, the per capita consumption in Australia as a whole nation has been relatively low when compared with other countries.

In a recent survey[2] conducted in the Australian capital cities, the per capita consumption of seafood was 10.1 kg, comprising 7.8 kg of fish and 2.3 kg of shellfish. Brisbane had a consumption rate of 10.4 kg, second only to that of Sydney. However, within the rest of Queensland this rate varies significantly depending on geographical aspect, and socioeconomic and behavioural characteristics of the population.

This article examines the present attitudes and consumption patterns of seafood in a cross-section of Queensland towns. The analysis is based on consumer and marketing surveys carried out by the author in select coastal and inland towns of Queensland (see Bibliography), and the Department of Primary Industry survey of Brisbane and other capital cities, referred to earlier. These urban centres provide a representative cross-section of the economy of Queensland with populations varying between 700,000 and 2,000 accompanied by widely fluctuating growth rates (Table 1).

Consumption Patterns

Consumption Form

Irrespective of the geographical location of the town and hence access to fish supplies, the proportion of households consuming any form[3] of seafood was relatively high — above 82 per cent (table 2).

The relatively lower percentages at Charters Towers (86 per cent) and Hughenden (82 per cent) can be explained with reference to their inland locations, pastoral economies and demographic structures. In contrast, Mt Isa, a city of predominantly young people, and having direct access to the Gulf of Carpentaria, had a consumption rate of 90 per cent.

Table 1 Population[1] and per capita consumption[2] of select Queensland towns

Urban Centres	Population (1976)	Population (1971)	Population change 1971-1976 (%)	Annual per capita consumption (kg)
Brisbane	700,671	696,740	-0.56	10.4
Townsville	68,591	78,653	14.67	8.2
Cairns	32,747	39,305	20.03	8.6
Rockhampton	48,213	50,132	3.98	8.0
Bowen	5,880	6,707	14.06	10.4
Mt Isa	25,497	25,377	-0.47	8.0
Charters Towers	7,518	7,914	5.27	5.5
Hughenden	1,916	1,811	-5.48	4.7
Mareeba	5,160	5,776	11.94	7.6

Source: [1]Queensland Year Book, 1980
[2]DPI Survey, 1978 (Brisbane). Author's survey for all other towns

Table 2 Consumption of fish and shellfish by form

Urban Centres	Any form (%)	Fresh (%)	Frozen packaged (%)	Smoked (%)	Canned (%)
Brisbane	86	na*	na	na	na
Townsville	91	97	42	32	87
Cairns	92	76	39	40	79
Rockhampton	95	81	47	23	77
Bowen	98	76	32	28	78
Mt Isa	90	70	51	28	65
Charters Towers	86	66	42	21	69
Hughenden	82	68	62	20	75
Mareeba	100	92	31	11	74

*na—not available

Overall consumption in the form of "fresh" and "canned" supplies were most popular. "Smoked" or "cured" varieties of fish and shellfish were found popular among smaller ethnic groups, at Cairns and Townsville. Brisbane too exhibited a similar trend in preference for the various forms of seafood. Thus the overall trend, in the forms of consumption, is the same throughout most of Queensland and Australia.

Consumption Situation

More than three-fourths of the households preferred home consumption to eating seafood at a restaurant or from a takeaway outlet (table 3). As expected, in the urban centres of Townsville, Cairns and Rockhampton where the number of restaurants is greater, the frequency of restaurant consumption was relatively higher. Consumption via takeaway outlets was more popular in smaller towns like Bowen (74 per cent) and Mareeba (72 per cent). The incidence of high consumption frequencies in both takeaway outlets and at home is consistent with the high per capital consumption at Bowen.

The existing consumption situation together with the socioeconomic and demographic characteristics of a town are important aspects in the future planning of seafood restaurants or takeaway outlets. For instance in rapidly growing cities like Townsville and Cairns it would be most feasible to increase the number of restaurants and fast food outlets serving seafood.

Consumption Frequency

Urban centres with a coastal location, in most cases having ready access to direct supplies of seafood, had a relatively higher per capita rate of consumption, for example, Townsville (8.2 kg) and Cairns

Table 3 Consumption situation in various urban centres

	Home	Restaurant	Takeaway
Brisbane (kg)	5.99	0.93	1.10
Townsville (%)	88	12	61
Cairns (%)	87	13	60
Rockhampton (%)	86	14	61
Bowen (%)	98	2	74
Mt Isa (%)	91	9	41
Charters Towers (%)	79	5	62
Hughenden (%)	75	7	32
Mareeba (%)	92	8	72

(8.6 kg) (table 1). In contrast, inland towns like Charters Towers (5.5. kg) and Hughenden (4.7 kg) had low per capital rates of consumption. For reasons given earlier, Mt Isa had a relatively higher rate of consumption (8.0 kg) than other inland towns. Economically it would be feasible to air freight supplies of seafood to a rapidly growing town such as Mt Isa. However, it would not be profitable to engage in similar marketing techniques at Hughenden or Charters Towers owing to the size of these towns and their immediate hinterland.

The high per capita rate of consumption at Bowen (10.4 kg) is partly explained by the high incidence of recreational fishermen (71 per cent) in this town.

Recreational Fishermen

Participation in fishing activity is another index of measurement of consumption which is often overlooked by official statistics. In the towns surveyed it was found that a third of the households were engaged in fishing activity, mainly for recreation. In the inland towns of Mt Isa, Charters Towers, Hughenden and Mareeba approximately one-fourth of the households were engaged in fishing. At Rockhampton, Townsville and Cairns just over a third of the households were engaged in fishing activity and at Bowen as much as 71 per cent were recreational fishermen.

In Brisbane 38 per cent of the households were engaged in recreational fishing. The majority of these fishermen were found to be of Greek descent.

Reasons for Nonpurchase

Seafood competes with other forms of protein and meat in the normal diet. Although the incidence of seafood consumption is at present reasonably satisfactory in Queensland, there is no guarantee it will be the same in the future.

From table 4 it is evident that the main reason for nonconsumption was the "dislike" of the commodity. This means either there was a total dislike of the product or there was a preference for other forms of seafood or meat. The large percentages recorded in the "other" category was mainly due to the prevalence of recreational fishermen who had their own supplies. The "poor availability" of fresh seafood was a significant indicator of low consumption frequencies in remote inland towns like Hughenden (25 per cent). A smaller incidence of this same factor was recorded at Charters Towers (6 per cent), Mt Isa (6 per cent) and even Townsville (6 per cent), an indication of unsatisfied demand in these areas.

Apart from the "dislike" of the commodity and "other" reasons

Table 4 Reasons for the nonpurchase of different forms of fish and shellfish

		High price (%)	Poor availability (%)	Low quality (%)	Dislike (%)	Other (%)
Townsville	Fresh	19	6	11	41	24
	Frozen	92	–	5	59	27
	Smoked	8	1	1	65	25
	Canned	6	–	–	74	21
Cairns	Fresh	–	–	–	16	84
	Frozen	6	1	9	67	37
	Smoked	2	2	3	66	27
	Canned	5	–	–	83	12
Rockhampton	Fresh	–	–	–	7	93
	Frozen	5	–	6	83	15
	Smoked	3	1	2	70	27
	Canned	10	–	–	82	11
Bowen	Fresh	9	–	–	18	73
	Frozen	3	–	18	36	42
	Smoked	3	3	–	66	29
	Canned	10	–	–	50	50
Mt Isa	Fresh	19	6	6	3	56
	Frozen	11	–	7	97	14
	Smoked	11	–	1	75	19
	Canned	7	–	–	59	40
Charters Towers	Fresh	6	6	–	50	50
	Frozen	7	2	14	66	28
	Smoked	3	5	–	70	19
	Canned	18	–	–	65	24
Hughenden	Fresh	–	25	12	25	38
	Frozen	–	–	8	83	17
	Smoked	–	–	–	–	100
	Canned	–	–	–	100	–
Mareeba	Fresh	–	–	–	–	100
	Frozen	7	–	24	58	27
	Smoked	5	–	3	58	39
	Canned	10	–	–	40	50

given for nonconsumption, the high price of the commodity was an important deterrent to consumption. Quite a significant proportion (92 per cent) of the nonconsumers of frozen seafood in Townsville in particular, attributed the high price of the product as the main reason for nonconsumption.

It is noteworthy that in Mt Isa, "high price" is one of the major reasons for nonpurchase. This is a result of the extra air transport costs incurred in obtaining fresh seafood supplies from the Gulf of Carpentaria, an inevitable situation in interior locations.

Overall, the general availability of seafood appeared fairly satisfactory, except in the case of isolated inland towns like Hughenden. The complete dislike of the commodity, owing to preference for other forms of seafood, other kinds of meat, dietary reasons, and so forth were the most predominant reasons for nonpurchase.

Restraints on Further Purchases

The effect of high price on purchasing habits is further highlighted in table 5.

"High price" was the most important or second most important factor affecting additional purchases of fresh seafood at all centres. This factor was more of a problem in the larger cities of Townsville, Cairns, Rockhampton and Mt Isa than in the smaller urban centres. A fairly significant group of consumers felt they were unable to purchase further supplies of seafood since they were at the maximum level of consumption. This however may not necessarily be correct; it could be an illusion or a means of concealing the honest reason for restraints on additional purchase. Once again in inland towns like Charters Towers and Hughenden, the "poor availability" was a leading reason for restricting additional purchases. The "dislike" of the product itself or the option for other forms of seafood were the main restraints to additional purchases of frozen packages supplies.

Sources of Supply

The proportion of fresh seafood purchased from different retail outlets varied widely among different towns, depending on the availability and efficiency of the organizing retail units. Overall, the "fish shop" was the major source for purchases of fresh seafood (table 6). The two exceptions to this were Mt Isa (35 per cent) and Hughenden (41 per cent) where private suppliers were more important. At Charters Towers, "private agents" (24 per cent) supplied a considerable fraction of the fish supplies.

Table 5 Restraints on further purchases of fresh and frozen supplies

		High price (%)	Poor availability (%)	Low quality (%)	On maximum consumption (%)	Prefer other forms (%)	No special reason (%)
Townsville	Fresh	41	5	8	26	–	21
	Frozen	13	8	–	15	52	15
Cairns	Fresh	38	11	4	34	–	24
	Frozen	23	3	–	20	63	12
Rockhampton	Fresh	40	5	7	41	–	15
	Frozen	32	–	–	27	55	6
Bowen	Fresh	24	13	3	47	3	31
	Frozen	12	–	–	44	31	19
Mt Isa	Fresh	44	4	10	51	–	9
	Frozen	23	2	–	65	14	18
Charters Towers	Fresh	26	32	6	23	–	33
	Frozen	12	2	–	7	44	42
Hughenden	Fresh	37	61	2	20	–	10
	Frozen	19	–	–	54	44	3
Mareeba	Fresh	36	11	6	14	–	34
	Frozen	33	–	–	8	67	34

Table 6 Sources of fresh, frozen, smoked and canned supplies (Percentage)

		Super market	Hotel/ pub	Fish shop	Delica- tessen	Fish board	Friends, relatives, self	Fisher- man	Private supplier	Neigh- bourhood store	Mobile unit	Fish market	Other
Brisbane	Fresh	19	3	36	3	11	33	3	4	–	–	6	25
Townsville	Fresh	–	–	40	–	5	15	–	–	–	–	–	1
	Frozen	91	–	1	–	–	–	–	–	–	–	–	1
	Smoked	82	–	–	16	–	–	–	–	2	–	–	1
	Canned	96	–	–	2	–	–	–	–	–	–	–	–
Cairns	Fresh	27	2	33	6	12	24	1	2	–	1	5	–
	Frozen	91	–	5	5	–	–	–	–	–	–	–	–
	Smoked	79	–	1	24	–	–	–	–	13	–	–	–
	Canned	87	–	–	3	–	–	–	–	–	–	–	–
Rockhampton	Fresh	7	2	64	–	29	16	1	3	–	1	–	–
	Frozen	93	–	1	1	5	–	–	–	–	–	–	–
	Smoked	89	–	7	4	1	–	–	–	6	–	–	–
	Canned	97	–	–	1	–	–	–	–	–	–	–	–
Bowen	Fresh	5	3	55	–	13	8	13	3	–	–	–	–
	Frozen	75	–	25	21	19	–	–	–	–	–	–	–
	Smoked	86	–	7	–	–	–	–	–	8	–	–	–
	Canned	97	–	–	–	–	–	–	–	–	–	–	–
Mt Isa	Fresh	25	7	27	3	1	2	1	35	–	–	–	7
	Frozen	88	–	–	1	–	–	–	–	–	–	–	–
	Smoked	40	–	3	57	–	–	–	–	19	–	–	10
	Canned	77	–	–	4	–	–	–	–	–	–	–	–
Charters Towers	Fresh	9	12	47	–	6	12	5	24	–	–	–	2
	Frozen	93	–	–	–	2	–	–	–	–	–	–	7
	Smoked	100	–	–	–	–	–	–	–	4	–	–	–
	Canned	94	–	–	–	–	–	–	–	–	–	–	–
Hughenden	Fresh	29	2	19	–	2	41	27	2	–	2	–	5
	Frozen	92	–	3	–	–	–	–	–	–	–	–	3
	Smoked	100	–	–	–	–	–	–	–	–	–	–	–
	Canned	100	–	–	–	–	–	–	–	–	–	–	–
Mareeba	Fresh	26	–	32	–	5	5	5	8	–	16	–	3
	Frozen	100	–	–	–	–	–	–	–	–	–	–	–
	Smoked	100	–	–	–	–	–	–	–	–	–	–	–
	Canned	90	–	–	–	–	–	–	–	10	–	–	–

It is noteworthy that Queensland's prime official channel of marketing, the "Queensland Fish Board", was not very popular among the consumers. The varying significance of the Fish Board as a retailing outlet was probably due to the varying efficiency of the units in each town and its degree of competitiveness with other fish retail units.

Irrespective of the size of the town, the "supermarket" was a fairly popular outlet among most towns. Approximately one-fourth of the purchases were made here. The "mobile unit" or fish van which conveyed supplies of seafood was a common feature in the inland towns of Mareeba and Hughenden. A major limitation in this system was the restriction in the choice of species and limited availability to the purchaser.

The "fish market" is not as yet a developed source of retailing fish and shellfish in most Queensland towns. A small percentage of the purchases in Brisbane (6 per cent) and Cairns (5 per cent) were made at the fish market. In Brisbane, as with the rest of Queensland, the fish shop was patronized by little over a third of the households. In addition, another third of the households obtained their supplies in the form of personal catch or gift.

Other sources of supply such as the "hotel" or "pub" and direct purchases from the fishermen were of lesser importance. It may be noted, however, that it is conceivable that a few consumers were unwilling to admit their purchases were made direct from fishermen, owing to problems of legality of those purchases. Some of these responses may be recorded under "other" in table 6.

With reference to the major supply sources of frozen packaged, smoked and canned seafood there was a clear dominance by one or two types of retail outlets.

The "supermarket" predominated in a significantly large proportion of sales in frozen, smoked and canned seafood. In frozen packaged fish, the next most important retail outlets were the "fish shop" and the "Fish Board". The "fish shop" and the "delicatessen" were moderately popular retail outlets of smoked fish. The "neighbourhood store" was next in importance to the supermarket in the retailing of canned seafood. These trends in frozen, smoked and canned seafood retailing were found to be similar elsewhere in Queensland.

Availability

The availability of a product to the consumers is another leading factor influencing the purchasing behaviour of a consumer. Table 7 illustrates the availability of seafood by form in each of the towns listed.

With regard to the availability of fresh fish, Hughenden in

Table 7 Availability of seafood by form

	Fresh (%)			Frozen (%)			Smoked (%)			Canned (%)		
	S	U	N	S	U	N	S	U	N	S	U	N
Townsville	66	20	14	57	37	6	83	15	2	93	6	1
Cairns	80	20	–	82	10	8	73	17	10	91	7	2
Rockhampton	82	15	3	73	25	2	88	9	4	96	1	2
Bowen	71	29	1	37	12	50	71	21	7	97	–	3
Mt Isa	87	12	1	89	5	5	40	54	6	81	14	5
Charters Towers	61	39	–	62	19	19	85	15	–	93	3	4
Hughenden	39	61	–	97	3	–	75	25	–	98	2	1
Mareeba	81	16	3	83	8	8	100	–	–	93	7	–

Satisfied (S)
Unsatisfied (U)
No Opinion (N)

particular remains unsatisfied (61 per cent). Of the larger cities, Townsville's level of satisfaction with regard to the availability of fresh seafood was only moderately satisfactory (66 per cent). In contrast, the consumers at Cairns (80 per cent) and Rockhampton (82 per cent) and even Mt Isa (87 per cent) had higher levels of satisfaction. In Townsville, whilst there is a fairly high demand for fresh seafood, the retail outlets have been rather restricted until very recently.

With reference to frozen packaged seafood, once again Townsville (37 per cent) expressed its dissatisfaction, together with Rockhampton (25 per cent), Charters Towers (19 per cent), and Bowen (12 per cent) to a lesser extent. In contrast there was a general consensus of opinion regarding the satisfactory level of availability in canned seafood at all the towns.

Popular Varieties

When examining consumption patterns, it is interesting to note that favourite species of the consumers on the one hand, and the species that are actually consumed on the other. Among all the urban centres in Queensland, excluding Brisbane, barramundi was the most popular variety, followed by coral trout, whiting and salmon. Of the shellfish, prawns were the most popular, followed by crabs. It is noteworthy that in all towns fish were more popular as a favourite dish than shellfish. Even at Mt Isa where prawns rank as the second most preferred species, there was a wide difference in the degree of popularity between barramundi which ranked first and prawns which ranked second (7 per cent).

The most favoured species among consumers need not necessarily be the most frequently consumed species. The latter would depend greatly on availability of the product. Tables 8A to 8E give the five most frequently consumed species for all capital cities, for Brisbane, and for each of the other towns surveyed.

It is also noteworthy that there was little association between the local production and the most popular species served in each town.

According to table 8A, the most popular fish species consumed at home in all capital cities including Brisbane were predominantly tuna (18 per cent) and salmon (17 per cent). Prawns (52 per cent), oysters (16 per cent) and crabs (13 per cent) were the most popular shellfish species served at home in Brisbane. However, the trends in the towns outside the capital cities were quite different (table 8B). Of the fresh fish, barramundi was by far the most common species consumed and prawns the most popular shellfish species. Mackerel and coral trout were next most popular in these towns, despite the incidence of ciguatera poisoning associated with these two species.

Table 8A Most popular species served as a percentage of consumption occasions for all capital cities and for Brisbane

		Served at home Rank	(%)	Dining out Rank	(%)	Takeaway Rank	(%)
All Cities		1 Tuna	18	1 Whiting	17		
		2 Salmon	17	2 Flounder	11	na*	
		3 Fish Fingers	9	3 Snapper	8		
		4 Sardines	8	4 Bream	6		
		5 Cod	6	5 Salmon	5		
Brisbane	Fish	1 Salmon	18	1 Barramundi	26	1 Cod	21
		2 Tuna	14	2 Whiting	8	2 Whiting	10
		3 Fish Fingers	9	3 Salmon	4	3 Mullet	9
		4 Sardines	8	4 Bream	4	4 Bream	7
		5 Mullet	8	5 Flounder	3	5 Snapper	6
	Shellfish	1 Prawns	52	1 Prawns	42	1 Prawns	71
		2 Oysters	16	2 Seafood Cocktail	28	2 Scallops	12
		3 Crabs	13	3 Lobster	10	3 Crabs	10
		4 Seafood Cocktail	8	4 Oysters	10	4 Seafood Cocktail	2
		5 Scallops	7	5 Crabs	9		

Source: Department of Primary Industry, Canberra, 1978

na* — not available

Table 8B Most popular fresh fish and shellfish species served as a percentage of total households

	Rank	Species	(%)		Rank	Species	(%)
Townsville	1	Barramundi	54	Mt Isa	1	Barramundi	65
	2	Prawns	50		2	Prawns	36
	3	Mackerel	38		3	Oysters	23
	4	Coral Trout	38		4	Coral Trout	16
	5	Crabs	37		5	Crab	16
Cairns	1	Barramundi	61	Charters Towers	1	Barramundi	48
	2	Coral Trout	54		2	Bream	16
	3	Prawns	39		3	Mackerel	14
	4	Crab	32		4	Jew Fish	13
	5	Mackerel	30		5	Prawns	7
Rockhampton	1	Prawns	63	Hughenden	1	Barramundi	65
	2	Barramundi	57		2	Prawns	32
	3	Crab	46		3	Crab	22
	4	Sweetlip	37		4	Yellowbelly	17
	5	Oysters	28		5	Whiting	12
Bowen	1	Prawns	60	Mareeba	1	Barramundi	67
	2	Mackerel	52		2	Mackerel	46
	3	Barrumundi	48		3	Coral Trout	41
	4	Crab	48		4	Prawns	21
	5	Whiting	42		5	Salmon	18

Table 8C Most popular frozen fish and shellfish species served as a percentage of total households

	Rank	Species	(%)		Rank	Species	(%)
Cairns	1	Fish Fingers	25	Mt Isa	1	Fish Fingers	41
	2	Fish Cakes	13		2	Fish Cakes	20
	3	Coral Trout	11		3	Cod	15
	4	Whiting	7		4	Prawns	12
	5				5	Whiting	5
Rockhampton	1	Fish Fingers	42	Charters	1	Fish Fingers	35
	2	Whiting	14	Towers	2	Cod	6
	3	Cod	5		3	Fish Cakes	5
Bowen	1	Fish Fingers	28		4	Whiting	5
	2	Whiting	10		5		
	3	Fish Cakes	8		1	Fish Fingers	53
	4	Prawns	4		2	Fish Cakes	22
	5	Scallops	4	Hughenden	3	Whiting	20
Mareeba	1	Fish Fingers	21		4	Flounder	8
	2	Whiting	8		5	Prawns	5
	3	Fish Cakes	5				

Table 8D Most popular smoked fish and shellfish species served as a percentage of total households

	Rank	Species	(%)		Rank	Species	(%)
Cairns	1	Coral Trout	18		1	Herring	12
	2	Haddock	13		2	Haddock	12
	3	Herring	9	Mt Isa	3	Sprats	6
	4	Flounder	5		4	Cod	5
Rockhampton	1	Cod	12	Charters	1	Haddock	16
	2	Haddock	10	Towers	2	Cod	9
Bowen	1	Haddock	22		1	Haddock	18
	2	Cod	6	Hughenden	2	Cod	5
	3	Kippers	4				
Mareeba	1	Cod	3				
	2	Haddock	3				
	3	Herring	3				

Among the shellfish, crabs and then oysters were the most favoured.

The frequency with which some of these species is consumed would depend greatly on the availability and the price of the product. Whilst barramundi is one of the more expensive species of fish, it is extremely palatable and it is also somewhat "prestigious" to be identified with the consumption of this product. On the other hand, coral trout and mackerel would suit more easily the average consumer's budget. Prawns, a much desired species of shellfish, can

Table 8E Most popular canned fish and shellfish species served as a percentage of total households

	Rank	Species	(%)		Rank	Species	(%)
	1	Salmon	61		1	Salmon	43
	2	Sardine	50		2	Tuna	43
Cairns	3	Tuna	42	Mt Isa	3	Sardine	35
	4	Herring	25		4	Oyster	28
	5	Oyster	21		5	Anchovy	12
	1	Salmon	54		1	Salmon	44
	2	Sardine	47	Charters	2	Sardine	36
Rockhampton	3	Tuna	44	Towers	3	Tuna	24
	4	Herring	22		4	Herring	15
	5	Oyster	13				
	1	Salmon	62		1	Sardine	67
	2	Sardine	56		2	Salmon	50
Bowen	3	Tuna	50	Hughenden	3	Whiting	48
	4	Herring	30		4	Herring	32
	5	Oyster	12		5	Oyster	20
	1	Tuna	54				
	2	Sardine	49				
Mareeba	3	Salmon	46				
	4	Herring	15				

be described as an elastic commodity where consumption fluctuates with fluctuations in price.

The three most popular varieties of frozen packaged fish were fish fingers, whiting and fish cakes in almost all the towns. As illustrated in table 2, smoked fish was the least popular form of seafood. The species available were also limited. Haddock and cod were the more popular species of smoked fish (table 8D).

Of the canned fish, salmon, sardines and tuna were the most popular varieties served (table 8E). Among the shellfish varieties, oysters were by far the most popular.

Preparation for Consumption

As illustrated in table 9, there was little variety in the methods of cooking fish at home. In Brisbane on 39 per cent of occasions fish was served without cooking, mainly in sandwiches and salads, and on another third of the occasions, fish was fried.

In the towns outside the state capital, frying of fish was the most popular cooking method. This method varied in popularity from just over two-thirds of the households in Townsville and Cairns to more than 80 per cent of the households in Mt Isa and Bowen. The next

Table 9 Preparation of seafood (cooking methods)

	Brisbane*1	Townsville*2	Cairns	Rockhampton	Bowen	Mt Isa	Charters Towers	Hughenden	Mareeba
Fry %	33		67	79	86	80	77	73	78
Bake %	3	25	27	16	43	40	16	14	10
Salad %	39	20	17	5	22	55	7	2	8
Grill %	6		53	38	49	39	34	50	49
Boil %	3	6	10	8	18	9	8	2	8
Other %	15	4	7	-	-	11	6	2	13

*1 Percentage of occasions fish and shellfish were served at home
*2 All other towns excluding Brisbane, percentage of households using a particular cooking method

most popular preparation was grilling where approximately a third to a half of the households used this method.

As for shellfish, most of it was obtained in a form which could be consumed direct, such as in a salad. When further preparation was done by a few consumers, it was served as a mornay, a cocktail, or a quiche, etc. On the whole, there was a lack of enthusiasm in experimenting with fish cookery.

There was also a general reluctance to purchase whole fish. Filleted fish was preferred by a majority of the consumers owing to convenience of handling the product.

Seafoods are usually consumed at all meals, but it was found to be most popular at the evening meal, and least popular at breakfast. On many occasions smoked fish was eaten at breakfast and canned fish mainly at lunch. Shellfish was eaten at lunch for almost a fourth of the occasions and hardly ever at breakfast.

Socioeconomic Factors

In addition to the geographical location of a town — i.e., coastal or inland — demographic and socioeconomic factors were expected to influence consumption patterns. Therefore the following variables were also looked at in terms of consumption patterns:

  a. household size
  b. household structure
  c. occupation
  d. income
  e. religion
  f. previous residential location
  g. period of residence in present towns.

Occupation and income were closely related. Occupation was used as a surrogate measure for income which on many occasions remained undisclosed. As expected, consumers having higher household incomes ate more seafood than those with lower incomes. Table 10 illustrates this feature for Mt Isa.

In Brisbane, households with adult males only, consumed about twice as much seafood as any other group. They ate more from restaurants and takeaway outlets.

It was found that migrants from the Mediterranean and Asian countries and also northern Europe consumed larger quantities of fresh seafood irrespective of their income grouping.

The high incidence of frozen packaged fish among the middle income earners was purely a function of convenience among a group of white collar workers where often both husband and wife were employed. Most British migrants were found to consume relatively larger quantities of smoked fish than any other community, probably

Table 10 Frequency of fish and shellfish consumption at home, by household income (in Mt Isa)

Income class ($)	Mean consumption frequency (per mth)	% in each income class
2,001– 4,000	1.0	3.3
4,001– 6,000	2.8	3.3
6,001– 8,000	3.0	2.2
8,001–10,000	3.3	7.2
10,001–15,000	4.7	37.1
15,001–20,000	4.8	30.9
more than 20,000	5.3	16.0

due to a tradition brought over with them. There was no marked differentiation among the income groups in the consumption of canned seafood.

What was significant here was the very low consumption of canned seafood by people of Greek extraction who preferred mainly fresh seafood.

Among the 9 per cent of nonconsumers of seafood in Townsville, 52 per cent had an income of less than $6,000 per annum. Here a major factor influencing their consumption habits could be monetary considerations. By way of occupation most of them were pensioners, retired widows or students. Forty three per cent of the remainder had an income of between $6,000 and $15,000 and came from different walks of life. A small percentage (5 per cent) of nonconsumers belonged to the higher income groups. The latter households had a distinct dislike for seafood even though they could afford it.

Although religion did not have a direct influence on consumption, it can be suggested that some of the more traditional Catholic households still prefer to consume fish on Fridays in preference to meat, probably as a matter of habit. This trend is more apparent among Catholics of overseas ethnic origin.

Future Demand

Future demand for seafood in Queensland depends to a large extent on rates of population growth and marketing strategies adopted.

Population Growth

With the exception of the two smallest statistical divisions in Queensland, in all other divisions the rates of population growth are

Table 11 Population by statistical divisions of Queensland

Division	Major cities	Population 1971	Population 1976	Population change 1971-1976 (%)	Estimated population 1979	Population change 1976-1979 (%)
Brisbane City	Brisbane	700,671	696,640	−0.56	702,000	0.75
Greater Brisbane	Ipswich	870,287	957,745	10.05	1,014,700	5.95
Moreton	Gold Coast	162,441	213,235	31.27	256,290	20.19
Wide Bay-Burnett	Bundaberg	137,888	152,095	10.30	163,760	7.67
Darling Downs	Toowoomba	148,795	155,313	4.83	164,950	6.20
South-west	Roma	30,620	27,876	−8.96	27,600	−0.99
Fitzroy	Rockhampton	115,158	126,395	9.76	136,070	7.65
Central-west	Longreach	15,198	14,063	−7.47	13,770	−2.08
Mackay	Mackay	65,523	77,030	17.57	86,680	12.52
Northern	Townsville	127,018	150,605	18.57	156,650	4.01
Far North	Cairns	110,274	124,661	13.05	133,830	7.36
North Western	Mt Isa	40,198	41,058	2.14	42,000	2.29
TOTAL QUEENSLAND		1,827,065	2,037,197	11.50	2,196,300	7.81

Compiled from ABS Statistics, 1980

satisfactory (table 11). The rate of growth is highest in the division of Moreton, followed by Mackay.

However, overall there appears to be a slower rate of population growth in most major urban centres throughout Queensland. These features, together with the demographic structure, are an important consideration when projecting the future demand for seafood in Queensland.

Per Capita Consumption

In the more recent fish consumption surveys conducted by the Department of Primary Industry, Canberra, and by the author, the per capita consumption rates identified were much higher than previous estimates of between 6 and 7 kg.[4] It is conceivable that the average Australian is consuming more seafood than before. The discrepancy could also result from different techniques of calculating per capita consumption. For the purpose of this paper, it is not unreasonable to assume that there has been a general increase in seafood consumption over the past few years.

On average Queenslanders eat fish at home about once a week. Further, consumers appear more favourably disposed towards fresh fish (table 2). Therefore, the expansion of consumption of Australian fish in particular is quite likely in the future. There is always the danger that the more popular species of today could be in short supply in the future, as a result of increasing demand or diversion to overseas markets. Therefore there is the need to develop consumer tastes to other Australian species.

Marketing Implications

Future demand for seafood supplied will depend to a large extent on the marketing strategies that are adopted to encourage further consumption.

In the past the fishing industry has concentrated on supplying more expensive fresh seafood with relatively small increases in the quantity sold.

Marketing strategies are directly linked to biological and economic considerations. If the potential catch is restricted, either owing to resource limitations or commercial reasons, this would necessitate the altering of the marketing strategy. On the other hand, there could be changes in the cost of living and thereby the purchasing power of the consumer. Here, too, adaptive marketing strategies would be essential.

Competition from other forms of meat and protein has always been a problem to the developing fishing industry. When attempting to increase seafood consumption, local species should be encouraged.

Sometimes due to the influx of cheap foreign fish such as the current flooding of the market with New Zealand perch, there is always the danger of losing the market for local varieties of fish.

Future demand for seafood will depend much on the availability of supplies. It was noted that most consumers had a distinct preference for consuming seafood in its fresh form rather than in other forms. However the fresh fish market in Queensland is far from favourably organized. A compatible marketing system could be achieved through a centrally organized marketing organization controlled by the state, or through private enterprise.

Even though on an average, the largest proportion of a consumer's household budget is spent on food, price competitiveness is an important factor influencing consumption. Price will always remain a problem with export orientated species such as prawns, where the current retailing price fluctuates widely, depending on the international market.

The quality and the presentation of the product sold are equally important considerations. At the moment there are doubts among some of the householders regarding the quality of freshness of the product. This could affect sales adversely. Proper presentation of the product in the market is lacking in most retail outlets of Queensland. The current ingress of New Zealand perch to the Australian market is a good example of the possible boost in sales as a result of competitive pricing and an attractive, convenient form of packaging.

Owing to the increasing tendency for both husband and wife to be employed, it will be necessary to cater to ready packaging of filleted fish for quick preparation. This also means there is the possibility of an increase in the frozen packaged seafood consumption.

Unless fresh and frozen seafood are made more readily available, potential consumer demand will remain unfulfilled or be directed to competing forms of food. Availability can be increased, ideally through specialist fish shops located in shopping complexes.

In the past, the location of the fish shop has usually been away from the city centre in the cheaper rental areas or in the suburbs. This has restricted access to some degree. However, recently a few fish retailers, becoming more aware of ready access to the consumer, have located their shops in shopping complexes like the Westfield Shoppingtown at Indooroopilly in Brisbane and at North Town in Flinders Mall, Townsville. Yet this is more the exception than the rule. The future trend in consumer shopping behaviour is towards one-stop shopping centres. A number of urban centres in Queensland are experiencing the onset of this trend. If fish retailing shops were located in these shopping complexes it would be extremely convenient for the consumer to purchase groceries and other household items together with seafood at the same time.

In general, there is a lack of expertise in fish purchasing, handling, processing, storage and selling which acts as a major setback to the fish retailing industry.

Changes in demand may also be anticipated with the future exploitation of the 200 mile fishing zone for new species. Production statistics indicate that catches of the most favoured species in Queensland, the barramundi, are fast depleting. If this trend continues and there is no adequate replacement there is the danger that consumption rates could be reduced drastically. Coral trout and mackerel are next most popular species, especially in north Queensland. Here again if the incidence of ciguatera poisoning in these species spreads, there is the danger of lower consumption frequencies. This does not imply that the future of seafood consumption is bleak in Queensland, but these are some of the limitations that may have to be coped with in the future.

The provision of seafood supplies to isolated towns in the interior of Queensland can best be done through a centrally organized marketing unit controlled by the state government. Many private suppliers are hesitant to supply smaller markets, not being fully aware of its potential for seafood consumption. If they did, being a small business concern, the price of the product will necessarily be high. In contrast a statewide marketing organization with possibly a multiple-base pricing system may be able to rectify the situation to a large extent.

In order to increase the future demand for fish, promotion is necessary in the following areas—improving the limited knowledge of consumers regarding preparation of fish, and informing consumers about new or unfamiliar species introduced to the market and of the nutritional value of fish in the diet.

In a competitive economic system, the survival and growth of an industry requires accurate knowledge about consumers—how they buy, what they buy and where they buy. Once these factors are known it is up to the marketing agents to satisfy the demands of the consumers accordingly.

In conclusion it can be said that there is a great potential in the Queensland market, and if proper marketing strategies are adopted, and assuming there is a reasonable rate of population growth, the per capita consumption should increase further. One of the immediate changes required in Queensland is the organization of a proper marketing channel for fresh fish supplies in particular. Latent demand will not be realized unless the marketing of fish is improved with immediate effect.

114 S.D. Bandaranaike

Notes

1. In this article "Seafood" refers to fish and shellfish species. "Fish" refers to all species of freshwater and seawater fin fish including sharks, rays and eels. "Shellfish" refers to all species of crustaceans, molluscs and echinoderms.
2. *Fish and Seafood Consumption in Australia: A Consumer Survey 1976-1977* (Fisheries Division, Department of Primary Industry, Canberra, 1978).
3. Fish and shellfish were classified according to their form at the time they were obtained as — fresh, frozen packaged, smoked (including dried or cured), and canned.
4. *Fisheries 1975-1976* (Australian Bureau of Statistics, Canberra, 1977).

References

Bandaranaike, S. D. "Preliminary Investigations in Seafood Consumption Patterns in North Queensland". *Northern Fisheries Research Session*, Brisbane (July 1977).
—— "Case Study: A Socio-economic Study of Seafood Consumption in Townsville". Monograph Series, *Occasional Paper* No. 2. Department of Geography, James Cook University of North Queensland, Townsville, 1978.
—— "Patterns of Seafood Consumption and Marketing in Townsville". *Australian Fisheries* 37, 6 (1978).
—— "Some Aspects of Seafood Retailing in North and Central Queensland". *Northern Fisheries Committee Research Session*. Townsville, 1978.
—— "Consumer Attitudes and Purchasing Behaviour in Seafood Consumption of an Inland North Queensland Town: Charters Towers". *Northern Fisheries Committee Research Session*. Townsville, 1978.
—— and Hampton J. W. "Seafood Purchasing Behaviour in Mt Isa". *Australian Fisheries*. 38, 8 (1979).
Fish and Seafood Consumption in Australia: A Consumer Survey 1976-1977. Fisheries Division, Department of Primary Industry, Canberra, 1978.
Fisheries 1976-1976. Australian Bureau of Statistics, Canberra, 1977.
Fisheries Statistics, Queensland, 1979-1980. Australian Bureau of Statistics, Queensland, 1981.
Queensland Year Book 1980. Vol. 40 Australian Bureau of Statistics, Queensland, 1981.

9

The Commercial Fisherman's View of Management: Past — Present — Future

D.F. Bryan

The Past

From the independent producer's point of view, fisheries management in Queensland has to date (1981), in the main been a disaster for the industry, primarily because there is not, and never has been, any master plan, and any attempts at management in the past have proved to be "too little too late".

The first management strategy introduced was in Moreton Bay, and I think I can safely say, it has as yet been the only successful management method. It has been successful because that fishery still survives. Independent producers can still make a living and the general public still has access to fresh seafood from that area. The method used in this management was centred around controlling the fishing effort by mesh and gear size regulations and the protection of the nursery areas. As fishermen are generally neither academic nor scientific, we can only assess the success of management by results. It should be emphasized that this type of management has obviously been the most effective in the past, but only because of the geographical location of the area which allows reasonably easy access to the fishery by the enforcement service.

Similar management methods have had no effect whatsoever in the rest of the state, and the situation will not improve unless there is a complementary commitment from government to implement the necessary enforcement service to ensure the management's effectiveness.

Gulf Management Regime

By the early 1970s the potential of the fishery was being realized at both government and large investor levels.

At this time, participants involved in the fishery agreed that some form of management was required. It was felt that the maximum level of exploitation had now been reached and the sustainable yield of the known banana prawn resources was being decreased.

The "lip service" paid to management control in the following year now seems to contain a certain irony, in that the commonwealth government called for the need to improve and regulate management of the gulf fishery.

It was of no surprise to independent fishermen that in the same year the government called for a report on northern fisheries, and in particular the gulf prawn fishery. The investigation was hurriedly completed and the report presented during 1976 to the authorities who were, by this time, operating under a new government. This change of government should be stressed, because it is understood that when the report was put forward for consideration, the recommendations for future gulf prawn management were put forward to be adopted in their entirety. As only some recommendations were adopted, this, in time, set off a chain of circumstances which only worked towards lowering the efficiency of the management plan, as well as bringing about adverse effects jeopardizing the entire Queensland fishing industry.

It can only be assumed that the reason why the recommendations were adopted in part was because of a conflict of political views between the various governments, which somehow overrode the true aim of fisheries management and any consideration for the then independent fishermen who pioneered, participated in, and were an essential mainstay of the fishery at that time because of their knowledge of the fishery. The report stated that northern fisheries would be best developed under a constituted joint regime made up of the three states—Queensland, Northern Territory and Western Australia.

The joint regime was desirable for management as the resource base was spread over both commonwealth and state waters, and the Gulf of Carpentaria fishery was shared in common interest by Queensland and the Northern Territory, although it was halfheartedly agreed that Queensland possessed, by geographical location, a major portion of the banana prawn resources. Obtaining maximum and sustainable yields would appear at first sight to be a practical proposition. However, the report warned that the management plan had inherent dangers.

When observing the sudden changes that took place in the gulf prawn fishery to 1980, it is now obvious that these warnings were not considered but passed over as either being of no importance or deliberately overlooked.

Two areas would have to be studied for the management plan to be fully effective. The first area was the shipbuilding subsidy in force at the time. The independent fisherman generally cannot afford to build a vessel to the size required to attract the subsidy and has the attitude that these vessels will prove to be too large to remain viable in the long term. The second area lay within the monetary aspect of selling limited entry licences.

The plan released upon the fishery a framework of incomplete restrictive regulations. Companies with solid financial backing were quick to perceive the opportunities and set about controlling the industry. The independent fisherman's future in the gulf was immediately limited. Control of the fishery by companies was swift and dramatic. The change has later proved to lower the degree of efficiency of fishing operations in the area and has produced side effects never before experienced in the Queensland fishing industry. By the end of the decade, of the 287 licences in force, 29 were still held by independent fishermen, the balance being held by companies. The total market value of gulf licences had reached 30 million dollars in the space of three years. This had already brought to the fishery an unnecessary element of overcapitalization.

The management plan concentrated on the fishery itself and at no time considered the effect the proposal would have on fisheries in neighbouring areas, such as the east coast. However, in later years another report was drafted by the industry which contained a warning that problems directly attributable to the Gulf Management Plan were developing on the east coast. These warnings were ignored. It can only be assumed that the original investigators did not anticipate any such effects.

Implications

At the same time, problems on the east coast were to deepen. The east coast fishery had been expanding with the natural increase of boats being built in the state's shipyards. The fishery was also absorbing the steady influx of boats leaving the gulf fishery. To complicate matters further, some fishermen who sold out from the gulf zone also sold their old vessels to new fishermen on the east coast and with the capital acquired from the two distinct sales, moved to build bigger boats for themselves. They had no choice but to join the east coast fleet together with the new owners of their former vessels and the already disheartened east coast fishermen.

This uncontrolled fishing pressure was further intensified by various gulf participants who exercised their dual fishing rights and conducted trawling operations on the eastern seaboard. This occurred mainly between seasonal fishing peaks in the gulf fishery.

With the entry of each new additional, not replacement, fishing unit into the industry (and this applies to all sections) the known resource was further divided and existing units were forced to increase their fishing effort to maintain their position of viability in the industry.

In an endeavour to remain viable, a direct result of the number of trawlers operating in the industry, the deliberate taking of immature prawns and small scallops escalated, thereby depleting the known resources and further compounding the issue.

Of course everything will not be altogether sweet-sailing in the gulf zone considering the price of fuel, the current position of overcapitalization, and the results of international experience which shows that once a fishery has reached peak development a notable slide back to smaller vessels follows.

Many of you will oppose the statements and viewpoints put forward as being either inaccurate, misinformed, or not indicative of the true situation. There are many areas of gulf and east coast management which have not been covered. There should be more input so that solutions can be found to achieve true fisheries management to the benefit of the industry as a whole.

These past events described did not necessarily occur in their order of description. The detrimental forces were all silently interacting, year by year, between the gulf and the east coast fisheries.

The Gulf of Carpentaria zone, which was not a wise decision in the first place, is insured in some respects by its size, which does allow at least a certain amount of flexibility and mobility of fishing operations in that zone for the moment, but it, too, is surely destined to go the same way, and one day will, unfortunately, become a disaster area, because those controlling the fishery are governed by their economic and marketing commitments and are unable to reduce their ever-increasing fishing effort in the area. Those participating in gulf fishing operations will one day be faced with a number of options involving auctions and ballots. This particular fishery is now pressuring for nursery area protection. Is it again going to be "too little too late"?

Hopefully I have been able to establish clearly that the situation that now exists on the east coast fishery is a direct result of uncontrolled massive expansion caused by the shipbuilding subsidy and the selling of limited entry licences.

Any further plan for fishery management must ensure that government assistance of any kind that affects that fishery must apply equally to all participants. The present shipbuilding subsidy favours the fishing companies to the detriment of the independent fishermen. This position must be rectified either by: (i) applying the shipbuilding subsidy to all new fishing vessels; or (ii) abolishing the shipbuilding subsidy on all fishing vessels. If independent fishermen are to survive in competition with the fishing companies in any fishery, managed or otherwise, there are no other alternatives.

The Present

Apart from conservation measures on crabs and other specific species, the major management controls are: Moreton Bay, weekend closure; northern fishing zone; otter trawl entitlement (east coast);

gulf barramundi management plan; barramundi endorsement (east coast); beam trawl; Pumicestone Passage permits.

Already on the east coast we have a number of management controls, set up in a piecemeal fashion over a period of time. Most fisheries have some form of management with one thing in common, that is, they are all entirely different. Added to these management controls we also have the Great Barrier Reef Marine Park Authority, and now trying to get into the act to add to the confusion is the Queensland National Parks and Wildlife Service.

Recognizing the need for the management of a fisheries resource indicated immediately that restrictions and/or limitations are required on the catching effort in the fishery. Controls on a fishery are instigated by pressures on the government from bodies outside the commercial fishing industry or by fishermen themselves from within the industry.

Unfortunately, we very often find that many of the controls and limitations placed on commercial fishermen by the government come from bodies outside the industry, and, as always, it appears that these bodies are able to exert more influence on government thinking than we in the industry can.

There are massive problems facing the industry today and an East Coast Management Plan is vital for the survival of the industry and the independent fishermen. Some of the major problems are: fuel price issue; effect on the northern fishing zone on the east coast fishery; the declining resource; too many vessels competing for a limited (declining) resource; harvesting of immature prawns and scallops; detrimental effects of the shipbuilding subsidy to the east coast; the massive inroads into the market of cheap imported seafoods; too many fishermen.

Zoning

Fishermen are already plagued by rules, regulations and restrictions and truthfully, and let's not deny it, once government (the manager) draws an imaginary line across a stretch of water for a purpose, it becomes an enforceable regulation. Any regulation in the fishing industry is therefore a restriction on total fishing operations. The purpose of the regulation is usually just an uneducated excuse to attempt to bring economic stability to those fishermen concerned, when in fact, it is a form of protection being afforded to those fishermen from other fishermen.

Once this form of protection is afforded to an industry it has a chain reaction with multiplies and breeds further regulations to protect fishermen from other fishermen. Thus our fisheries are not being correctly managed but are seen to be managed under the guise of a complex network of rules, regulations and entitlements, restrictions

which, in effect, are only regulating one fisherman against another
fisherman. The whole situation ends up in an impractical
unworkable, total fishing plan of mismanagement. As fishermen we
find ourselves back at base one trying to pull down fences which
now contain no resource, with no stable future for our industry. This
has already happened in America and in South Australia.

The only acceptable regulation, and this should be the only
regulation in the industry, is one which protects the resources. Any
regulation so adopted should be truly aimed in this direction and
should not pit one fisherman against another fisherman.
Unfortunately in reality the only defence against a zone is another
zone.

Everyone in industry and government agrees that such a dangerous
situation, once established, gains momentum and eventually gets out
of control. This then applies pressure on the government to
implement more restrictions on fishermen, and industry ends up in
a situation whereby our whole fishery is based on a farm ownership
principal of one fisherman fishing one paddock for one species. It
could be that our future Queensland waters will be a crisscrossing
of survey lines regulated by a government rule book of do's and
don'ts in our own paddock, and we find that as a result of our
attempts to manage a fishery we regulate ourselves out of the
industry. This has happened in other parts of Australia.

Fuel

The fuel crisis will ensure advances in gear technology and in
economic propulsion to such a degree that if all past improvements
and the improvements of the next ten years were incorporated, the
catching capability of the fleet could increase by up to 50 per cent.
In any fishery management this must be a consideration. This fact
without any added units means that the catching capability of the
present fleet could be increased by 50 per cent in ten years.
Indications are that the known resource cannot sustain the present
level of fishing effort, let alone an increase of this nature.

It has been suggested that we should introduce some sort of "buy-
back" licence scheme to reduce the number of vessels in the fishery.
This has worked in other countries with similar problems; Denmark
is an example. Such a scheme would be financed by both state and
federal governments as well as by fishermen themselves, and is the
best long-term solution to the present problem.

Today part of the industry is looking to government for financial
assistance and it has been suggested by our organization that a
suitable method of funding areas such as a buy-back licence scheme
or research and development of new fisheries would be to use the
government grant given unwisely to the industry in the form of the

shipbuilding subsidy. Instead of using this money to build more boats and compound the problem even further, the funds should be used to try to alleviate the problem which has arisen as a result of this grant.

There are approximately thirty Gulf entitlements which have not as yet had new vessels constructed for them. This means there should be aproximately $2.2 million now available for the benefit of the whole industry.

Such a policy cannot be properly formulated or implemented unless it is supported by a united industry front or management, combined with a genuine interest by the various government departments responsible for contributing to the well-being of the Queensland industry.

East Coast Fin Fishery

By far the greatest problem this fishery is experiencing is the operations of the illegal operators and "shamateurs". Until the government is prepared to face up to this fact by effectively policing the fishery and preventing the sale of fish by other than the holders of a master fisherman's licence, any form of management imposed by the government, other than that requested by master fishermen, is an unjust action singling out the commercial fisherman.

The Declining Resource

Unfortunately, the contribution made to the fishery by the Queensland coastal estuarine areas has never been scientifically evaluated. Research in America indicates that the decline in the inshore fishery in that country is directly related to estuarine wetland destruction.

It is reasonable to assume that the same position exists here. In Queensland we have seen the continual destruction of estuarine areas, from Moreton Bay to Cape York. In the past decade, the destruction has raged like an uncontrolled bushfire, condoned by state government and local authority alike. It continues with an air of frightening finality for all fishermen — amateur and commercial — ignored alike by most supposedly responsible persons in authority at all levels of government. There are hundreds of examples, the best for this purpose being the development in the Cairns inlet.

For the long-term benefit of the nation we need to evaluate and conserve these resources and it is a responsibility of the industry to initiate action by government in this regard.

The Declining Markets

The Queensland industry cannot compete with imports. This is an unpleasant fact. The industry is not equipped to present the product to the consumer at the same cost or quality. Nor do we have the continuity of supply necessary to compete. These combined factors result in an unstable market when the consumers prefer to have top quality product at a stable price available for their convenience at all times.

Too Many Fishermen

The otter trawl industry is creating pressures on all branches of the fishing industry. Under present regulations, to be in charge of a vessel engaged in fishing a person must be the holder of a Queensland master fisherman's licence. Trawlers must have licence holders on board. Consequently many skippers and deckhands have licences as well as the owner. That licence entitles any holder to set up business in any fishery. The trend seems to be to the low investment fisheries, and usually these fishermen do not have the skills to succeed in these fisheries. The regulations are forcing both companies and independents on an industry self-destruct course by creating unnecessary master fishermen.

Diversification

Now that all the parties concerned can appreciate our current situation it should be obvious why there is a necessity for diversification of the total Queensland fishing effort.

The only true and immediate solution to our whole industry situation is firstly, to maintain a complete freeze on licences and secondly, to diversify a certain section of our fishing into a new fishery, such as longlining and offshore gill netting. This, it is hoped, will decrease the effort being applied on the existing fisheries and restore economic viability to the remainder of fishermen.

Such diversification has to be developed on an industry understanding that the diversity is being encouraged in order to halt the snowballing effects of further restrictions and maintenance of the status quo, as well as to ease the pressure on our existing fisheries and bring stabilization to the industry.

This is easier said than done. But what has been surfacing from discussion is the complexity, challenges, and uncertainty of such development, and more importantly, a better understanding that if such development is to proceed successfully, it will require a well coordinated and preplanned fishery management policy.

In any action we take we must place the interest of the genuine Queensland fishermen ahead of all others. Investors, as well as fishermen from other states, must take second place. Our motto should be "Queensland waters for Queensland fishermen". It would be desirable to reduce the number of units in the fishery by placing some units in other unexploited fisheries that exist in the Northern Territory and the northwest coast of Western Australia if possible.

The biggest single overriding factor which has made a major contribution to the problem that exists today, is that no one in authority in Queensland has in the past had the courage to make the necessary decisions to preserve the industry. The reason given for this failure is that the industry is not united. Our organization is confident that the new advisory committee to the minister will promote the forum for a united effort.

I venture to say that half the number of units could catch the same amount of produce much more efficiently with a massive saving in fuel, man-hours, constructive effort and capital investment. Instead, at present, the Queensland fishing industry is destroying itself from within. A lack of direction, planning and management, together with the mindless pursuit of sectional interests by both corporate and independent sectors, is ensuring the long-prophesied disaster.

Until all people involved in the Queensland industry begin to take a more long-term view, and to shun considerations of short-term economic benefit and/or survival, the destruction of the industry will continue, and we can anticipate little cooperation from governments. One message the industry is getting loud and clear is that the government will not again allow a section of the industry to evolve around the price of an entry entitlement or licence.

Gulf Barramundi Management

On the initiative of the fishermen themselves the Gulf Barramundi Management Plan has been completed. All affected fishermen were consulted and advised throughout the resolution process. The plan embodies a philosophy of total management of the fishing effort on each particular species by legislation and regulation. The industry will have divided ôpinions as to whether this philosophy will achieve its designed aims or develop into another fiasco.

One aspect has been clearly established. The barramundi producers in the gulf are in control of their own destiny. It is now necessary for the east coast producers to decide if they intend to develop their own strategy, or continue to permit outside influences to dictate the mismanagement of our industry for them.

I have made enquiries as to the government attitude and have learned that we must make our own decisions on this subject and advise them accordingly. We should all be aware of the present trend of dividing the industry and imposing specific species entitlements and regulations. We should also realize that if no firm plan is developed this process will continue. It has been shown that as soon as a species becomes endangered, political pressure from the industry and the community will force the issue, regardless of all attempts to prevent further fragmentation of the industry.

The Future

Representing approximately three thousand master fishermen in Queensland and, I am confident, with support of the company section as well I would like to ask: "has our industry any future?"

We have been told that we are a "Cinderella" industry with untold potential. I doubt very much if the practising fisherman or fishing company administrator presently trying to balance the books would agree.

The main problem seems to be with academic people who have a different perception of the extent of the available resource along the Queensland coast than we the fishermen have. A total lack of liaison between these two groups is aggravating the misunderstandings.

I would like to suggest that an idealistic forecast of the industry's future will be of no benefit and that a realistic understanding of our present problems would be of greater value and is the area which should receive all available effort and resources.

Fuel Tax

Before the last two fuel price increases, the economists warned that the industry had reached a stage of economic instability. The federal government is now considering the next fuel price increase, not when or whether, just how much.

This will cause the following chain reaction:
A percentage of fishermen will drop out of the industry; the survivors will become far more efficient resulting in an increased fishing effort; the fisherman's inherent ability to survive will ensure that the percentage of increased effort will far outweigh the effort lost by the number dropping out; this will, in turn further endanger the resource; this will result in increased unprofitability and desperation to survive; the final destruction to the resource breeding stocks will be inevitable.

The industry certainly cannot afford to supply the funds to develop new fuel-efficient fisheries, and the federal government does not seem to recognize the need. The fishing industry is desperate for new and alternative fisheries; examples as previously mentioned are offshore gill netting and longlining. At present any benefits from these alternatives would be lost in increasing production costs.

However, let us assume that a miracle does occur and the authorities decide to return a small portion of the fuel tax to the industry for some meaningful development. At the same time, for this development to be of any use, the government would also have to make it possible for this industry to compete with foreign countries (such as, Taiwan, Russia and India) on both the domestic and international markets. In our present economy this seems like a pipedream, unless the government changes its attitude towards market replacements or tariffs. So much for the future of the fuel intensive sea-based section of the industry.

Turning now to the inshore fishery, there are two very distinct conflicting pressures ensuring the demise of this section of our industry. Firstly, the state government, local government and, in fact, the community, because of the need for development, is effectively destroying the life-support system of this fishery. Every time the wetland area is interfered with by the community another section of this industry dies. The second factor is the reliable supply of New Zealand sea perch, a quality product at an acceptable price that is readily available to the consumer.

One school of thought is that the industry needs promotion to encourage more of the community to eat fish. I believe that if the claims being made by the Cattlemen's Union that the consumption of beef is declining in favour of fish and poultry, are correct, we do not need promotion.

The community is eating more fish. What the Cattlemen's Union does not realize, and for certain the estuarine fishermen do, is the fact that Queensland produced fish is not being sought in the market place by the consumer. Any promotion would only ensure that the community consumes more imported fish.

As our industry cannot supply local fish in the same quantity or quality, sea perch would need to be retailed at a similar price to barramundi and coral trout to have any effect. This effect would probably favour the beef industry. Therefore, the estuary fishermen must now look toward becoming an importer and a retailer of New Zealand sea perch. There is a healthy margin available in this trade which could be a method of surviving.

We have the government trading offshore fishing rights to the east. In the north our traditional grounds are being traded to the New Guinea Government. To the west the community is destroying the habitat, and elsewhere National Parks are cutting it up into sections.

The community is acquiring the habit of purchasing imported sea perch, because that is the best value for money available, and the industry itself is staggering under ever-increasing production costs.

This is a summary of the reasons. I have asked the question — what is the future of the Queensland fishing industry? The members of our organization believe that our industry has a future.

The traditional fisherman of the past is being forced by economic necessity to evolve from an activity that is a way of life to becoming fully professional in all attitudes and it is these professionals who will survive. All that we ask is that we be given the opportunity.

We have learnt from experience that sectional management is not in the best interests of the industry. We do not have the answers in the Queensland east coast situation and the Queensland Commercial Fishermen's Organization is presently seeking direction in this regard.

Certainly, if there is not an immediate general awareness of the industry's situation resulting in a coordinated total industry management policy supported by government at all levels and by all sections of the industry, the survival of the industry must be considered to be in doubt.

10

Recreational Fishing in Queensland: The Eighties and Beyond

C.T. Russell and P. Saenger

Man's utilization of fish resources can be traced to the beginnings of history, and even at a very early stage the evidence suggests that this activity was motivated by one or more of the following: survival, barter or recreation. With the appearance of more highly organized communities, "governments" generally accepted the responsibility for overseeing and partitioning this commonly owned resource on behalf of its subjects. Acceptance by "governments" of this role was almost certainly not altruistic, but fostered by a desire to prevent conflict within the community and to ensure that some part of the resource was available to those government members who, because of their governmental duties, no longer had the time or inclination to supply their own needs. At the community level, this arrangement was undoubtedly a highly efficient division of labour.

This pattern of governmental responsibility is firmly entrenched in the English common law, which still forms the basis of Queensland's legal, social and political institutions. Under the common law, all members of the public had a common right to fish in tidal waters and rivers to the point where the tide ebbs and flows, although this right was exercisable at the pleasure of the sovereign who, it might be added, reserved certain rights to himself. Thus, whale and sturgeon, when thrown ashore or caught near the coast, became the personal property of the sovereign. The common law right to fish in tidal waters by the general public was gradually eroded by a succession of sovereigns who granted exclusive rights to individuals as a revenue-raising measure. When this erosion of common law right was finally recognized and challenged in the courts in a series of cases, the Crown's view was, not surprisingly, upheld (*Malcolmson v O'Dea* 10 HLC 593).

At this point, as far as Queensland is concerned, the fish resources of this state had achieved their modern status, and from The Pearl-shell and Beche-de-mer Fishery Act of 1881 to The Fisheries Acts of 1976 the Crown has demonstrated a jurisdictional willingness to oversee and regulate the fish resources of this state for the people of Queensland.

Within this framework, the fisherman, whether commercial or recreational, occupies a position of privilege. He is granted that privilege by the people through the Crown to harvest some of the state's fish resources. The commercial fisherman clearly performs a very valuable function within the community by providing fisheries products for those unable to catch their own and it is acknowledged that the commercial fishing industry contributes to the local economies. However, it must be emphasized that the right to harvest is a privilege and privileges carry responsibilities — for the commercial fisherman there are responsibilities to the stocks they harvest, to the environment and, not least, to the people of Queensland.

The role, impacts and responsibilities of the recreational fisherman are less clear and until recently, these have been largely ignored. Established in 1977, the Queensland Amateur Fishing Council has attempted to assist in the definition of the role, interests and future of the recreational fisherman in this state and these aspects form the basis of the ensuing discussion.

Recreational Fishing: Extent and Economic Impact

No definitive assessment of recreational fishing activities is available; Queensland, with its marlin and reef fishery, is probably in a better position than the other Australian states. Nevertheless, comparisons and extrapolations from existing survey results are of dubious validity largely because of the differing parameters employed, and any such attempt must be considered to be of "order of magnitude" only. Be that as it may, recreational fishing is probably best summed up as a popular participatory sport with a cast of thousands.

Table 1 Participation, effort and expenditure for recreational fishing

Country	Survey Year	Angler (%) Pop'n	Annual Effort (mandays/ year)	Annual Expend. ($/ angler)	Source
USA	1975	27	24.5	282	US Fish & Wildlife
Canada	1976	31	11.6	140	Fisheries & Environment Department, Canada
NSW	1977	30	22.5	–	NSW State Fisheries
Victoria	1977	36	17.3	–	Fisheries & Wildlife Department, Victoria
Queensland	1978	54	19.0	155	QAFC pilot study

Some comparative data on recreational fishing participation, effort and expenditure is given in table 1. However, a greater insight into the extent of the recreational fishery in Queensland can be gleaned from the following data:

1. in 1977, 70,000 powerboats were registered in Queensland with

a 1977 market value of $200 million; with an annual maintenance expenditure of $50 to 100 million;
2. 20,000 Queenslanders are members of fishing clubs;
3. the North Queensland Black Marlin Game Fishery is estimated to be worth up to $20 million per year to the regional economy;
4. QAFC estimates fishing activity in the Southport Broadwater at 780,000 man-hours per year fishing from boats during daylight;
5. QAFC estimates fishing activity in the Tweed River to Cape Moreton region at 153,500 man-days per year fishing from boats and beach, generating a yearly trade of at least $4.5 million.

Taken together, these data suggest that the recreational fishery in Queensland is a popular, significant and sizeable activity.

The Need for Management

If the participation rate in recreational fishing remains relatively constant, then with the state's present population growth the number of participants will continue to increase. Based on crude estimates from mangrove productivity studies, the present harvests of edible fish (20,000 tonnes in 1978-79) may not be too far from the upper limits of animal sea life produced annually in Queensland's coastal region, presently estimated at 40,000 tonnes. While these figures are estimates only, they serve to emphasize that the fish resources of this state are finite.

Queensland's population is not evenly distributed but rather is concentrated largely in the coastal zone. Historically, the coastal plains were the first areas to be densely populated and most major cities are sited on rivers or foreshores, with the coastal plains highly favoured for agriculture and grazing. More recently, industrialization has created a greater demand for coastal land and has generated its own population growth.

These factors operate against the maintenance of a stable coastal zone environment, whilst the increasing population (and fishing participants) continues to demand increasing productivity from the coastal zone.

Clearly, this cannot continue indefinitely and the recreational fisherman, together with his commercial colleague, has a responsibility to ensure that some socially acceptable position can be attained which balances the various competing pressures on the fish resource. This can, in all likelihood, only be achieved through sound, scientifically based fisheries management.

Prerequisites for Effective Management

To have effective management of this state's fish resources, there are several prerequisites. Of utmost importance here is the collection of basic data on much of our coastal and riverine biota.

During the long process of evolution, much of our aquatic biota adjusted to the specific environmental conditions prevailing in our coastal waters, including salinity, temperature, turbidity, river discharges, flooding frequencies and droughts. Seasonal changes in the environment guided and controlled the biota's migrations, sexual maturations, spawning, growth and competitive relationships with other species. Many of the environmental conditions to which our aquatic biota has become adapted are now environmental requirements. Species-specific data of this type forms the basis for successful management.

A second essential data set is the response of our biota to manipulation. Manipulative research in this state is in its infancy but the effects on our biota of environmental manipulation, varying fishing techniques and other forms of regulation, must be known in the long term.

Finally, on the human side, effective management requires the availability of experienced, motivated scientists and the existence of an informed, cooperative public and courageous, far-sighted politicians, who will implement and work towards the acceptance of the resultant management schemes.

Objectives of Management: The Recreational Fisherman's View

Three broad aspects should be considered as basic to effective management of this state's fish resources – protecting, partitioning and enhancing the resource.

Protection of the Resource

Regulations can be of value for protecting aquatic life resources, for preventing overfishing, and for ensuring equal opportunities to harvest and enjoy the recreational species, but regulations alone do not produce crops of the desired species. To increase the production of desired species, it is necessary to maintain or restore not only a favourable physical and chemical environment but also their biological environment; that is, to maintain a favourable and desired balance among species.

Management of aquatic life resources may include the establishment of habitat reserves, marine parks and refuge areas, the protection of spawning migrations and spawning areas, and other regulations. In the management of recreational species, however, the basic requirement is to protect, restore and improve the environmental conditions for the desired species so that these may remain viable, and hopefully comprise a large percentage of the biota. In this way, a large proportion of the productive capacity of the water is utilized for the production of desired species.

The maintenance of a favourable environment for all species consists of two main activities: preventing its physical destruction, particularly for nonessential alternative uses and the elimination of pollution in its many, often insidious, forms. Maintaining a viable environment must be of prime concern, as emphasized by Dr D. Francois, Director of NSW State Fisheries in an address dated 25 September 1980. He states:

> Natural mortality is the key to modern fisheries management, for it is through a full understanding of natural mortality that we can safely allow huge yields to be taken from fisheries without reducing future yield or the regenerative capacity of the populations. Because fishes have such high reproductive rates and grow so quickly, they are particularly resilient if, and this is the big if, the environment remains viable. In fact, if we make a mistake and allow a fishery to be over-exploited, the worst that can possibly happen is that anglers have some poor fishing for a few years or commercial fishermen do not catch as much as they did . . . We can place the necessary restrictions on the fishery and it will bounce back in a very short time. Damage to the environment, on the other hand, where irreparable harm can be done, causes fisheries managers many restless nights.

Partitioning of the Resource

There have been conflicts of interest between recreational and commercial fishing, as well as between practitioners of different fishing methods. Every effort should be made to reduce or eliminate real adverse effects of one fishery on another, and where supposed fears are unfounded, to enlighten the respective groups. A thorough understanding of the basic facts of production and the proper use of regulations can go a long way towards this end.

Commercial fishermen are already limited in some recreational fishing areas as to their activities and to certain periods of the year. In prime recreational fishing areas, commercial fishing should be gradually phased out in such a way that no hardship is engendered (for example, Pumicestone Passage). Where it appears desirable, the taking of valuable recreational species by commercial fishermen may also be prohibited (for example, commercial spearfishing for coral trout in the Capricornia Marine Park). In the same context, certain areas or species may need to be set aside for commercial operations only.

Enhancement of the Resource

This is the area of management in which the QAFC and other recreational fishermen have concentrated most effort in the past year or two and a few examples would seem to be in order.

Artificial Reefs.   In Queensland, the construction of artificial reefs is not seen as a government responsibility. It has therefore fallen to the lot of public-spirited fishermen, divers and boating clubs. However, artificial reefs in Hervey Bay, off Cowan, in the Southport Broadwater and near the Rous Light are all reported to be doing well, with rapid build-up in quantities of fish, and numbers of species. In view of this, it would seem desirable to have a scientific evaluation of these structures and if found feasible, some governmental initiatives.

Midwater Fish Attractors.   Over the last few years, considerable data on the efficacy of these structures has become available from a number of localities. Wherever these devices have been tried, they have been acclaimed for vastly improving pelagic fish populations in their immediate vicinity. While they might add little to the overall productivity of an area, they appear to reduce the distances spent in search of aggregations of pelagic fish; in an energy-conscious society, this would seem to be of real value. It is hoped that a pilot midwater "reef" will be functioning in Queensland waters within a year or so as a research project initiated by the QAFC, and it is hoped that significant governmental assistance would be available.

Stocking of Dams.   Queensland's large freshwater impoundments have created a new environment unsuitable to any native food or sport fish. QAFC has lobbied for the introduction of nile perch for scientific evaluation under quarantine conditions, as a potential inhabitant of this newly created environment. Nile perch are similar to barramundi in sporting attributes and table quality, are commonly caught up to 50 kg, and do not require access to salt water to spawn. If this species turns out to be favourable for stocking, our dams could produce something of the order of $10 million worth of prime table fish per year.

Barramundi Management.   QAFC has supported measures aimed at a regeneration of depleted barramundi stocks. These measures include an amateur bag limit of two fish per day, with five in possession at any one time. There is also a closed season covering the spawning period and closure to fishing of certain hatcheries. The commercial fishermen have also accepted restrictions on their gear and activities in relation to this species. Some recreational fishermen from north Queensland report apparent benefits from the initial closures. However, management of a species such as barramundi must be flexible and responsive to resultant changes in the fish stocks in either direction.

Marlin Fishery.   The role of the QAFC in relation to the Japanese longline fishery in our northern waters is now a matter of history. As a result of the longline closure, the area closed to longlining off north Queensland can be expected to reduce the take of black marlin by about 95 per cent. It should be noted that the Japanese still have access to the tuna stocks by dropline fishing—a method that is more selective and less wasteful of unwanted species.

Aquaculture.   While aquaculture projects are probably inevitable on a coastline as suitable as that of this state, any proposal involving the loss of natural fisheries habitats should be carefully evaluated, and the natural fish production loss taken into consideration in calculating aquacultural production. Thus, while aquaculture promises an easy enhancement of the resource, experience elsewhere has shown this not to be the case.

Summary

Queensland has the potential to become the recreational fishing focus not only of Australia, but of the world—but it all depends on what happens here in the eighties. We are faced with a choice: we can continue our depredations on the environment, particularly our coastal regions, or we can maintain and enhance its attractiveness, including its fishing potential. What direction we take depends on the public and our politicians and, to a large measure, on the specialists in the field. A little has been done but much remains to be done, and time is running short.

11
Management-Orientated Research: Penaeid Prawns

W. Dall

Fisheries research may be seen as having a number of functions. The simplest, and perhaps the oldest, view is that the scientist's role is to help the fisherman find new grounds and to maximize his catch. Early in Australia's fishing history this approach was predominant, but as the sophistication of the industry increased it tended to take over these roles itself since a well-organized fishing fleet is far more effective at fish finding and catching than a single research vessel. In recent years this role has become restricted to normally inaccessible areas such as the outer continental shelf or fisheries involving specialist gear such as purse seining. Once serious exploitation of a fishery begins, management becomes necessary and scientific research becomes largely management orientated.

The research role by CSIRO reflects these trends, except that the declaration of the 200 nautical mile economic zone has temporarily placed an emphasis on fish finding. Thus the role of CSIRO in fisheries management has been defined as "providing scientific advice for management when called on to do so". This is a broad charter and, since research funds are normally very limited, it is essential to adopt a systematic approach in planning management-orientated research. A number of approaches are possible, but one that is perhaps most appropriate to CSIRO uses the total harvest or yield of a given fishery as a starting point. The next step is to examine the broad concepts of management which contribute to this yield and maximize them, and finally the levels of knowledge necessary to base management on a firm scientific foundation. Research on the western rock lobster developed *ad hoc* along these lines over a long period and proved successful. The start of the Tropical Prawn Research Project, centred on the Gulf of Carpentaria, in 1974 gave the opportunity to plan systematically the research from the start and the scheme shown in figure 1 was drawn up.

The yield of any animal harvest is made up of numbers of individuals multiplied by the size at which they are harvested. These are the two basic parameters studied by the population dynamicist, namely survival and growth. The yield should be controlled by scientific management so that the resource is exploited rationally and this in turn depends on a proper stock assessment being made. Where well-established, closely comparable fisheries exist, the parameters of stock assessment equations may be estimated, but at the best, this should be regarded as a first approximation and real data from the particular fishery should be obtained. Estimates of mortality need to be made from the fished population (normally adults or near-adults) and growth rates found from tagging or cohort analysis. Tagging also serves to determine the extent of migration, if any.

At the pragmatic level of fisheries management, research could stop here, and legislation framed to ensure that the catch does not exceed the sustainable yield. This rarely suffices because management is normally faced with a number of other problems.

Natural fluctuations in abundance are usual and a very poor year is likely to lead to accusations from industry that overfishing has been allowed to occur and there may be pressure for further restrictive legislation. The extent of annual fluctuations becomes known only after a fishery has been established for some time, but intelligent use of statistics may enable estimates of the poorest possible year to be made. This only serves to reassure industry that a poor year is within expected limits, and a more valuable estimate is prediction of the actual magnitude of a coming season's catch. Stock prediction is difficult and demands an intimate knowledge of the biology of a given species (figure 1). Obviously accurate measurements need to be made of the number of recruits to the coming season's fishery, that is, the juveniles and postlarvae. This alone is not sufficient because these recruits do not automatically and quantitatively transfer to the fishery. Environmental factors such as temperature and predation will affect mortality, and rainfall may affect rate of migration. The population of juveniles is determined by the postlarvae which immigrate into the nursery grounds, and hence knowledge of the mechanisms which control this immigration and knowledge of the ecology of the larvae and reproducing adults is desirable.

Information on the biological environment is also necessary. In many of the nursery ground environments macrophytes may be abundant. The primary value of these may be for cover from predators, but the production of macrophytes may have an influence, via microorganisms, on the production of the small animals that comprise the food of prawns. Predation is, of course, a major cause of mortality in prawns, and common predators at least should be known. This is an area that tends to be neglected in management-orientated research, but is a possible cause of sudden population depletion of small juvenile prawns. For example, a large influx of cubomedusae, a known predator of sergestids and small prawns, into an estuary could decimate the population of juvenile prawns.

Compared with the "survival" part there is a less on the "growth" side of figure 1, apart from measurement of growth rate, that can be directly applied to stock assessment models. Temperature will

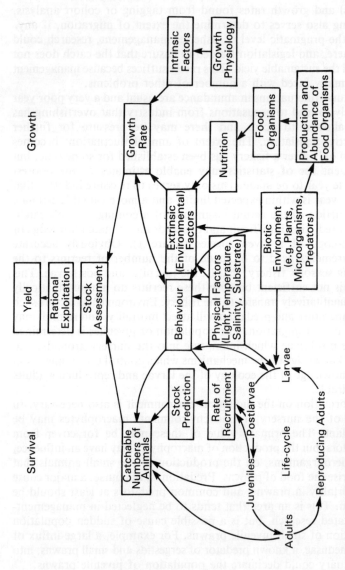

Figure 1 Model for management-orientated research based on yield.

obviously affect growth rate and needs to be taken into account in growth estimates at different latitudes. Food abundance has not yet been identified as a limiting factor in prawn growth, but is a possible factor in regions of high population density such as nursery grounds. A catalogue of the components which make up nursery grounds is necessary, however, to enable nursery grounds to be defined, since it is highly desirable that legislation should be introduced as early as possible to protect the nursery grounds from the effects of fishing and other man-made influences. Apart from these considerations, research on areas which affect growth rate must necessarily be more basic, and from the management point of view, less urgent than those affecting survival. Nevertheless, it should not be forgotten that in the longer view a knowledge of the extrinsic and intrinsic factors affecting growth rate is critical for aquaculture.

Finally, reference again to figure 1 will show that "behaviour" occupies a central position and indeed affects almost all major parts of the model. For a start the fisherman is an empirical behaviourist. Understanding all stages of the life-cycle demands at least some knowledge of the animal's behaviour. Responses to the various environmental factors will determine where a population is at a given time and its rate of recruitment into the fishery and is thus perhaps the most critical factor in stock prediction. In spite of its overall importance, systematic studies of behaviour are sadly lacking in management-orientated research, although admittedly some understanding of an animal's behaviour is acquired during field studies of populations.

The Tropical Prawn Research Project employed a total of twenty-one professional and technical staff an was thus a major research programme by any standards and probably the most comprehensive that has been mounted anywhere for prawn research. Because of this it is worth recounting some of the difficulties that arose. These fall into two broad categories—general problems, and those specific to particular sections.

General problems

Vessels

Operation at sea is always difficult and vessels are always expensive to run. Initially CSIRO owned a new 22 metre prawn trawler, modified for research. It proved unsuitable in a number of ways, and after a couple of years of operation the vessel was sold and subsequent seagoing operations were done by charter. This is even more expensive than running a vessel and caused the field work to be terminated in 1979 due to lack of funds.

Volume of Data Gathered

One of the problems often not forseen or even recognized in marine research is that a properly run research vessel is a very efficient data gathering device. In most research institutions time at least equal to that of the field work needs to be allotted for working up the data. Access to a large computer with backup personnel (programmers, statisticians) is usually necessary because of the large volume of complex data. All of the field programmes have had problems in data processing. The larval ecology and juvenile ecology sections have had their data processing problems exacerbated by the need for plankton sorting of a large number of samples (a labour-intensive process) before data processing could even begin.

Difficulties of Working in a Remote Tropical Area

Transport costs for personnel, equipment and samples are high and contributed materially to the cost of the programme. The administrative difficulties in working from Brisbane as a base were considerable. The most serious problem, however, was with personnel. The alternatives were for field personnel to spend fairly long periods away from home (tours of three to four weeks) at regular intervals or for families to move to the area (Kurumba). In practice both alternatives were used, but high staff turnover should be expected in such situations.

Specific Problems

Lack of Background Data

This was most keenly felt in the larval ecology section. There were almost no descriptions of the larval stages of most of the commercially important species in the Gulf of Carpentaria. This required time-consuming rearing of prawn larvae so that larvae plankton catches could be identified.

There was also very little environmental data. A tentative tidal model, based on very little data, had been developed and water masses identified from a few hydrological cruises. A concomitant oceanographical study was not started until the final year of the field work.

The larval ecology group also had to collect their own environmental data for the Norman River.

Differences in Progress of the Various Areas of Work

In the adult ecology programme, detailed data was tabulated and completed by the end of each cruise. In contrast those in the larval ecology section had a series of plankton samples with many man-weeks of work ahead before the larvae were even separated from the plankton. Such problems are inherent in any biological programme of this nature, but need to be recognized at the outset.

This project was necessarily very expensive for three principal reasons: the number of scientific personnel employed; the logistics of operating in the Gulf of Carpentaria; vessel operating or vessel charter costs. There are various ways in which costs could be reduced in future programmes of this nature and some of these will be briefly discussed.

A reduction in number of personnel can be achieved by restricting the number of areas investigated as discussed previously, or by giving each researcher a broader area for investigation. Either course leads to less useful information being obtained and the net effect is to reduce the scope of the research.

Secondly, a pilot study of a population of appropriate species in a more accessible area would reduce logistic costs and, if successful, enables a suitable model to be developed which can then be tested in the area of question.

Thirdly, vessel costs can be reduced by making the maximum use of commercial vessels or catch samples. These provide only limited information, however, and some kind of research vessel is usually necessary. Again the pilot project concept is worth considering. In this case a small part of the area of interest is selected for intensive study. Probably a smaller and much cheaper vessel will suffice and operating time will be reduced. Eventually, the results of this study will have to be tested over a larger area.

Overall the Tropical Prawn Research Project has been successful. A detailed stock assessment model has been developed for banana prawns. A stock prediction model for the same species has been completed and over forty papers and articles published on the biology of prawns and their environment.

While the model developed for management-orientated research in figure 1 was for prawns, the principles are of course applicable to other exploited marine groups of animals. One drawback is that some knowledge of the biology of the animal in question, particularly the life history, is needed before such a flow diagram can be constructed. This is, however, rarely a serious problem today. Usually something at least is known of related species, but where uncertainty exists provision should be made for modification of the relevant areas of research as knowledge accumulates.

12
Private Enterprise Research Programme[1]

G. Kesteven, J. Stratton and D. Carter

As any industrial enterprise grows a stage is reached when the manager's personal knowledge and experience are no longer adequate as a base for sound management decisions.

A transition then must be made from seat-of-the-pants management to what is often called scientific management.

Often this transition can be a gradual, continuing process. But there are times when the changes in industry are major in character and when important innovations are made in managerial practice, such as when serious use begins to be made of the techniques now available from operations research. At such times a manager is required to adjust himself to new ways of working. This is the kind of change we are concerned with in this article.

Operations reserach previously has found little place in Australian fishing enterprises; indeed, with few exceptions, the scale of operation has been too small to warrant it except at a quite elementary level. But Australian fisheries are now very different, technically, from what they were, say, twenty years ago and the situation is changing rapidly.

One of the many changes taking place involves the "information revolution" brought about by developments in radio, television, satellites and computers.

We do not need to dwell on the effect that such equipment has had on people generally or on fishermen in particular. What is important in the present connection is its effect on the collecting, assembling, analysing and interpreting of technical information.

In this article we outline the changes occurring in the operations of KFV Fisheries. The company operates a fleet of prawn trawlers in the Gulf of Carpentaria, on prawn stocks about which relatively little is known as yet. This year (1981) it has twenty-five trawlers in the fleet.

Operating costs are high and are rising rapidly, particularly with the frequent increases in fuel prices. Good management decisions can bring good profits. Bad management decisions can bring disastrous losses.

The company has recognized that if it is to continue to be successful its managers will require much more information than they have had in the past about various facets of the company's operations. It has reached a stage in its growth when serious operations research is needed.

Proposed Research, Monitoring Programme

The central aim of any fishing enterprise is to take the greatest possible catch with the least possible expenditure of effort.

Put another way, every commercial fisherman tries to schedule his operations to apply fishing effort where and when there is the greatest concentration of fish (or in this case prawns). He seeks to reduced searching time to a minimum, to quit fishing on a ground when the catch rate has fallen below a satisfactory level, and then to move to another ground as quickly as possible.

Every fleet manager seeks to ensure that his vessels are fully operational at the best fishing times and strategically placed to enable them to fish the most productive grounds.

Successful fishing skippers get to know quite a lot about the distribution and behaviour of the species they hunt, and the prawning skippers in the gulf have already acquired a great deal of information about the stocks of banana prawns and other prawn species.

But we have to recognize that, compared with what is known about the resources of many other fisheries, our knowledge of gulf prawns is only rudimentary. Hopefully government research now in progress will, in time, fill many of the gaps in our knowledge. But what can we in the industry do to improve the knowledge base from which we operate?

Let's look at the "state of the art" in fisheries research, or at least at some of its relevant features.

From the experience of the past hundred years of research has emerged a set of procedures for estimating the catch that can be taken from a stock. In such research the structure and dynamics of each fish population is studied on a base involving the life history and distribution of the species.

It is now virtually traditional among fisheries biologists that this total array of information — life history, distribution, population structure and population dynamics — should be developed before advice can be given on the level of catches that can be taken to avoid wasteful reduction of the stock. Much of this work is anchored to a concept of maximum sustainable yield, a concept being seriously questioned in many quarters.

Development of the total account of a resource requires years of research. This traditional approach therefore is unlikely to be of immediate help to anyone working in a new fishery. What can they do while they wait for applicable results?

We believe there is a great deal they can, and indeed must, do in their own interest. In saying this we have in mind the value of observatons made by fishermen and the importance of an accurate record of their operations, primarily the catch and effort statistics but including other items.

Let's begin with catch and effort statistics; these lie at the heart of the practices of fisheries biology. These statistics, especially the derived statistics such as catch per unit effort, are very informative about the stocks from which the catches are taken.

In the normal practice of fisheries biology such statistics are collected and compiled over extended periods—months and years—and the derivative indicator statistics (mean catch, catch per unit effort and so on) are published after the event, often long after the event. Often they do no more than merely remind the fishermen of their own experience.

Instead of continuing in that way we believe we can profit from such information day by day, as events are happening, interpreting the behaviour of the statistical series to understand what is happening in the stocks.

Of course this is what an individual fisherman does, but what KFV is doing is making use of modern equipment to draw together as quickly as possible the information that can come from many fishermen, process the information at once, and interpret the results of the analysis. These results then are made available to the

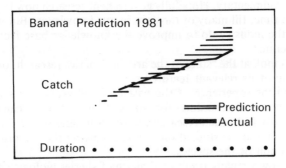

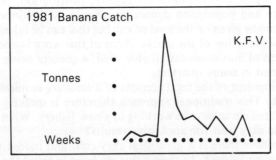

Figure 1 The top graph shows KFV's banana prawn catch prediction for 1981. The prediction, made in mid-March, was a very useful management tool. The weekly catch graph (bottom) shows that the best catches were taken in the week after March 15 and then declined as the season progressed.

fishermen, and at the same time used for managerial decision making.

This much we are doing already, and in fact did with marked success during the recent banana prawn season (figure 1). But we intend to further develop the system, and are even considering cooperative operation of the system to serve other fleets in future.

The practice so often adopted in the past of lumping statistics of operations and calculating long-period averages — yearly or perhaps monthly — is dangerous. These averages are sometimes about as far from reality as the concept of the mythical "average man in the street".

The analysis must be much more detailed, made day by day, for each locality separately; that is, it must be in real time with respect to real place. We must be able to monitor operations as they take place.

The basic component of the system we are developing is a monitoring of catch and effort data from our boats. This component is already in operation. In some ways it resembles the practice of statistical quality control employed in manufacturing industries. (We refer to the practice as SQR.)

Here, a manufacturer identifies a measurable characteristic of his product and then sets the value that this characteristic should have in each item; this average value is marked on a graph. He then determines tolerance limits for the acceptance of items, and these limits too are marked on the graph. Next he establishes a procedure, generally of sampling, to measure items coming off the production line, and each result is entered on the graph. As long as the observation points remain within the limits he is assured that his production system is functioning as he wishes. But if the points take a trend and move out of the limits he is alerted to a change having occurred in production.

In our system the average, or central control line is not horizontal, but traces out a curve, and the limits are not set at a fixed distance from the control line. These features of our control chart — the shape of the control line and the width of the band about it — are set by us from analysis of statistics from the past, subject to biological considerations. Moreover we work with more than one control chart and will enlarge the number over the next year, after which we may find that some may be discarded as being less helpful than others.

From the start of its operations the company has kept daily records of catch by species and locality. These data have been edited and stored on computer, together with a range of data relating to vessel characteristics and vessel operations.

Possibly the most vital data that are lacking, with regard to banana prawns, are those that would provide some indication of the number of schools. The company's skippers have now been asked to record the occasions on which they make the first encounter of a school and from this we hope to get some idea of the number of schools on a given day. Meanwhile we have formulated a hypothesis about the number, size and average density of schools, and the current interpretation of catch data is being made in accordance with that hypothesis.

With regard to other species, we are aware that some questions concerning exact identification of species remain, but the more immediate problems relate to measuring effort and identifying individual stocks.

As we have described the monitoring system so far, it is little more than a within-season operation to yield early forecast of the whole season outcome, and to give some help in decisions on the grounds to be fished and the timing of gear changes.

However we expect the analysis of statistics from the past, now in progress, to increase the power of the system, especially in detecting between-season changes. The ongoing analysis will make full use of all the published data we can lay our hands on, and we hope to gain access to unpublished material.

A further result we expect from the ongoing analysis is an evaluation of other components of this fishery that could usefully be monitored. These include:

1. fluctuations in recruitment — and here we will be looking at ways to obtain data by direct means, such as observations of juveniles in the rivers, and by indirect means such as size composition of the catches;
2. allowance for the different capabilities and performances of fishing units in terms of their fishing power; and
3. environmental conditions (such as moon phases, ocean currents and rainfall).

Some of these data are already available elsewhere; all we have to do is gain access to them and put them into our data storage system. Collection of some data — size composition of catch, for example — will mean extra work and involve some cost. However KFV believes the time has come when expenditure of this kind must be regarded as a normal part of operating costs.

The next component of our system is a set of statistical procedures for testing the significance of results from the monitoring system and for evaluating each of the different courses of action open to the company at different times. This will be a version of linear programming with special emphasis on sensitivity analysis.

Government and Industry

To the best of our knowledge KFV's proposed monitoring system will be the first of its kind in Australia. It marks a new stage in the development of Australian fisheries; both industry and government should be asking themselves whether this new stage should be accompanied by changes in relative responsibilities.

We believe that some changes will be highly desirable.

In fisheries research, we see the respective roles developing along these lines:

1. government research will be essentially of a long-term nature, leading to a description of the distribution and abundance of the species being studied, and to stock assessments that will provide a basis for management of the fishery as a whole; and

2. industry will itself carry out operations research and monitoring to help it make economies in its operations and improve its profit margin; some such research and monitoring will be limited to the operations of a particular firm but much of it will be carried on or financed jointly by industry operators on a cooperative basis.

Therefore government programmes will be directed towards those results that will give a basis for overall and long-term strategy for conservation of the resource. The industry's programmes will aim at results that will assist it to reach high levels of efficiency while supporting, and conforming to, the general strategy.

Notes

1. Published in *Australian Fisheries* 40, 10 (Oct. 1981), as "KFV Launches Private, Enterprising Research Program".

13
Management of the Queensland East Coast Otter Trawl Fishery: An Historical Review and Future Options

B.J. Hill and A.J. Pashen

History

Commercial prawn fishing in Queensland commenced in the mid nineteenth century in the Brisbane River and soon extended to nearby rivers such as the Albert and the Logan, Noosa Lakes District, the Mary River (Maryborough) and the Fitzroy River (Rockhampton).[1] Prawns were caught by means of various nets but the beam trawl gradually became the most common equipment used. The early beam trawlers were limited in their operations because boat length was restricted to 18ft and engine capacity to 5 hp. It was not until 1952 when the use of otter trawl gear was legalized that prawning grounds in more open waters were exploited. Initially otter trawl gear was used in offshore areas of Moreton Bay. Later during the 1950s additional offshore fishing grounds were developed at Gladstone, Keppel Bay, Sarina, Mackay, Proserpine, Bowen, Townsville, Cairns and Princess Charlotte Bay. In the 1960s the Gulf of Carpentaria prawning grounds were opened and these now provide about half the state's landings. Finally in the latter half of the 1970s, increasing numbers of trawlers began working in the Torres Straits. The opening of these distant grounds was accompanied by the introduction of larger and more sophisticated vessels. Numbers of vessels also increased rapidly in the late 1970s giving rise to concern in the industry about the introduction of excess capacity. This resulted in a limited entry fishery being introduced in northern waters in 1977 and a freeze on east coast trawlers in 1979.

Management of Otter Trawl Fisheries

Queensland has three "managed" otter trawl fisheries — Moreton Bay fishery, east coast fishery and the northern prawn fishery (NPF) in the Gulf of Carpentaria which is under the joint control of the Queensland, Northern Territory, West Australian and Commonwealth governments.

Moreton Bay

Limited entry as a management regime was introduced into this fishery in 1970 because of a decline in landings in the late sixties and an increase in the number of trawlers, particularly large offshore trawlers which fish these waters during the peak of the season. Fishermen with a three-year history in the fishery were issued a permit to otter trawl in the bay during a closed season. In 1971 further restrictions on the length of existing and replacement boats were implemented but in 1978 the area was opened to all vessels of 14 metres and under.

As far as controlling the numbers of boats operating in the fishery is concerned, the permit system could not be regarded as a success. At the time of the introduction of the limited entry regime, records did not provide sufficient information on the number and size of boats which had operated in the Moreton Bay region, let alone those with a three-year history in the fishery.

Whilst it was evident that landings had declined and industry had suffered a financial setback, fisheries managers were unable to judge the economic performance of individual vessels in the fishery because of lack of relevant data. The problem was ". . . essentially one of economics, and yet the attempted remedy was spawned without the assistance of any economic data or studies."[2] An economic survey conducted by the Commonwealth Department of Primary Industry in 1975 failed to provide insight into the fishery because of difficulties caused by understatement of income by fishermen.

As an exercise in fisheries management, the Moreton Bay permit system demonstrated that decisions must be made within the limits of the information currently available and if gaps in this information exist, then steps should be taken to improve the data base for future management of the fishery.

Northern Prawn Fishery

During the 1960s banana prawns were found in commercial quantities in the Gulf of Carpentaria. The growth and development of this fishery and the management philosophy adopted by the governments involved were to have important ramifications for the east coast otter trawl fishery.

Initially the fishery was worked mainly by trawlers of Queensland origin. These were "wet" boats in which product was stored in chilled brine. The vessels were usually 12 to 14 m in length and of timber construction. Although they were of limited endurance, they were well suited to the east coast fishery where grounds lay in close proximity to the coastline and points to unload product were easily accessible.

However conditions in the gulf were entirely different. Prawning grounds lay further offshore and the method of storing product in brine tanks meant that the vessels had to unload their catch either to a mother ship or to a shore based operation in a matter of days after being caught.[3] Valuable fishing time was therefore lost in steaming to a receival point.

The gulf fishery initially centred around banana prawns (*Penaeus merguiensis*). These prawns are different to other species in that they form dense schools or "boils" and once a school is located large quantities of prawns can be taken in a short period of time. These factors led to the development of large steel trawlers having greater endurance and dry freezing facilities capable of handling large quantities of product.

Good catches in 1971 and 1974 were followed by a build-up in the number of dry freezer vessels. These vessels required catches at least five times that of smaller trawlers for viability and their continued entry into the fishery aroused fears of "overcapitalization".[4] On 1 January 1977 a limited entry scheme was imposed in the area from Cape York in Queensland to Cape Ford in Western Australia. Some 292 vessels were endorsed to fish in the NPF and entry was generally open to trawlers which had previously fished in the gulf, trawlers under construction or under contract before May 1975 for use in the fishery and trawlers that had not fished in the NPF but whose owner had worked in the NPF in the past.

Whilst the number of fishing units able to operate in the fishery was restricted, provisions for the replacement of vessels allowed for expansion in fishing effort. The replacement policy introduced at the time of the closure allowed vessels less than 12 metres to upgrade to 12 metres and vessels greater than 12 metres to be replaced "on a one for one equivalent characteristic basis". No further guidelines on the replacement length of vessels were stated, with the result that both industry and the managers interpreted the term "equivalent characteristics" fairly loosely. A 15 per cent increase in length on replacement became the norm and many approvals exceeded this. The replacement policy caused more problems to management than any other single factor and as a result of industry pressure a new replacement policy was developed. This policy took into account the fact that the Commonwealth Government in an effort to stimulate the local shipbuilding industry had introduced a 25 per cent subsidy (increased to 27½ per cent from 1 January 1981) payable to shipbuilders for the construction of vessels greater than 21 metres at the designed load waterline length. In order to take advantage of the subsidy, industry requested a relaxing of the replacement policy. This was done and from November 1979 vessels under 21 metres were permitted to upgrade to this size.

Because of the limitation on vessel numbers, entry could be gained only by procuring a gulf endorsement. The rents or "abnormal profits" being generated by vessels within the fishery (MacLeod reports that 44 per cent of vessels made returns in excess of 20 per cent in 1976–77 whilst 31 per cent made similar returns the following year) were capitalized into the licence value. Gulf endorsements were reportedly trading for up to $100,000. The large sums of money required to finance both the licence and the new gulf vessel were more readily available to companies, especially processors, than to individuals. A company purchasing an endorsement attached to a small wet boat, transferred it to a new dry freezer vessel. The owner of the still functional wet boat now "sold" it on the east coast and used the proceeds of the sale together with the funds from the sale of the gulf endorsement to finance a new east coast vessel. In this way the replacement of one boat in the gulf generated two additional boats on the east coast (prior to the 1979 freeze on otter trawlers).

East Coast Fishery

Since the east coast fishery was the last significant open-access otter trawl fishery in Australia it became the dumping ground not only for former gulf boats but also for trawlers from other limited entry fisheries. This contributed to an acceleration in the number of east coast trawlers.

A major problem in analysing the east coast trawl fishery is the absence of logbook data. Licensing records can be used to define the number of otter trawlers having Queensland licences, but prior to 1980 these did not differentiate between vessels operating in the declared management zone (DMZ) of the northern prawn fishery, in the present case mainly the Gulf of Carpentaria, and those which operated solely on the east coast. There are three categories of trawlers carrying Queensland licences: firstly, a small group (24 in 1982) which were restricted to the Gulf of Carpentaria; secondly, a group which can operate in the gulf and on the east coast (268 in 1982); and thirdly the largest group which can operate only on the east coast (1,002 in 1982). The second group appears to split its effort fairly evenly between the two areas; thus an estimate of *the total boat year effort* on the east coast in 1982 is 1,002 + 134 (half of the fleet eligible to fish both gulf and east coast) = 1,136. Similar adjustments to the numbers of Queensland licensed trawlers have been made to give an estimated east coast fleet from 1971 to 1982 for the purpose of the present review. This estimate is an approximation only, since Somers and Taylor[5] have shown that commitment of trawlers in the DMZ has been increasing annually since 1970.

Figure 1 shows the number of trawlers licensed to operate in Queensland waters between June 1970 and July 1982 as well as an estimate of the potential east coast fleet. Overall there has been a steady increase in the number except in 1976 when a number of

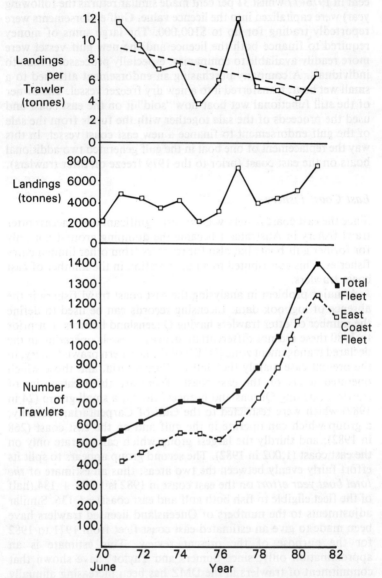

Figure 1 From bottom to top, the number of Queensland trawlers, estimated number of east coast trawlers, east coast prawn landings and estimated landings per east coast trawler. The broken line in the top graph indicates a trend in landings per trawler.

owners failed to renew licences following poor landings. At that time nonrenewal of a licence in one year did not prevent its being renewed at a subsequent date. From 1977 the numbers rose very rapidly until 1981 when they levelled off as a result of a freeze in licences introduced in 1979. This freeze took time to become effective because allowance was made for vessels under construction to be completed.

At the same time that the number of otter trawlers was increasing, the total quantity of prawns landed each year was also rising although there were considerable year to year fluctuations (figure 1). There is no catch and effort data available for the east coast but a relative index can be obtained by calculating the average landings per trawler (figure 1). The period 1974–75 to 1976–77 saw a massive increase in landings per trawler, from 3.7 tonnes to 12.3 tonnes. Nevertheless, over the decade, average landings per trawler showed a downward trend, from a mean of around 11.8 tonnes in 1971 to 6.9 tonnes in 1981.

Most of the prawns landed in Queensland are exported to Japan. Because the Australian share of the Japanese market is very small (4-7 per cent), the supply of prawns from countries such as India has a far greater effect on Japanese prices. Accordingly, the Australian industry is in a price-taking rather than a price-making situation. Until 1975 prawn prices had been fairly static but between mid 1975 and 1976 they doubled. Since then, prices have tended to fluctuate around the 1976 level due to changes in demand, interest rates and exchange rate variations.

Whilst the money value of the catch has increased quite substantially since 1976 a much smaller increase occurred in real terms (figure 2). The average real value of catch per trawler (real value of landings per number of trawlers), however, declined in the early 1970s with a dramatic rise in 1976–77, but has declined subsequently.

Periods of high prices in the mid to late seventies coupled with good landings attracted many newcomers with no prior involvement in the fishing industry. Whilst trawlers can land thousands of dollars worth of catch at one time, most people outside the industry were ignorant of the high costs of catching the product. A picture of the economics of the operation is given by a break-even analysis, which estimates the level of catch which must be landed to equate total revenue to total cost, that is, to "break even". Total revenue is taken to be the value of product sold by fishermen. Total costs comprise those costs incurred in the normal operation of the fishing unit as well as "imputed" costs for the use of the owner's labour and capital employed.

Costs can be divided into two categories — fixed and variable. Fixed costs remain the same regardless of the level of output, for example, depreciation, insurance, licence fees, etc. On the other hand variable

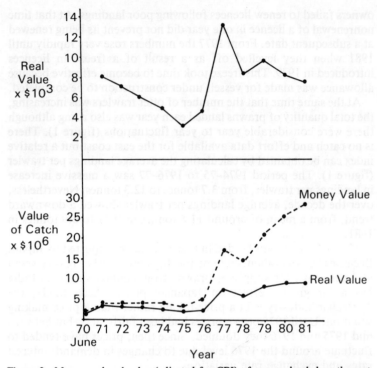

Figure 2 Money and real value (adjusted for CPI) of prawns landed on the east coast of Queensland. The upper graph shows an estimated real value of landings per boat obtained by dividing total real value by the number of east coast trawlers licensed each year.

costs vary directly with the level of output, e.g., crew payment. Some costs, for example, fuel, oil and a proportion of repairs and maintenance are related to fishing effort rather than catch of prawns. However in the absence of catch and effort data to the contrary it will be assumed that catch is directly related to effort, and such items will be considered as variable costs.

The cost and earnings data was taken from taxation returns of trawler owners (with east coast entitlements only) in the Port Douglas–Mackay region surveyed during 1981. The Queensland average weekly earnings per employed male unit were used as an estimate of the opportunity cost of the skipper's labour. A 10 per cent return on capital funds employed for 1977–78 and 1978–79 and a 12 per cent return in 1979–80 were used as a measure of the opportunity cost of capital. Higher returns to capital would result in much larger break-even catches.

Table 1 Cost analysis data derived from a survey in 1981 of east coast trawlers from 12 to 14.9 metres in length.

Cost items	1977–78	1978–79	1979–80
Fixed costs	5,208	7,310	9,491
Variable costs	13,105	21,230	23,129
Skipper's allowance	10,514	11,305	12,189
Return on capital funds employed	3,206	3,705	7,310
Total	$32,033	$43,550	$52,119
Average price paid for prawns (per kg)	$3.56	$4.74	$4.90
Catch required to break even (kg)	8,998	9,188	10,637
Actual landings (kg)	6,797	8,357	7,654
Value of landings (Total revenue)	$24,197	$39,612	$37,505

Over the three-year period trawlers in this length category failed to land sufficient product to cover costs; the shortfall in 1979–80 was approximately 3,000 kg. From 1977–78 to 1978–79 the increase in prawn prices more than compensated for the increase in costs, hence the break even catch was lower than in 1979–80. During this year increases in costs (particuarly fuel which increased more than two and a half times during the survey period) exceeded increases in prawn prices with the result that more product had to be landed to break even.

A survey of the prawn/scallop trawlers in the Capricornia section of the Great Barrier Reef by the Institute of Applied Social Research showed that these trawler operators fared better than their northern counterparts. A return to capital and labour of 27.9 per cent was calculated for 1978–79, and allowing for a payment for the owner/skipper's labour the return on capital funds employed would be 12.4 per cent which is slightly higher than the normal return to capital for the year.

Although high returns on capital were not made in the fishery over the three years, this did not deter contracts to construct vessels from being entered into. Boat building boomed as a result and the increased demand led to an increase in the price of trawlers. These became a form of capital investment; even without working, a trawler tied up at a wharf represented a rapidly appreciating asset which, in the absence of a capital gains tax, was likely to yield a good profit when sold. The process was facilitated by the ready availablity of loan money although at high interest rates.

The basic cause of the rapid increase in vessel numbers appears to lie in a few years of good landings coupled with high prices for prawns. This combination in the particular investment climate of the time encouraged a massive flow of capital into the industry. In the light of the growth of the number of trawlers on the east coast of Queensland and, in particular, industry concern about the influx of large interstate trawlers and rumours of some 300 trawlers in the "pipeline", a freeze on the number of otter trawlers able to fish the east coast of Queensland was introduced in September 1979. Vessels with current Queensland licences were granted entitlements. Provision was made for applicants who, previous to the announcement, notified the Queensland Fisheries Service of their intention to operate in the east coast otter trawl fishery and to those Queensland residents or registered companies who could produce documentary evidence that prior to the announcement (a) they had commenced construction of a particular vessel; or (b) had entered into a firm contract for construction of a vessel.

By 1982 the total number of licences had fallen, due to a combination of a stricter attitude from the managers and the difficult economic conditions. Licences which were not renewed within six months of expiry date were cancelled, vessels seized by creditors had to be transferred to a new owner within six months or the licence was forfeited, and vessels which had been under construction but not completed two and a half years after the freeze were refused licences. In addition a number of "ghost ships" which either did not exist or were in a very early stage of construction were struck off the register.

Under the conditions of entry, commitment to the fishery was established if the vessel held a Queensland licence. On constitutional grounds there was a need to avoid any restrictive policy based solely on the place of residence of the applicant. Since a history of participation in the fishery could not be established from licence records, no account was taken of the actual involvement of trawlers in the east coast fishery. Consequently vessels in the gulf were granted entitlements for the east coast by virtue of their Queensland licence whether or not they had fished on the east coast. Subsequently this led to a practice of licence splitting whereby a gulf entitlement could be transferred to a new vessel while the east coast entitlement was retained with the replaced vessel. Licence splitting allowed an avenue for an additional 250 trawlers to be added to the east coast fleet.

Objectives of Management

In the case of the Queensland otter trawl fishery there are several different and in some cases conflicting objectives which could be pursued by management. The objective of maximizing economic rent has been dealt with by Meany.[6] To restate Meany's argument briefly: Fishermen will continue to enter the industry whilst revenue is greater than costs and a "profit" can be made, i.e., in figure 3 up to point Y at fishing effort E_1. At a much lower level of fishing effort the

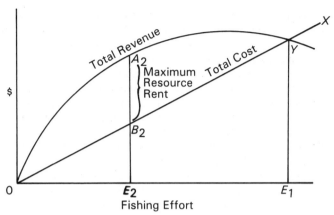

Figure 3 Theoretical cost and effort curve.

difference between revenue and costs will be maximized, and this difference or "very high profits" represents the maximum resource rent available to the fishery, i.e., A_2B_2. From an economic point of view therefore we will be making the best use of our resources if fishing effort is restricted to the point where "profits" can be maximized, i.e., at the point of maximum economic yield at fishing effort, E_2. An important method of limiting effort is through control of numbers of boats. A reduction in fleet size could lead to a decline in the total quantity of product landed, which would disadvantage processors. Thus boat owners and processors would have different ideas on the ideal number of vessels in the fleet. The boat owner will achieve maximum profitability with a smaller fleet than that which is necessary to provide a large throughput for a processing factory. This difference was borne out by the arguments put forward by processors when requesting additional vessel entitlements for the Gulf of Carpentaria prawn fishery. They repeatedly pointed out that they needed more vessels in order to ensure sufficient product for their processing plants. Limitation of the east coast fleet was also opposed by the Queensland Fish Board on these grounds. It is evident also that provided adequate profit can be made at the processing stage, a processor owned vessel need not make a profit. Licence limitation therefore is not favoured by processors whether or not they own vessels.[7]

Leaving the question of the efficient use of capital aside, maximizing the number of trawlers is favoured in some quarters as a method of increasing employment. East coast trawlers up to around 18 metres in length seldom have more than two crew. Much of the time the vessel is steered by an autopilot. Increasing the number of vessels will not significantly affect total employment. More importantly, if the opportunity cost of labour is higher, that is, if crew are able to earn higher wages in other sectors of the economy then they would be better off seeking employment elsewhere.

The maintenance of stocks is one of the prime objectives of fishery management. There are numerous examples of overfishing leading to decline in stocks and collapse of a fishery. Despite high fecundity and rapid growth, prawns are not immune to overfishing, as illustrated by the fishery in the Arabian Gulf. Overfishing takes two forms, growth overfishing and recruitment overfishing.[8] Growth overfishing is associated with the taking of juveniles or animals before they have reached their most valuable size. This trend is already occurring increasingly along the Queensland east coast and numerous requests are being received by the authorities to close "nursery areas" to prevent the taking of small individuals. The main effect of growth overfishing is to reduce the value of the catch since small prawns are worth less than large ones. Recruitment overfishing occurs where the number of adults remaining after fishing activities is insufficient to provide an adequate number of recruits to sustain the population. This effect can occur rapidly in a population where the animals live for only one year, and its initial effect may be obscured by variability in population numbers from year to year.

The existing fleet has considerable capacity for increase in fishing effort. This can come about even if numbers are pegged, since vessels can increase the time spent fishing. Williams[9] has pointed out that this trend is already occurring, with trawler operators in 1980 spending 10 per cent more time fishing than they did in 1979, more nets are being towed, and new areas such as the northern east coast and the Torres Straits have been opened up. Despite all these factors, total landings have not increased in direct proportion to the number of trawlers.

One of the major objectives of the management scheme for the northern prawn fishery was to prevent overcapitalization but, as pointed out by MacLeod[10], this objective was not achieved. In the case of the Queensland trawl fishery the large influx of trawlers represents a massive capital inflow. Although this has now been checked partially by the freeze it appears that the capital investment is in excess of the amount required to maximize economic rent. Upgrading of existing trawlers and replacement of old vessels by new ones also represents an avenue for further capital inflow. At this stage the managers have not clearly stated their objectives. Nevertheless the freeze and the one-for-one replacement policy indicate that the main concern is to restrict further capitalization and potential fishing effort.

Further increased effort is unlikely to result in a proportional increase in landings. Thus one of the objectives which should be pursued is to restrict effort. Fisheries managers have several ways in which they can restrict effort. Some of these can be used to control the operations of the existing fleet whilst others relate to restrictions on the number and size of new vessels entering the fleet.

To date there has not been a swing to large vessels on the east coast. Between 1970 and 1979, the numbers of Queensland trawlers between 9 and 18 metres increased from 400 to 832, but the average length rose only from 13.2 metres to 13.5 metres and the modal size class (12 to 15 metres) remained unchanged. By contrast in the DMZ modal size changed from under 14 metres in 1971 (94 out of 292 vessels) to 21 metres and over in 1980 (163 out of 287 vessels).[11] Present replacement policy in the DMZ allows for any vessel to upgrade to 21 metres whereas on the east coast an increment of only 1 metre is permitted on replacement.

Quotas

In this technique an estimate is made of the total allowable catch, this quantity is shared out between the vessels in the form of quotas and each operator then decides how best to take his share. Unfortunately the method is not applicable to prawn fisheries because of the large year-to-year variation in population size and the impossibility at this stage of predicting the size of the stock. The problem is compounded by the fact that the east coast prawn fishery is a multispecies one with populations of prawns varying independently of each other. An additional problem with this system is that quotas would be difficult to enforce on the east coast of Queensland and would inevitably lead to an increase in illegal sales.

Closed Seasons

A closed season has the effect of limiting the amount of time for which fishing can be carried out. It has been applied for example in the barramundi fishery in Queensland in order to reduce fishing pressure on this valuable fin fish. The east coast prawn fishery is a multispecies one and there are considerable differences in the peak fishing season for the different species. Thus a closed season could result in no dimunition of effort on one species whilst providing excessive protection for another. In general the major prawn season in the south of the state is in summer whilst it is in winter in the north. Different closures for different areas would result in vessels travelling from one open area to another, considerably increasing pressure on the open stock. Prevention of the movement of trawlers along the coast would be resisted strongly by the operators who are opposed to any form of zoning. At this stage, therefore, it does not

appear that seasonal closures could be used to control effort in the
east coast prawn fishery. Seasonal and area closures can be of benefit
in protecting stocks of juveniles. A closure of this nature operates
each year in the southern and eastern Gulf of Carpentaria in order
to allow banana prawns to achieve a size for maximum economic
value. This closure does not however prevent the fleet from fully
exploiting the stock once the season opens.

Gear Restriction

Two restrictions presently apply to the gear used by trawlers. Firstly
the prescribed minimum mesh size of net used in trawls is 38 mm.
This size was chosen in order to allow juvenile prawns to escape.
Unfortunately because of net clogging and the elongation and closing
of meshes when the net is under tension, minimum mesh sizes are
not very effective in preventing catches of juveniles. The second gear
restriction relates to the headrope length of the net. In Queensland
waters (three miles from the low water mark) maximum headrope
length of an offshore otter trawl is 40 metres. In certain specified
inshore areas such as Moreton Bay the headrope length is 20 metres.
These restrictions do not apply in Commonwealth waters. Deepwater
prawns appear to be one of the last prawn resources which are not
fully exploited in Queensland, and thus it may be inadvisable to apply
a 40 metre headrope restriction to those vessels capable of working
in deep water although the ban on large opening nets in Queensland
waters should be retained.

Gear restrictions in limiting elements of fishing power attempt to
limit fishing effort. Restrictions on some elements of fishing power
may lead to an increased use of other elements of fishing power not
regulated. However as Crutchfield suggests, there is a limit to the
amount of additional capital which can be invested in a vessel to
increase its catching power if key dimensions of fishing power are
constrained.[12] At present the only restriction on the replacement of
vessels otherwise removed from the fishery deals with length, and
even this is relatively modest since an increase of up to 1 metre is
permitted. A tighter policy will be necessary in the future if managers
do not want to see an increase in the average size of the vessels with
an accompanying increase in fishing capacity and the need to land
more produce. The major factor in determining the fishing capacity
of an east coast trawler is the size of the vessel and the horsepower
of the engine. This suggests that controls on the engine power might
be used to prevent further increases in effort.

Engine Size and Towing Power

There is a direct relationship between the length of a trawler and the power of the main propulsion engine (figure 4). There is also a great deal of variability in engine power in similar sized vessels; engine power of trawlers of 13.7 metres constructed in 1978 ranged between 120 and 250 hp. Over the last twenty years the average power of trawlers has increased, as shown by the regression lines in figure 4. On average, trawlers constructed in the period 1960 to 1971 had a lower power than those constructed between 1972 and 1977 and the latter had lower power than trawlers constructed between 1978 and 1981.

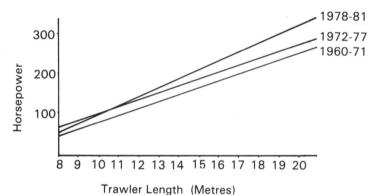

Figure 4 Regression lines showing the relationship between horsepower and length for vessels constructed in different periods.

Refrigeration equipment on trawlers is usually run by an auxiliary engine, leaving the main engine to propel the vessel and to operate the winches used for operating trawl nets. Increases in the power of the main engine have enabled the vessels to tow a larger quantity of net and to increase towing speeds for certain species such as tiger prawns, i.e., to increase fishing power. Williams showed that there was a strong trend for vessels to increase the number of nets towed.[13] In 1979, 24 per cent of trawlers towed three nets, and by 1980 this proportion had increased to 37 per cent.

The change from double to triple net rigs is not solely to increase the quantity of net towed. A double rig is really two separate single nets, each with its own pair of otter boards. By connecting the two nets by means of a third between them, the two inner otter boards can be replaced with skids or slides which have a far lower towing resistance. Thus a triple rig may require less fuel to tow than a double, even though there is more net. Triple nets are more difficult to handle, however, and in areas where the bottom is rough operators prefer the double rig. Vessels fishing in deep water tend to use a triple rig since this arrangement avoids the problem of two separate nets becoming entangled. Accordingly, as shown by Williams, the number and arrangements of nets varies along the coast.[14]

A combination of restrictions on horsepower and headrope length would help to curtail increases in effort resulting from more and more net being towed. In order to allow for the large variation in horsepower, the horsepower of the replaced vessel would need to be restricted to no more than the average for that size. This figure could be obtained by fitting a line to data for the whole fleet or for vessels of a particular age class. This restriction would not necessarily result in a decrease in average horsepower; in order to achieve such a reduction, a line below the average would have to be chosen.

There is a possibility that if no restrictions are placed on engine sizes, those of new vessels will decrease because of the high cost of fuel. It is easy to monitor trends such as these from existing licensing records and to place checks on power should it be necessary.

Because the advantages and disadvantages of various arrangements of nets differ along the coast it is suggested that the present practice of specifying a maximum headrope length and allowing fishermen to choose for themselves the best method of towing be continued.

Consideration should be given to the possibility of an introduction of pair trawling; in this method two vessels are used to tow the net. This allows much wider nets to be towed without the use of otter boards for spreading. No vessels other than entitled otter trawlers should be permitted to pair trawl, and the headrope length of net towed should not exceed the combined quantity available to the two vessels unless a corresponding reduction in effort can be achieved through other methods.

Licence Limitation

This option was introduced into the east coast otter trawl industry in 1979. Although the numbers of east coast trawlers increased slightly following the freeze, they levelled off by 1982. The trawlers added to the fleet after the start of the freeze represented vessels which were either under construction at the time of the freeze or for which a contract to construct had been signed, or they represented cases where people had informed the Fisheries Service of an intention to build a new vessel. An increase of this type following a freeze is inevitable where the industry is undergoing rapid expansion at the time of the freeze and has occurred in many limited entry fisheries. There now remains only one avenue whereby additional vessels can be introduced into the east coast fleet, and that is through splitting of "gulf" licences as described above.

Simply freezing the number of trawlers will allow fishing effort and capitalization to continue to increase through vessels carrying more equipment, spending more time fishing and becoming more powerful. Methods of reducing effort are required.

An effective method of reducing fishing effort in the prawning fleet is to lower the number of vessels operating in the fishery. At present boats do not have to engage in fishing to retain their licences and there is no way of identifying nonfishing vessels. When the freeze was introduced all vessels that had been licensed in the past were granted entitlements. Removal of vessels that do not trawl full time will not greatly affect fishing effort; but if they are left in the fleet there is a latent potential to increase fishing effort. Consequently, vessels would have to be categorized, for example, according to the amount of time spent otter trawling, income derived from the fishery, etc., to determined which vessels should be removed. This process has been used successfully in the limited entry gill net fishery in the Gulf of Carpentaria where only those fishermen who could prove that they spent more than a certain minimum time in the fishery and who obtained 70 per cent of their income from the fishery were given an entitlement. While fishermen may agree that a reduction in the number of vessels is desirable, the matter of who drops out is a difficult problem. Although 87 per cent of fishermen in the southern zone of the South Australian rock lobster fishery agreed that there were too many boats in the fishery, only 16 per cent were interested in selling to a buy back.

Buy Back

A system of buying back licences has been used in some fisheries in order to reduce the numbers of fishermen or vessels. Attractive sums of money have to be offered to fishermen to induce them to leave the fishery and considerable finance needs to be made available for the purchase of vessels and entitlements. The buy back could also allow for the purchase of east coast licences in the case of vessels with entitlements to operate in the gulf and the east coast fishery.

In the case of old trawlers, it may be possible to separate the licence from the vessel for buy back. For example, northern prawn fishery entitlements are offered for sale with no vessel attached. In the case of the east coast it should be possible to purchase entitlements from vessels which are to be scrapped. At present these vessels are offered for sale for replacement. This method should certainly be considered since it allows for some vessels to be removed at low cost.

The buy-back authority would need to consider whether licences should be transferable. It appears that the transferability of licences was one of the downfalls of the buy-back scheme in the Canadian salmon fishery.[15] Licence values increased because of the expectations of speculators of the benefits of the buy-back scheme, with the result that during the period October 1971 to April 1974 the net cost (i.e., after recovery of auction revenue) to the committee per ton capacity removed from the salmon fleet rose from $800 to $3,900. Only 5.1 per cent of the total salmon fleet as measured by the 1970 actual catch performance has been bought out and removed from the fleet. The question remains as to who should actually pay for the scheme. In a fishery situation where there is no control over the inputs into the fishery or in a limited entry fishery where there are too many inputs such as capital and labour, resource rent is dissipated. With a reduction in the numbers of vessels operating in the fishery and no subsequent gear rush, fishermen will be able to retain a greater share of the resource rent, in which case it is only appropriate that the buy back of vessels should be financed by the benefactors of the scheme, that is, remaining fishermen, through higher licence fees. It is unlikely that additional revenue could be raised through the sale of the trawlers which have been "bought back", since their design makes them unsuitable for alternative uses.

Licence Leasing

The current licensing procedure for both trawlers and fishermen allows for an annual renewal, suggesting that the right to fish extends for one year. In practice, however, unless the fisherman fails to renew a licence or it is cancelled or revoked by the Minister, it is renewed indefinitely. In the case of fishermen there will clearly be an attrition through retirement from the fishery. In the case of a vessel, however, if the licence can be transferred freely from one boat to another, there is no attrition and theoretically the licence becomes perpetual. Thus the establishment of a limited entry scheme with free transferability and no time limit on licences tends to result in a fixed number of vessels. It would, for example, be difficult for government now to alter the number of vessels entitled to operate in the northern prawn fishery. Entitlements have become valuable, making new entry expensive, and it is unlikely that existing operators who have paid around $100,000 for entry would accept that additional licences be granted to new operators without a similar payment. Alternatively any attempt to reduce the number of operators would require payment of large amounts of compensation.

Because fisheries are dynamic it is inappropriate to manage them by means of a static system such as a freeze on vessel numbers. The management policy should allow the licensing authority to vary the number of fishing units in the best interests of the industry. This control should make it possible to reduce or increase the number of vessels, depending upon the performance of the fishery.

Meany pointed out that a fishing boat is a deteriorating asset with a finite economic life.[16] The economic life will depend on the rate of physical deterioration, the cost of maintenance and the rate of obsolescence which in turn will be determined by the rate of technological change. He proposed that instead of a one-year licence with an apparent perpetual renewability, a contract should be entered into between vessel owner and licensing authority permitting the vessel to be used for a fixed period of time. Meany proposed that this period should be sufficient to make the investment in the vessel economically viable but should not exceed the expected economic life of the vessel.[17]

Table 2 Percentage of vessels in each age category for the years 1970 and 1979

Year	Number of vessels	Percentage in each age category			
		10 yrs	10-15 yrs	15-20 yrs	20 yrs
1970	1,629	70	12	8	10
1979	4,220	73	14	7	5

Restricting the contract period to a maximum of fifteen years would probably cover the economic life span of most vessels. Data on the age of vessels are presented in table 2. At the end of this period it may be possible to negotiate an extension for a limited time, for example, two years where the vessel is still in good condition. When the contract period finally runs out the vessel has to be removed from the fishery. If the owner wanted to continue fishing he has two options, either to purchase an existing vessel with an entitlement, or to apply to the licensing authority for permission to introduce a new vessel.

With a fleet of 1,300 trawlers and assuming an economic life of fifteen years, on average eighty-six vessels could be retired each year. If the licensing authority wishes to reduce the size of the fleet then the number of new licences issued each year would be less than the number terminated. If it was decided to maintain the existing fleet size then the number of licences issued would be the same as the number terminated. In the event of more requests for licences being received than the number available for issue, preference could be given on the basis of factors such as length of time in the fishery, size of vessel to be introduced, and so forth.

If a vessel was removed from the fishery before the termination of the contract period, the issue of a contract for a new vessel would also be subject to approval by the licensing authority. Thus at no stage would reissue become an automatic process unless the licensing authority wishes it to be so. This restriction is essential if the two objectives of gaining control over numbers and preventing the licences from attracting a large premium are to be attained. A leasing system may not be well received by trawler owners if they think that their licence continuity would be endangered. The system would, however, have advantages even if granting a licence for a replacement vessel were automatic. One advantage would be a considerable simplification of annual licence renewal. A second advantage is that the licence would at most have a reducing value, the nearer the expiry year the smaller the premium which owners would be prepared to pay.

Conclusion

Fisheries managers cannot guarantee the profitability of a fishing unit since factors such as fuel costs, interest rates, product prices and the size of the exploitable stock are beyond their control. Large differences in efficiency of skippers further compound the matter of profitability, and even in good years some operators will lose money while in bad years a few will make a profit. Nevertheless, decisions by management can affect the economics of the industry. As shown above, part of the present problem of the east coast prawning fleet lies in an inability to land sufficient product. Total landings have risen only marginally despite an increase in numbers of boats, more time spent at sea, improvement in gear and the opening up of the Torres Straits fishery. Landings per vessel have declined and it appears that this is related to the expansion in the fleet size. Continuing to freeze the number of trawlers at its present level will therefore merely perpetuate the problem. Initially, therefore, management should aim at reducing the number of vessels. It is difficult to estimate what the ideal number of vessels would be, but it has to be related to catch per vessel. A 40 per cent increase in landings in 1979–80 was shown above to be the quantity required for average size east coast trawlers to reach a break-even point. Any large reduction in the number of trawlers presents a massive problem since there are very few methods of removing vessels, and managers will have to utilize every opportunity offered. The process has started by preventing additional vessels from entering the fishery, but the loophole of splitting of gulf licences remains.[18] There appear to be two methods whereby the numbers can be reduced, firstly through a buy-back scheme and secondly through changing the licence system from a perpetual right to a fixed period related to the life of the vessel.

The introduction of a buy-back scheme is a final step since it officially puts a value on a licence. The more successful the scheme the more expensive the licences become and thus ultimately the buy back becomes too expensive. It encourages the concept of the licence gaining a value, an aspect of limited entry which has attracted a great deal of criticism since it represents an additional cost to the fisherman and benefits only the first generation of fishermen. Buy back should therefore be considered as a last resort when all other methods of reducing fleet size have failed.

Leasing of licences rather than granting them in perpetuity does offer a method of phasing out vessels as they reach the end of their economic life. It additionally reduces the value of the licence without interfering with transferability. The major drawbacks are its acceptability to fishermen and the fact that with the recent influx of new vessels, it would take a long time to reduce fleet size significantly. This system does not place an additional financial load on fishermen nor does it require the government to contribute funds—a potential difficulty with buy backs.

Finally, with the depressed state of the industry many operators are being forced out. If an objective of management is to increase efficiency and reduce effort, then vessels which do not work should have their licences cancelled. If the vessel is relatively new, it could be purchased and put back into the fishery as a replacement vessel, bearing in mind the present allowable variation of 1 metre.

Once the numbers of vessels were decreased, management would need to introduce a replacement policy which would allow for replacement of vessels when they were no longer economic to operate. Restrictions on gear and other elements of fishing power for vessels on replacement and existing fleet would need to be strictly enforced. Otherwise it is envisaged that owners would invest further capital into their vessel in an attempt to increase their share of the total available catch.

Notes

1. N.V. Ruello, "An Historical Review and Annotated Bibliography of Prawns and the Prawning Industry in Australia", in *National Prawn Seminar* edited by P.C. Young (Australian Government Publishing Service, Canberra, 1975).
2. N.M. Haysom, "The Moreton Bay Permit System. An Exercise in Licence Limitation", in *National Prawn Seminar,* edited by P.C.Young.
3. I.F. Somers, "Management of the Australian Northern Prawn Fishery" (M. Sc. Thesis, School of Australian Environmental Studies, Griffith University, 1977).
4. N.D. MacLeod, "Limited Entry Management for the Northern Prawn Fishery". A Review of Its Development." in *Policy and Practice in Fisheries Management* edited by N.H. Sturgess and T.F. Meany (Australian Government Publishing Service, Canberra, 1982).
5. I. Somers, and B.R. Taylor, "Fisheries Statistics relating to the Declared Management Zone of the Australian Northern Prawn Fishery 1968-1979," (CSIRO Marine Laboratories Report 138, 1981).

6. T.F. Meany, "The Nature and Adequacy of Property Rights in Australian Fisheries", in *Policy and Practice in Fisheries Management* edited by N.H. Sturgess and T.F. Meany.

7. T. Kailis, "Limited Entry—An Industry View" in, *Policy and Practice in Fisheries Management* edited by N.H. Sturgess and T.F. Meaney.

8. D.H. Cushing, *Marine Ecology and Fisheries* (Cambridge University Press, Cambridge, 1975).

9. M. Williams, chapter 5 in this volume.

10. MacLeod, ibid.

11. Anon, *Development and Management of the Northern Prawn Fishery* (Department of Primary Industry, Australian Government Publishing Service, Canberra, 1982).

12. J.A. Crutchfield, "Economic and Social Implications of the Main Policy Alternatives for controlling Fishing Effort", *Journal of the Fisheries Research Board of Canada*, 36, (1979).

13. Williams, chapter 5 in this volume.

14. Williams, ibid.

15. P. Copes, *Resource Management for the Rock Lobster Fisheries of South Australia* (South Australian Department of Agriculture and Fisheries, Adelaide, 1978).

16. Meany, ibid.

17. Meany, ibid.

18. Splitting of licences is no longer permitted. Separation of a Gulf and an East Coast entitlement results in forfeiture of the East Coast entitlement. Replacement provisions have also been changed. Otter trawlers less than 9 m can upgrade to 9 m. Vessels greater than 9 m can be replaced by a vessel of the same size as the one being replaced.

The Effect of Variation in Prawn and Scallop Stocks on the Behaviour of a Fishing Fleet

M. Dredge

In this article a case history of a Queensland trawl fishery is examined. The fishery is one of relatively few in this state for which any amount of detailed information on both the biology of the target species and on the fishery itself exists, and it gives a particularly good example of the complexities involved in the management of trawl fisheries in Queensland.

A trawl fishery aimed at saucer scallops, *Amusium japonicum balloti* (Bernardi), has existed in Queensland waters since the mid 1950s. The fishery presently operates in waters between latitudes 22°S and 26°S, with most scallops being taken in water depths of between 30 and 55 metres. Vessels engaged in the fishery are typical east coast trawlers with lengths ranging between 12 and 20 metres. These vessels operate from the ports of Yeppoon, Gladstone, Bundaberg, Urangan and Tin Can Bay and in addition to scallops, trawl for stocks of king prawns (*Penaeus plebejus* Hess) and banana prawns (*Penaeus merguiensis* de Man). Vessels also land sand crabs (*Portunus pelagicus L*) and Moreton Bay bugs (*Thenus orientalis* Lund) which are caught as nontarget species.

Scallops occur in beds with peak densities in the order of 1 per m². Two unfished beds which have been studied covered areas of approximately 40 km² and 50 km². Beds are separated by areas of low or zero scallop density. Fishermen working for scallops spend a certain amount of time searching for suitable concentrations if other vessels have not already started working on a bed. Once fishing (as opposed to searching) begins, trawlers remain working on a particular bed for periods of up to four to five days unless the density of scallops (and subsequent catch rates) fall below a given level or the refrigerated space is filled. Scallops are held as whole animals and processed ashore.

The biology of saucer scallops can be summarized as follows. Following a winter-spring spawning and a larval phase of unknown duration, settlement occurs between July and October. Growth is rapid, and individuals attain a size of 85 mm shell height in a period of six to eight months, at which time they recruit into the fishery.[1] Their life span is relatively short: on the basis of tag returns few scallops appear to survive beyond three to four years of age, which agrees with conclusions made by Heald and Caputi for the same species.[2] The species is gonochoristic and animals first spawn at the age of one year. Individuals appear to spawn more than once in the winter spawning season and fecundity is high, with individual females carrying as many as a million mature oocytes at one time.[3]

Scallop fisheries are notorious for irregularity in landings,[4] but the extent of variability in the Queensland fishery is exceptional (figure 1). Investigations which commenced in 1976 were designed to give some insight as to why such variability exists, and possibly to supply advice to management so that the excessive fluctuations might be dampened.

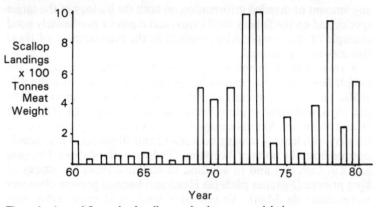

Figure 1 Annual Queensland scallop production: meat weight in tonnes.

The following reasons can be hypothesized as inducing variation in landing of scallops: variation in recruitment from year to year, leading to changes in abundance of $0+$ and $1+$ scallops from year to year; changes in exploitation levels in previous years, determining the abundance of $2+$ and $3+$ scallops.

Variation in exploitation rates can be caused by:
1. variation in the number of days available for fishing as determined by weather;
2. changes in fleet composition, again leading to a variation in the amount of fishing effort available to work on the scallop stock;
3. changes in effort expended on the scallop stock induced by trawlers working on prawn stocks as an alternative. Williams has shown that very few trawlers rely on scallops as a primary source of income, thus implying that prawns act as a major income source of most trawlers involved in this fishery.[5]

The indirect role played by changes in fleet composition, prawn landings and weather upon scallop exploitation will be examined, followed by a discussion of the availability of effort for exploitation of the stock.

Data Sources

Data sources used in subsequent discussion have been derived from the Australian Bureau of Statistics, the Commonwealth Bureau of Meteorology, from processors' records, and from individual logbooks issued by the Queensland Fisheries Research Branch and which have been kept by most fishermen who participate in the scallop fishery. Logbook data cover up to 70 per cent of annual landings of scallops and give details of catch/trawl shot, duration of trawl shots, and distribution of effort. The logbooks made provision for fishermen to give details of prawn catches but the proportion of prawn data held is appreciably less than for scallop landings. Data presented is restricted to that from the ports of Yeppoon, Bundaberg and Tin Can Bay.

Results

Fleet Composition

The composition of the trawl fleet from the ports of Yeppoon (and Rockhampton), Bundaberg and Tin Can Bay is given in table 1. While there has been an increase in numbers of trawlers with time, the proportional increase in numbers is far less than for the whole Queensland trawl fleet.[6] The mean size of trawlers has not changed in the five years of data collection.

Weather

Trawlers involved in the scallop fishery normally continue fishing until wind speeds exceed 15-20 knots. The amount of workable weather per month in the years 1976-1980 was determined by a review of daily Meteorology Bureau records from stations in the fishing area. These records include a twice daily (0900 and 1500) wind speed measurement. Records taken at Lady Elliot Island, which were considered representative of the area in which scallop fishing occurs, were used to give an estimate of the number of workable days in the area presently fished for scallops. If recorded wind speed in any one day was less than 18 knots, the day was said to be workable. A summary of these data is given in table 2.

There was no demonstrable statistical association between either monthly scallop landings and the available number of working days, or between annual landings and the number of workable days in any one year (figure 2).

Table 1 Trawler fleet: numbers and size composition: 1976-1980

Size (m)	9-12.5	12.5-15.0	15.0-18.5	18.5	Total	Mean Size (m)
Port and Year						
Tin Can Bay						
1976	4	14	5	1	24	
77	5	14	4		23	
78	3	15	8		26	
79	4	16	6		26	
80	6	17	4	2	29	
Bundaberg						
1976	11	18	6	1	36	
77	8	25	10	2	45	
78	11	20	7	2	40	
79	16	25	14	4	59	
80	14	25	10	7	56	
Rockhampton & Yeppoon						
1976	21	12	8	1	42	
77	25	16	12	2	55	
78	24	16	17		57	
79	36	16	16	1	69	
80	23	14	7	1	45	
All ports						
1976	36	44	19	3	102	13.5
77	38	55	26	4	123	13.7
78	38	51	32	2	123	13.7
79	56	57	36	5	154	13.6
80	43	56	21	10	130	13.8

Table 2 Number of days per month in which recorded wind speed (0900, 1500) was less than 18 knots. All data from Lady Elliot Island.

Month	January	February	March	April	May	June	July	August	September	October	November	December	
Year													
1976	18	17	18	20	15	22	15	21	23	27	27	23	246
1977	21	17	22	22	25	11	15	25	28	29	27	23	265
1978	30	22	21	26	17	25	20	19	26	18	25	26	275
1979	14	10	22	19	18	15	18	19	21	22	28	25	231
1980	22	11	19	16	20	16	15	19	26	31	25	24	244
Mean	21.0	15.4	20.4	20.6	19.0	17.8	16.6	20.6	24.8	25.4	26.4	24.2	252.2

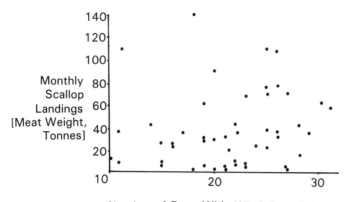

Figure 2   Relationship between available working weather and monthly landings of scallops for Yeppoon, Bundaberg and Tin Can Bay.

Relationship between Banana Prawn, King Prawn and Scallop Landings

Monthly landings of king and banana prawns show seasonal maxima (figures 3a, 3b) which in the light of published information on the fishery for banana prawns and king prawns is not unexpected.[7] Scallop catches are made throughout the year, but peak in the latter part of the year (figure 3c). Stephenson and Williams and Dall have suggested an association between rainfall and king prawn and banana prawn landings, respectively.[8] No such relationships, even when time lags were considered, have been found between scallop landings and rainfall[9]

The relationship between monthly landings of scallops and king prawn and banana prawn is shown in figures 4a and 4b. There is a statistically significant inverse relationship between monthly banana prawn landings and scallop landings using log transformation ($R^2 = .38$, $p < .001$), but no statistically significant relationship between monthly landings of scallops and king prawns. There is no clear relationship between annual scallop landings and annual prawn landings.

Fishing Effort expended on Scallop and Prawn Trawling

Data in table 3 summarizes total effort, and catch per unit effort expended in the banana prawn, king prawn and scallop fisheries in the period 1977–1980. The data have been extrapolated from logbook catch and effort statistics and can be used only as a guide for total effort expenditure for each component of this multitarget trawl

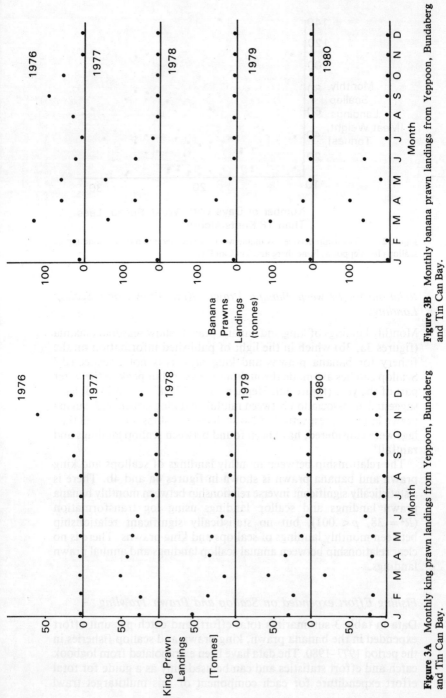

Figure 3A Monthly king prawn landings from Yeppoon, Bundaberg and Tin Can Bay.

Figure 3B Monthly banana prawn landings from Yeppoon, Bundaberg and Tin Can Bay.

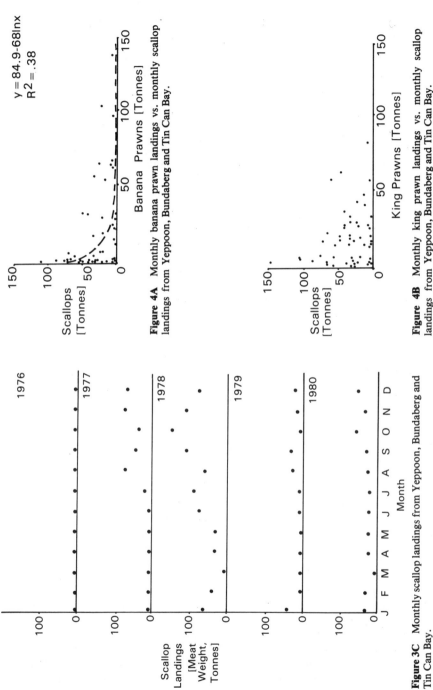

Figure 4A Monthly banana prawn landings vs. monthly scallop landings from Yeppoon, Bundaberg and Tin Can Bay.

$y = 84.9 - 68\ln x$
$R^2 = .38$

Figure 4B Monthly king prawn landings vs. monthly scallop landings from Yeppoon, Bundaberg and Tin Can Bay.

Figure 3C Monthly scallop landings from Yeppoon, Bundaberg and Tin Can Bay.

fishery. The estimate of effort expended on banana prawns is not accurate since the banana prawn fishery includes a component of searching time, and this was not shown in the particular format required in the logbook. Nevertheless, the format used was constant from year to year and suggests that relative effort expended in each fishery varied considerably from year to year. The data also show the total effort expended by trawlers from the three ports being studied varied greatly in the period of data collection.

Table 3A Estimate of fishing effort (boat hours) expended by trawlers from Yeppoon, Bundaberg and Tin Can Bay on scallop, king prawn and banana prawn stocks.

	f Scallops	f Banana prawns	f King prawns	Σf
1977	10,000	8,000	18,000	36,000
1978	25,000	14,000	25,000	64,000
1979	16,000	8,000	17,000	41,000
1980	32,000	25,000	25,000	82,000

Table 3B Estimate of catch (tonnes), based on incomplete processors' records, taken by trawlers working from Yeppoon, Bundaberg and Tin Can Bay.

	Scallops Meat weight	Banana prawns	King prawns
1977	320	550	250
1978	850	300	250
1979	180	250	250
1980	390	350	350

Discussion

If consideration is given to management, a distinction between what could be termed economic management and biological management needs to be drawn. If there is a close relationship between survival and subsequent recruitment, a case exists for regulating fishing activities in order to ensure that there is sufficient survival to maintain stocks at an acceptable level. But in some fisheries, such as those for penaeid prawns, recruitment can be highly variable and largely dependent on environmental factors. In such a fishery, management decisions are normally based on economic considerations rather than biological ones.

Evidence thus far obtained suggests that the fishery for *A. japonicum balloti* falls into the category of one which requires economic rather than biological management, if management is required at all. The species has great fecundity, and although fishing mortality may be high within patches, there will invariably be a residual population in areas where density is low.

Spawning occurs over at least a four-month period each year, and recent studies on water movements in part of the area occupied by scallops indicate that there may be substantial changes in water transport and hence larval transport.[10] Therefore changes in recruitment could mask the effects of varying exploitation levels.

The basis of earlier speculation was that the variation in annual landings of scallops could partially be attributed to the availability of "workable" weather, or that the total catch of, or effort expended on prawns could affect effort applied to scallop stocks through a shortfall in the availability of fishing effort.

Data in table 2 indicate that the variation in workable weather from year to year did not correlate with that of annual scallop landings. There is no reason to suggest that variation in available working weather significantly affects scallop landings.

The relationship between landings and effort expenditure on scallop and prawn stocks is not simple. Data in figure 4b suggest that there is a switch-over of fishing effort between banana prawns and scallops, with vessels fishing banana prawns during a relatively short season. But annual banana prawn landings appear to have little interaction with total scallop landings, and there is no statistically significant relationship between king prawn and scallop landings, either short or long term. Data presented in table 3 show that there is considerable variation in effort from year to year both in total, and that aimed at scallop stocks. Thus, at least in years of low effort there must be a residual pool of fishing effort available for working scallops if the scallops are available and motivation for working is there. Bearing in mind that searching and travelling time are not included in logbook data, the number of hours trawled per trawler (from table 1) is apparently quite low and thus it appears that there is adequate capacity in the existing fleet to fish the scallop stocks.

Part of the reason for variable effort input from year to year is that a number of trawlers from this area move to other ports, particularly during the winter months. Few trawlers are locked into the scallop fishery, and there appear to be few barriers to entry other than the ability of certain skippers to locate scallop beds.

Catch and effort information suggest that effort distribution has spread in the period between 1977 and the present, and thus that the stock is being more widely utilized. There is every possibility of recruitment variation from year to year, and if exploitation is heavy there will be little residual 2+ and 3+ scallop to act as a buffer against poor recruitment. For fishermen to retain any degree of stability of earnings they must have access to other fisheries. Therefore this scallop fishery cannot be considered in isolation by managers, but as part of a composite inshore trawl fishery.

Notes

1. M. Williams, and M.C.L. Dredge, "Growth of the Saucer Scallop *Amusium japonicum balloti* Bernardi in Central Eastern Queensland", *Australian Journal of Marine and Freshwater Research* 32 (1981): 657-66.
2. D.I. Heald, and Caputi, N., "Some Aspects of Growth, Recruitment and Reproduction in the Southern Saucer Scallop *Amusium balloti* (Bernardi 1861) in Shark Bay, Western Australia", *Fisheries Research Bulletin of Western Australia* 25 (1981): 1-33.
3. M.C.L. Dredge, "Reproductive biology of the Saucer Scallop *Amusium japonicum balloti* (Bernardi) in Central Queensland Waters", *Australian Journal of Marine and Freshwater Research* 32 (1981): 775-87.
4. M.J. Saunders and K.H. Beinnsen, "Managing Molluscan Production Systems", *Proceedings of the Ecological Society of Australia* 8 (1975): 84-94.
5. M. Williams, "Survey of Fishing Operations in Queensland 1980", *Queensland Fisheries Service Technical Report* No. 21, 1980).
6. B.J. Hill, and A. Pashen, pers. com.
7. C. Lucas, and G. Kirkwood and I. Somers, "An Assessment of the Stocks of Banana Prawns *Penaeus merguensis* in the Gulf of Carpentaria", *Australian Journal of Marine and Freshwater Research* 30 (1979): 639-657; C. Lucas, "Preliminary Estimates of Stocks of the King Prawn in South East Queensland", *Australian Journal of Marine and Freshwater Research* 25 (1974): 35-47.
8. W. Stephenson, and M. Williams "Analysis of South Queensland Prawn Catches Landed at Queensland Fish Board Depots", *Proceedings of the Royal Society of Queensland* 92, (1981): 57-74; W. Dall, "Northern Prawn Fishermen—Pray for Rain", *Australian Fisheries*, 39 (12) (1980): 3-4.
9. W. Stephenson, pers. com.
10. P. Woodhead, "Sea Surface Circulation in the Southern Region of the Great Barrier Reef, Spring 1966", *Australian Journal of Marine and Freshwater Research* 21, (1970): 89-102; Campbell, pers. com.

References

Dall, W. "Northern Prawn Fishermen—Pray for Rain". *Australian Fisheries* 39, 12 (1980): 3-4.
Dredge, M.C.L. "Reproductive Biology of the Saucer Scallop *Amusium japonicum balloti* (Bernardi) in Central Queensland Waters". *Australian Journal of Marine and Freshwater Research* 32 (1981): 775-87.
Heald, D.I. and N. Caputi. "Some Aspects of Growth, Recruitment and Reproduction in the Southern Saucer Scallop *Amusium balloti* (Bernard 1861) in Shark Bay, Western Australia". *Fisheries Research Bulletin of Western Australia* 25, (1981): 1-33.
Lucas, C. "Preliminary Estimates of Stocks of the King Prawn in South East Queensland". *Australian Journal of Marine and Freshwater Research* 25, (1974): 35-47.
Lucas, C. and G. Kirkwood and I. Somers. "An Assessment of the Stocks of Banana Prawns *Penaeus merguiensis* in the Gulf of Carpentaria". *Australian Journal of Marine and Freshwater Research* 30 (1979): 639-657.
Saunders, M.J. and K.H. Beinssen. "Managing Molluscan Production Systems". *Proceedings of the Ecological Society of Australia* 8 (1975): 84-94.
Stephenson, W. and M. Williams. "Analysis of South Queensland Prawn Catches Landed at Queensland Fish Board Depots". *Proceedings of the Royal Society of Queensland* 92 (1981): 57-74.
Williams, M. "Survey of Fishing Operations in Queensland 1980". Queensland Fisheries Service Technical Report No. 2 (1980).

Williams, M. and M.C.L. Dredge. "Growth of the Saucer Scallop *Amusium japonicum balloti* Bernardi in Central Eastern Queensland". *Australian Journal of Marine and Freshwater Research* 32 (1981): 657-66.

Woodhead, P. "Sea Surface Circulation on the Southern Region of the Great Barrier Reef, Spring 1966". *Australian Journal of Marine and Freshwater Research* 21, (1970): 89-102.

15
Recreational Fishing on the Great Barrier Reef: Research Findings[1]

W. Craik

Over the last twenty years there has been a belated international
recognition of the biological, economic and social significance of
the recreational component of fisheries. For example, in the USA,
the passage of the Fishery Conservation and Management Act of
1976 made it necessary for Regional Management Councils to
consider both recreational and commercial fisheries in the
development and implementation of each fishery management plan[2].
One reason for this increasing recognition has been the dramatic
increase in the number of people involved in recreational fishing,
presumably the result of a combination of increased leisure time and
disposable income, and the advent of outboard motors.

In Queensland, in the period from 1968 to 1979, registrations of
private motor boats increased from 20,638 to 72,801[3], an increase
of 350 per cent. Although no supporting figures are available, it is
reasonable to assume that recreational fishing activity in the Great
Barrief Reef region also increased substantially over this period.
Research undertaken over the last few years is beginning to provide
some "order of magnitude" figures on parameters of recreational
fishing and recreational fisheries for parts of the region.

Although recreational fisheries are the subject of this paper, it is
worth bearing in mind the view expressed at a 1964 Bureau of Sports
Fisheries and Wildlife regional conference in the USA by James W.
Moffett: "Biologically, there is little to be gained by considering sport
fishing and commercial fishing as separate entities. Both are methods
of harvesting fish, and the removal has but one effect. The two
activities differ only in the minds of people, but it is here that
difficulties arise in attitudes towards competition, harm, benefits,
value, and the use of the resources."[4]

Gordon puts forward the view that scientific biological enquiry
should not be judged or guided by "who catches the fish" but that
adequate stock assessment requires information on harvest by all
groups.

While direct assessment of the stock itself may provide information
on the effect of *all* fishing on the stock, it does not necessarily provide
any information on the quantity of fish caught. Because there are
a variety of groups harvesting fish in any one fishery and because
these groups usually have different methods of operation, it is

frequently necessary to approach the collection of data from the different groups of fishermen in different ways.

The demersal reef fish fishery in the Great Barrier Reef region is an example of a fishery exploited by a number of groups, including spearfishermen, commercial and recreational line fishermen and so-called recreational line fishermen who sell their catch. The recreational group fish mainly from private motor boats, charter boats, and cruising yachts.

This article addresses three aspects of the demersal reef fishery: first, direct evaluation of the effect of all fishing on the stock, and second, the catch of recreational line fishermen only. Part three compares the demersal reef fishery in the Great Barrier Reef region with fisheries in other tropical areas.

The former Queensland Fisheries Service (now part of the Department of Primary Industries) and the Institute of Applied Social Research at Griffith University have been working with the Great Barrier Reef Marine Park Authority in the investigation of the demersal fishery in the Great Barrier Reef region.

Direct Evaluation of Parameters of Populations of Recreationally and Commercially Important Species

With the assistance of fish biologists from State Fisheries, Universities and other research institutions, the Marine Park Authority has developed a technique which allows a rapid evaluation of the size frequency distribution and the relative density of the population of coral trout in the area surveyed. This enables comparison of populations between areas and/or between reefs. The technique is based on scuba divers swimming in a search pattern up and down the reef slope over a linear distance of 150 m and scoring the coral trout they observe into 10 x 10 cm size classes. These values are calculated to numbers per hectare.[5]

The technique was developed at a number of workshops held at Heron Island. Comparison of a number of underwater survey techniques showed an intensive search technique to yield the greatest numbers of fish, particularly where there were many fish. The workshop participants selected coral trout as the survey species because of its consumer appeal, quantities caught and its occurrence at depths accessible to divers. Subsequent development and assessment of the intensive search technique involved statistical evaluation of survey distance, number of dives, number of divers, range and number of size classes, tide and time of day effects on results.

An important variable assessed was accuracy in underwater fish length estimation. Initially all observers, including relatively "experienced" observers, exhibited a tendency to underestimate length, presumably overcompensating for their knowledge that objects appear large underwater. However, accuracy improved very rapidly when divers were informed of the direction and size of their bias. Over the course of the workshop, criteria were developed to indicate an acceptable level of accuracy in underwater length estimation. To assist in the training of divers using this technique, a series of plywood models of coral trout has been constructed. These are used for training before all surveys.

This technique has been used to survey coral trout populations on the leeward sides of the thirteen emergent Capricorn Group reefs and the seven emergent Bunker Group reefs (figure 1). The details of these surveys are soon to be published and only a summary of the results will be given here.

For each reef a mean population size frequency distribution and a relative density index were calculated. In the Heron–Wistari Reefs Marine Park, where fishing restrictions were introduced in November 1974, results represent single transects in areas of different fishing restrictions. Two of the areas, Heron unfished and Heron channel, have been protected from all fishing.

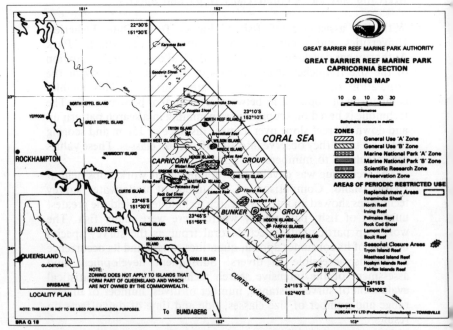

Figure 1 Location of emergent reefs in the Capricornia Section of the Great Barrier Reef Marine Park where *P. leopardus* were surveyed.

It is evident that at the Heron unfished and Heron channel areas, where neither spearfishing nor angling has been permitted for at least six years, coral trout are more numerous, and in most cases larger than at other areas of the Heron–Wistari Reefs Marine Park (figure 2). In comparison with the Heron unfished area, the other Capricorn

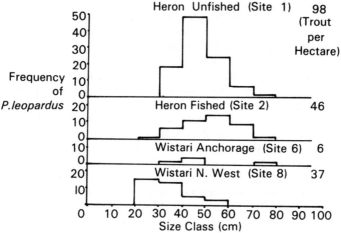

Figure 2 Population size structures and density indexes of *P. leopardus* at four reefs in the Capricorn and Bunker Groups, compared with the Heron unfished area.

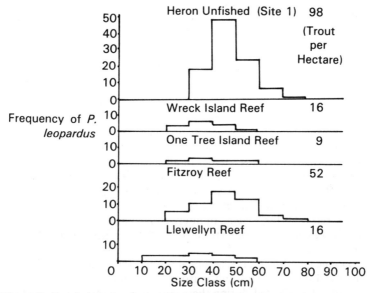

Figure 3 Population size frequency distributions and density indexes of *P. leopardus* at selected transects at Heron and Wistari Reefs.

and Bunker Group reefs support low densities of relatively small-sized coral trout (figure 3). All the reefs surveyed had similar coral trout populations apart from Fitzroy and Lamont Reefs. The reasons for the larger populations at Fitzroy and Lamont Reefs (although still smaller than the Heron unfished area) and the other reefs is not known.

Although habitat differences must play a role in determining population size structure and density, fishing appears to have had a considerable effect on the populations.

To determine the natural variation over time in these parameters, regular surveys of coral trout are being established at defined transects at four reefs in the Great Barrier Reef Region. This will give an indication of the degree of movement of coral trout over time.

Another programme which will provide more information on the degree of movement of coral trout is a reef fish tagging programme, which the Queensland Marine Parks staff and the Authority are undertaking. To date, approximately 2,400 reef fish have been tagged to determine if, where, and how far reef fishes move from the original tagging site. There have been 53 recaptures including 17 coral trout, the majority by the tagging teams. Most recaptured fish have been recovered in the vicinity of the tagging site.

Evaluation of Effort and Catch Data in the Great Barrier Reef Region Recreational Fishery

Two approaches have been used in this research. The first approach is the collection and analysis of catch records from deep sea fishing clubs and charter boat operators.

Deep sea fishing clubs keep records, for competitive reasons, of their fishing trips to the Great Barrier Reef. Several charter boat operators also keep catch records. Some of these records are particularly detailed and span a period of more than twenty years. The records refer to demersal fishes such as coral trout, sweetlip, emperor, cod, and they allow calculations of catch per unit effort (kg fish/angler day) for catches of all species, and in some cases for particular species[6] The nature of the records does not permit subtle changes in effort to be taken into account, for example, hours spent fishing, changes in bait and gear.

The second is the analysis of interviews from surveys at boat ramps which are launching points to the Great Barrier Reef. These surveys were designed to provide information on catch and effort, on economic investment in recreational fishing, some demographic data, historical data on trips and reasons for fishing.

The data collected during these surveys are used in conjunction with more detailed studies by the Institute of Applied Social

Research, using questionnaires mailed to random samples of registered boat owners in eastern Queensland and personal interviews covering the economic characteristics of both recreational and commercial fishing. This results in detailed data on average and total income and expenditures for various aspects of the fisheries in the area under consideration.[7]

For the purposes of this analysis, the Great Barrier Reef region has been arbitrarily divided into areas visited by anglers from the nearest coastal port (figure 4). The data refer to the most recent twelve-month period for which they are available. As will be indicated, some values should be regarded as order of magnitude values.

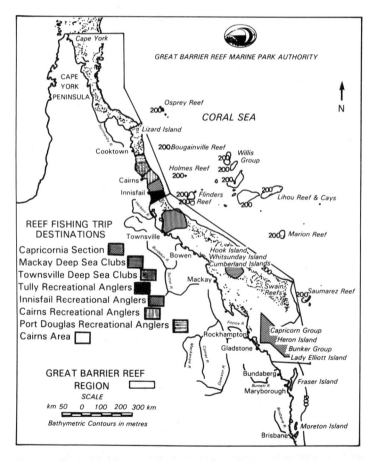

Figure 4 Reef areas fished by recreational anglers based at adjacent coastal ports.

Effort from Charter Boats

Numbers of charter boats making fishing trips to the reef vary with time. In 1978–79, from the ports of Gladstone, Yeppoon and Bundaberg, nine boats made regular charter fishing trips and three to four made intermittent trips to the Capricornia section.[8] Within the region, most charter boats fall in the 10 to 15 m length range, although Mackay deep sea fishermen used a boat of approximately 30 m (figure 5). For charter boats, the number of anglers per boat is proportional to the size of the boat (figure 5). Other than for Capricornia, where the data on mean number of anglers per boat

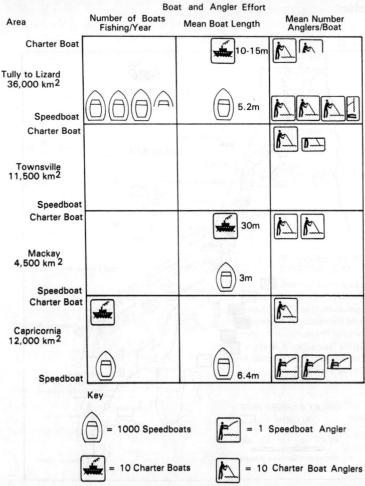

Figure 5 Charter boat, speedboat and angler effort in the Great Barrier Reef region.

refer to all trips in 1978–79 for the nine regular operators, the data for other areas refer only to deep sea club trips.[9]

Capricornia charter boats made an average of 17.5 trips per boat per year, for a total of 210 charter boat trips in the section in the year. Mean trip length was four days[10] (Hundloe *et al*, 1980). Data from the other three areas show a mean trip length of between one to two days. This reflects the timing of deep sea club trips, which were generally made on weekends or other statutory holiday periods (figure 6).[11]

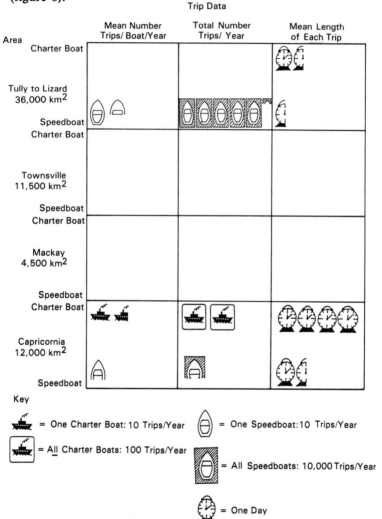

Figure 6 Trip data for charter boats and speedboats in the Great Barrier Reef region

The total number of charter boat angler days per year in Capricornia is 6,700;[12] approximately equivalent to 18.5 anglers fishing every day for one year in the section. Data are not available for charter boat angler days in other areas as yet (figure 7).

Effort from Speedboats

Reef fishing from some of the 73,000 privately owned motor boats is a popular activity in Queensland. Data are currently available for

Angler Effort

Area	Total Number Angler Days/Year	Mean Number Angler Days/km^2/Year
Tully to Lizard 36,000 km^2 — Charter Boat		
Speedboat	181,600	5.0
Townsville 11,500 km^2 — Charter Boat		
Speedboat		
Mackay 4,500 km^2 — Charter Boat		
Speedboat		
Capricornia 12,000 km^2 — Charter Boat	6,700	0.6
Speedboat	23,250	1.9

Figure 7 Angler effort from charter boats and speedboats in the Great Barrier Reef region.

the Cairns area and Capricornia and data are also presented from dories (small dinghies) carried on the "big boat" by deep sea club fishermen from Mackay and used to fish closer to the reefs than anglers in the "big boat" are able to do. As the dory data refer to fishing from small boats they are presented. However, it should be noted that the dories do not travel under their own power from shore.

There are quite striking differences in speedboat fishing effort between the Cairns area and Capricornia. In 1979–80 in the Cairns area, almost four times as many speedboats fished in the area as in Capricornia (figure 5). The Cairns area speedboats were smaller, carried more people, made more trips and made shorter fishing trips than Capricornia speedboats (figures 5 and 6).[13] These differences can be explained by the greater distance of the Capricornia section from shore compared with reefs in the Cairns area. The effect of distance on time spent fishing is also illustrated in the Cairns area for individual reefs (figure 8). Wind speed and day of the week are also important determinants of the number of boat launchings (figure 9).

Eight times as many fishing trips in speedboats were made to the Cairns section in 1979–80 compared with Capricornia (figure 6). This

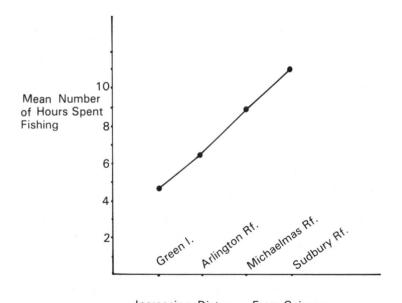

Distance Travelled and Hours Fished

Mean Number of Hours Spent Fishing

Increasing Distance From Cairns

Figure 8   Time spent fishing and distance of reef from Cairns.

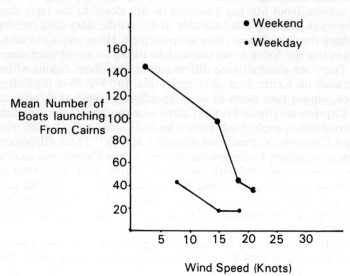

Figure 9 Wind speed, day of the week and number of speedboats launched from Cairns boat ramp (August 1980).

resulted in 181,600 angler days in speedboats in the year in the Cairns area compared with 23,250 angler days in Capricornia.[14] In terms of fishing effort per unit area, Cairns was much more heavily fished than Capricornia with approximately 5 angler days/km²/year compared with approximately 1.9 angler days/km²/year for Capricornia (figure 7).

Total Catch

Because sample sizes are small, values for catch per angler day for Cairns charter boats and Capricornia speedboats are not as reliable as other values. However, based on discussions and interviews with fishermen in both areas, they are believed to be of the correct order of magnitude.

Capricornia is the only reef area for which an estimate of total recreational catch is available. Based on catches per angler day of 11 to 15 fish,[15] total catch is estimated to be in the order of 390,000 reef fish, made up of 250,000 to 350,000 reef fish caught from speedboats and 70,000 to 110,000 reef fish caught from charter boats.[16] In Capricornia, fish numbers translated directly to total weight of the catch (mean fish weight of 1 kg)—see figure 11. The recreational catch is therefore believed to be approximately three times the size of the commercial catch in Capricornia, estimated at 130,000 kg reef fish.[17]

Total recreational catch from the Cairns area has not yet been determined, but total speedboat catch from this area was in the order of 770,000 fish in 1979–80 (almost twice the size of the Capricornia catch in an area three times as large).[18] Based on mean fish weight, the total weight of the Cairns area speedboat catch was in the order of 1,500,000 to 2,000,000 kg of reef fish — reflecting the greater mean weight of reef fish in the Cairns area (figure 10).[19]

The speedboat catch alone for 14 per cent of the Reef region is in

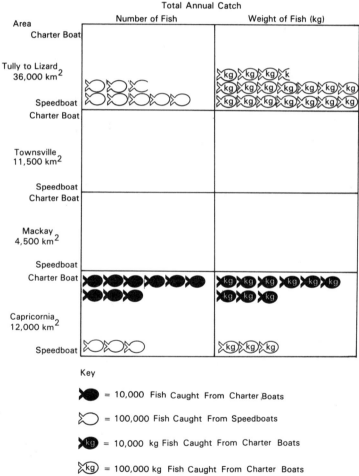

Figure 10 Total annual catch from charter boats and speedboats in the Great Barrier Reef region.

the order of 1 million reef fish (2 million kg). When total charter boat catches are added and catches from the Townsville, Mackay, and Swain Reefs areas are added, the total recreational catch for the Great Barrier Reef Region will be considerable.

Catch from Charter Boats

Comparison of catches from charter boats shows that the number and weight of fish caught per angler day decreased from south to north, although the mean fish weight shows a corresponding increase from south to north (figure 11). In the reef areas adjacent to Cairns and Innisfail, where some reefs are close to the shore, catches increased with increasing distance from shore (figure 12) (Craik, 1979). This was also found to be true for catches from speedboats from Cairns.

Off Townsville, mean catch (number of fish per angler day) remained steady since 1961 but mean fish weight has declined about 1 kg over that period (figure 13). This is in contrast with Capricornia, where both mean catch and mean fish weight remained relatively stable over the same period.[20]

Total catch for the year from charter boats in Capricornia was in the order of 70,000 to 110,000 (kg) reef fish (figure 10).

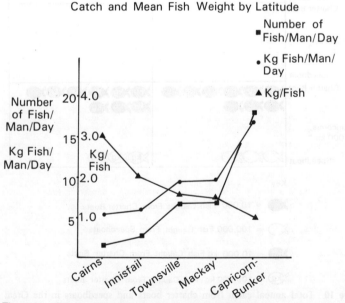

Figure 11 Changes in catch and mean fish weight with latitude.

Catch Vs. Distance From Cairns

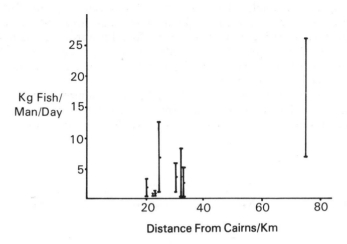

Figure 12   Catch and distances from Cairns.

Catch and Mean Fish Weight Over Time (Townsville)

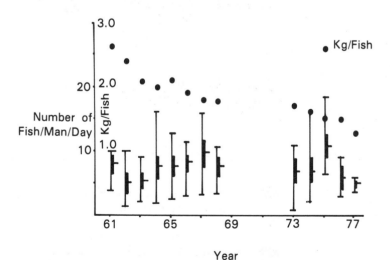

Figure 13   Catch and fish weight over time off Townsville (mean + 2 standard deviations).

Catch from Speedboats

Catches per angler day from small boats generally equalled or exceeded those from charter boats in the same area and increased numbers of fish per angler day were found towards the south and smaller fish towards the south. Mean fish weight caught by anglers in speedboats, however, was similar to that caught by anglers in charter boats (figure 10).

The total Capricornia speedboat catch was approximately three times the charter boat catch in Capricornia, and in terms of numbers, about one-third of the Cairns area speedboat catch.[21] In terms of

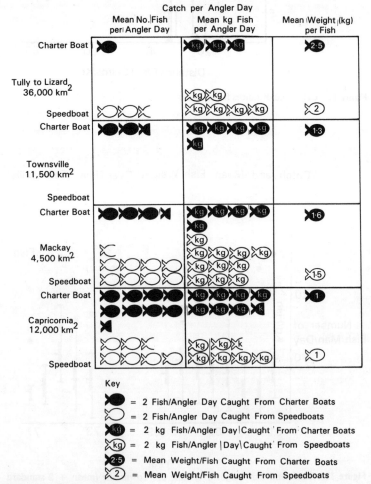

Figure 14 Catch per angler day.

numbers of fish caught per unit area, Cairns area and Capricornia speedboat anglers removed about the same number of fish, i.e., 21 to 24 fish/km²/year, but the greater mean weight of northern fish means that Cairns area anglers removed 40 kg/km²/year compared with 25 kg/km²/year in Capricornia (figure 14).

Catch Composition

For the three areas for which data are available, coral trout are a significant proportion of the catch (figure 15);[22] however, sweetlip are only significant in the Townsville and Mackay areas. The Cairns data are only for August and seasonal changes are therefore not

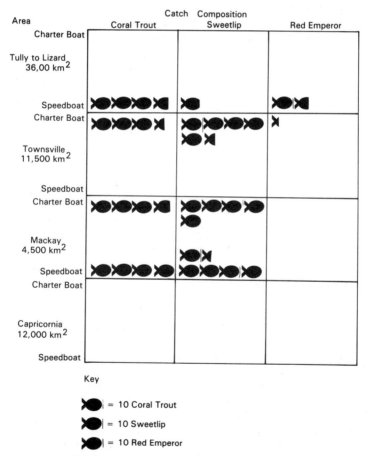

Figure 15 Catch composition from charter boat and speedboats in the Great Barrier Reef region.

represented. Catches at individual reefs in the Cairns area were found to vary considerably, with coral trout comprising 20-70 per cent of the catch.

Relative Angler Success

Data are available for Cairns area speedboat anglers and Townsville and Capricornia charter boat anglers.[23] They show that a small percentage of anglers take a large percentage of the catch; the top 10 per cent of anglers take approximately 30 per cent of the catch and the top 50 per cent of anglers approximately 80 per cent of the catch (figure 16). This means that the majority of people fishing catch very few fish; in the Cairns area the bottom 50 per cent of anglers catch, on average, 2.5 or fewer fish each day of fishing compared with a mean of 13 fish per angler day for the top 10 per cent of anglers. Similar results have been reported elsewhere.[24]

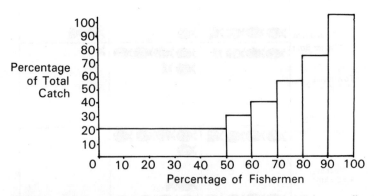

Figure 16   Relative angler success, based on rounded means from Cairns speedboat and Capricornia deep sea club fishermen.

Fishery Yields on the Great Barrier Reef compared with Other Areas

Yields of fin fisheries from reef areas and adjacent shallow water environments have generally been shown to be less than approximately 5 tonnes/km^2/year,[25] although recently reported yields of approximately 13 and 15 tonnes/km^2/year have been reported for reef fish in the Philippines.[26]

If the total area of Capricornia (12,000 km^2) is regarded as the shallow water area that is fished, the yield of reef fish (using the total recreational catch and the commercial catch of 130,000 kg/year) is in the order of 0.04 tonnes/km^2/year. However, much of

Capricornia is not fished. If the fishable area is the area shallower than 40 m, an estimate of the fishable area is approximately 4800 km².[27] The yield then becomes 0.1 tonnes/km²/year. Inclusion of the pelagic catch of 246 tonnes[28] and a similar estimated value for recreational fishermen might raise the yield up to 0.2 tonnes/km²/year. Marshall suggests that yields of fin fish far below 2 tonnes/km²/year may indicate the stock is either underutilized or overfished.[29]

Information on total yields is insufficient by itself to indicate the state of the fishery, particularly in multispecies reef fisheries where there may be a shift in the species composition of the catch before yields drop to levels indicating overfishing. Whether this has occurred in Capricornia, where mean catch per unit effort and mean fish weight have remained fairly stable since 1957[30] is not known, because there are insufficient data available on catch composition. If, however, the relatively low population levels and small mean sizes of coral trout at most reefs in the section are the result of heavy fishing, then stable mean catch per unit effort levels and fish weight could be maintained in spite of a change in catch composition. Management measures therefore would appear to be most beneficially directed towards increasing populations of most desired species. In this respect, the concept of closing off reefs or parts of reefs to allow recovery of populations of such species has been used by native inhabitants of Oceania.[31] In the Capricornia section, a number of replenishment areas will allow for rotational closures of reefs. During these periods of closure, population size frequencies and relative densities of target species will be closely monitored, as they will on nearby reefs to determine whether there is a "spin-off" effect, or whether the beneficial effect (assuming there is one) is confined to the closed reef. Catch and effort data will also be collected to see whether increased catches after reopening are a short-lived phenomenon or whether they persist over a considerable period of time.

Johannes has suggested that another opportunity exists for management of tropical reef species based on the reproductive behaviour of reef fishes.[32] If it can be shown that reef species of commercial and recreational importance form spawning aggregations which are as predictable in space and time as is reported for similar species in other reef areas of the world, the potential for both rapid stock assessment and relatively simple management, which has a minimal effect on the angler, is provided.

Conclusion

Research into the demersal reef fishery of the Great Barrier Reef has been and is being directed towards evaluation of the state of the fished stock and assessment of the catch and its composition. This is beginning to provide data on which decisions can be made as to whether management is necessary, and if it is necessary, the form it should take.

It does appear that fishing has had an effect on stocks in some areas. In the same areas it also appears that the recreational fishery makes a larger contribution to total catch than the commercial fishery and that, as in other fisheries, the majority of the catch is taken by relatively few people.

To date, management in the Marine Park has been directed at protecting all species in limited areas from all groups of fishermen. If, as more data become available, stocks appear to be overfished, other measures will become necessary.

Notes

1. *Acknowledgments.* The assistance of recreational fishermen in providing these data is greatly appreciated. T. Hundloe, S. Driml and P. McGinnity kindly provided early analyses of the mail questionnaire data. The efforts of those who participated in the workshops are appreciated, particularly D.A. Pollard, B.C. Russell and J.D. Bell who also participated in the coral trout surveys reported here. Volunteer anglers who participated in the tagging programme are also thanked for their effort.
2. W.J. Hargis, Jr, "Recreational Fishing Conservation and Management", in *Marine Recreational Fisheries 3: Proceedings of the Second Annual Marine Recreational Fisheries Symposium,* edited by H. Clepper (Sports Fishing Institute, Washington, D.C., 1978), pp. 5-8.
3. Queensland Marine Board, cited in A.K. Dragun, S.M. Driml & S.W. Lack, "The Economics of Fishing in the Capricornia Section of the Great Barrier Reef: Part A: a baseline study of the activity and resources of the Section" (IASR Research Report for GBRMPA 1979), 69 pp & appendices.
4. W.G. Gordon, "Federal View of Recreational Research Relative to Management", in *Marine Recreational Fisheries 3. Proceedings of the Second Annual Marine Recreational Fisheries Symposium,* edited by H. Clepper (Sports Fishing Institute, Washington, D.C., 1978), 151.
5. GBRMPA "Workshop on Reef Fish Assessment and Monitoring held at Heron Island, 18-28 November 1978" (GBRMPA Workshop No. 2, 1978), 64pp; GBRMPA, "Workshop on Coral Trout Assessment Techniques, held at Heron Island, 21 April to 4 May 1979" (GBRMPA Workshop No. 3, 1979), 85 pp.
6. W. Craik, "Survey identifies Trends in Reef Fish Catches", *Australian Fisheries* 38 (December 1979): 29-32.
7. T.H. Hundloe, S.M. Driml, S.W. Lack and G.T. McDonald, "Economic Characteristics of Fishing in the Capricornia Section of the Great Barrier Reef Marine Park" (A report prepared for the Great Barrier Reef Marine Park Authority, 1980), 134pp.
8. Ibid.
9. Ibid.; Craik, "Survey Identifies Trends in Reef Fish Catches".
10. Hundloe et al., "Economic Characteristics of Fishing in the Capricornia Section of the Great Barrier Reef Marine Park".
11. Craik, "Survey identifies Trends in Reef Fish Catches".

12. Hundloe et al., "Economic Characteristics of Fishing in the Capricornia Section of the Great Barrier Reef Marine Park".
13. Ibid; Hundloe, pers. com.; unpublished data,
14. Hundloe et al., "Economic Characteristics of Fishing in the Capricornia Section of the Great Barrier Reef Marine Park": Hundloe, pers. com; unpublished data.
15. Craik, "Survey identifies Trends in Reef Catches"; unpublished data.
16. Hundloe et al., "Economic Characteristics of Fishing in the Capricornia Section of the Great Barrier Reef Marine Park".
17. Ibid.
18. Hundloe, pers. com.
19. Hundloe, pers. com.; unpublished data.
20. Craik, "Survey identifies Trends in Reef Catches".
21. Hundloe, "Economic Characteristics of Fishing in the Capricornia Section of the Great Barrier Reef Marine Park"; Hundloe, pers. com.
22. Craik, "Survey identifies Trends in Reef Catches"; unpublished data.
23. Hundloe, pers. com.; unpublished data.
24. G. Henry, cited in *Professional Fisherman*, February 1981. B. Pollock, "Surprises in Queensland Angling Study", *Australian Fisheries* 39 (April 1980): 17-19.
25. D. Stevenson, & N. Marshall, "Generalisations on the Fisheries Potential of Coral Reefs and Adjacent Shallow-water Environments" (Proceedings of the Second International Coral Reef Symposium GBRC Brisbane, Oct 1974), 147-156.
26. A.C. Alcala, & T. Luchavez, "Fish Yield of the Coral Reef surrounding Apo Island, Negros Oriental, Central Visaya, Philippines (Abstract Only)" (Abstracts of Papers, 4th Coral Reef Symposium, Manila, Philippines 1981), 2; N. Marshall, "Fishery Yields of Coral Reefs and Adjacent Shallow-water Environments", in *Stock Assessment for Tropical small-scale Fisheries,* edited by S.B. Saila and P.M. Roedel (Proceedings of an International Workshop, Rhode Island, Kingston R.I. 1979), 103-129.
27. J.S. Jell, and P.G. Flood, "Guide to the Geology of Reefs of the Capricorn and Bunker Groups, Great Barrier Reef Province, with Special Reference to Heron Reef" (Papers, Dept. of Geology, University of Queensland 8, 3 1978): 85pp.
28. Hundloe, et al., "Economic Characteristics of Fishing in the Capricornia Section of the Great Barrier Reef Marine Park".
29. N. Marshall. "Fishery Yields of Coral Reefs and Adjacent Shallow-water Environments".
30. Craik, "Survey identifies Trends in Reef Catches".
31. R.E. Johannes, "Traditional Marine Conservation Methods in Oceania and their Demise", *Annual Review of Ecology and Systematics* 9 (1978): 349-464.
32. R.E. Johannes, "Using Knowledge of the Reproductive Behaviour of Reef and Lagoon Fishes to improve Fishing Yield", in *Fish Behaviour and Fisheries Management (Capture and Culture),* edited by J. Bardach, J. Magnison, R. Mayard, J. Reinhart (Published for Rockerfeller Fdn by ICLARM, Manila, 1980).

References

Alcala A.C. & T. Luchavez. "Fish Yield of the Coral Reef surrounding Apo Island, Negros Oriental, Central visaya, Philippines (Abstract only)". Abstracts of Ppaers, 4th Coral Reef Symposium, Manila, Philippines, 1981, p.2.
Craik, W. "Survey identifies Trends in Reef Fish Catches". *Australian Fisheries* 38 (December 1979): 29-32.
Dragun, A.K., S.M. Driml & S.W. Lack. "The Economics of Fishing in the Capricornia Section of the Great Barrier Reef: Part A: a Baseline Study of the Activity and Resources of the Section" IASR Research Report for GBRMPA, 1979, 66pp & appendices.

GBRMPA. "Workshop on Reef Fish Assessment and Monitoring held at Heron Island 18-28 November, 1978." GBRMPA Workshop No. 2, 1978, 64pp.

GBRMPA. "Workshop on Coral Trout Assessment Techniques, held at Heron Island, 21 April to 4 May, 1979." GBRMPA Workshop No. 3, 1979, 85pp.

Gordon, W.G. "Federal View of Recreational Research relative to Management". In *Marine Recreational Fisheries 3. Proceedings of the Second Annual Marine Recreational Fisheries Symposium.* edited by H. Clepper, 151-156. Sports Fishing Institute, Washington, D.C., 1978.

Hargis, W.J. Jr. "Recreational Fishing Conservation and Management". In *Marine Recreational Fisheries 3: Proceedings of the Second Annual Marine Recreational Fisheries Symposium.* edited by H. Clepper, 5-8. Sports Fishing Institute, Washington, D.C., 1978.

Hundloe, T.H., S.M. Driml, S.W. Lack and G.T. McDonald. "Economic Characteristics of Fishing in the Capricornia Section of the Great Barrier Reef Marine Park". A report prepared for the Great Barrier Reef Marine Park Authority, 1980, 134pp.

Jell, J.S. and P.G. Flood. "Guide to the Geology of Reefs of the Capricorn and Bunker Groups, Great Barrier Reef Province, with Special Reference to Heron Reef". Papers. Dept. of Geology, University of Queensland 8, 1978; 85pp.

Johannes, R.E. "Traditional Marine Conservation Methods in Oceania and their Demise". *Annual Review of Ecology and Systematics* 9 (1978): 349-464.

Johannes, R.E. "Using Knowledge of the Reproductive Behaviour of Reef and Lagoon Fishes to improve Fishing Yield". In *Fish Behaviour and Fisheries Management (Capture and Culture).* edited by J. Bardach, J. Magnison, R. Mayard, J. Reinhart, for Rockerfeller Fdn by ICLARM, Manila, 1980.

Marshall, N. "Fishery Yields of Coral Reefs and Adjacent Shallow-water Environments". In *Stock Assessment for Tropical Small-scale Fisheries* edited by S.B. Saila and P.M. Roedel. Proceedings of an International Workshop Rhode Island, Kingston R.I., 1979: 103-129.

Pollock, B. "Surprises in Queensland Angling Study". *Australian Fisheries* 39 (April 1980): 17-19.

Stevenson, D. & N. Marshall. "Generalisations on the Fisheries Potential of Coral Reefs and Adjacent Shallow-water Environments". Proceedings of the Second International Coral Reef Symposium GBRC Brisbane, Oct 1974, pp. 147-156.

16

The Effects of Selectively Fishing Reef Fish Stocks along the Great Barrier Reef

G.B. Goeden

Demersal reef fish surveys carried out between 1977 and 1980 were directed at establishing the extent and condition of commercial and recreational stocks along the Great Barrier Reef. Because there is a tendency for commercial and amateur fishing groups to blame each other for a reduction in catches,[1] the surveys were planned for areas ranging from entirely commercial to entirely recreational, and sampling included some species which are rarely taken by either party.

Methods

Representatives of four families (seventeen species) of demersal fishes were selected for visual surveys of population densities on seventy-six coral reefs.

These surveys were carried out by a team of two (one boat operator and one observer) from a 4 metre outboard powered boat. The observer followed the reef contours underwater with a manta-board while maintaining an altitude above the bottom of about 3 metres, noting distance travelled as measured by a log, and recording the number of individuals of selected species along a 5 metre wide track.

These data were used for the computation of population density indices which are estimates of the actual population densities of particular species.

Eight general areas were sampled from Melville Passage south to the Capricorn Group. Table 1 describes the sampling within each general area.

Tests for the difference between fish populations at each sample site combination were carried out using the Kolmogorov-Smirnov two sample test.[2] Correlation was tested using the Separman rank correlation coefficient, r_S.

The Heron-Wistari demersal reef fish community received only light fishing pressure during the five years prior to and during the survey period as the result of two closures of the grounds and the active discouragement of fishing by the local resort. The Heron-Wistari community provides a baseline measure for an area with only minimal fishing. This area is considered to be "undisturbed" for comparative purposes within this work.

Table 1 Description of the areas of sampling along the Great Barrier Reef

Area name	Date	Number of samples	Total sample area (ha)	Number of reefs sampled
Swains	12/1976 10/1977	151	94.2	30
Capricorns	12/1977	18	10.5	3
Heron-Wistari	12/1977	10	6.9	2
Wheeler	9/1977	5	6.2	1
Innisfail	11/1977	22	22.0	3
Cairns	2-5/1978	34	48.1	6
Melville	5/1978	20	10.0	3
Cooktown	1/1980	96	79.7	28
Total		356	277.6	76

Results

Plectropomids represent about 30 per cent of the demersal reef fish catch landed at the Queensland Fish Board and for the spearfishermen are "the most commonly-landed highly prized food fish in Queensland waters".[3] The relative proportions of the selected species within the undisturbed predator community were calculated and *P. leopardus* was found to be the most commonly encountered of the large demersal predators (66.6 per cent). As the result of its abundance and diverse feeding habits,[4] *P. leopardus* is likely to play a major ecological role in terms of competition with other predators for food and space and in helping to structure the fish community food web through preferential predation. In this sense *P. leopardus* may be regarded as a keystone species in the terminology of Paine.[5]

The ranked population density indices for Plectropomids at each reef area follow the descending order of Heron-Wistari, Swains, Melville Passage, Wheeler, Capricorns, Innisfail-Cooktown, and Cairns. The Cooktown samples covered such an extensive area (more than 6,000 km²) and included such a variety of reef types that they can not be readily compared with the other reef areas.

Heron-Wistari was significantly different from all other areas ($p < .05$). The remaining areas within the hierarchy were different when separated by one or more ranks. Adjacent ranks (excepting Heron-Wistari) were similar, i.e., $p > .05$.

There are now a large number of small boats of limited range associated with the amateur or recreation fishery. Increased fishing pressure resulting from the addition of their numbers to the fishing "fleet" appears to have been primarily directed toward those reef areas that are most accessible. Figure 1 shows the significant relationship ($r_S = 0.929$, $p < .05$) among the Plectropomid population

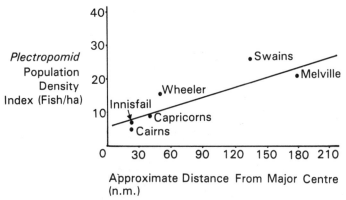

Figure 1 Plectropomid population density indices related to distance from the nearest major city for reefs between Cairns and Melville Passage.

density indices for the sampled reef areas along the Great Barrier Reef with their respective distances from major human population centres.

Extrapolation to the Heron-Wistari Plectropomid population density index (40.9 fish per ha) incidates that undisturbed populations could only exist more than 700 km from major centres. No large reef areas fall into this category and it appears likely that there are no large areas of the Great Barrier Reef that now support Plectropomid stocks in an unexploited condition.

Jones and Thompson found that "the ratio of relative abundance among the more commonly occurring (visible) suprabenthic species is representative of a given reef fish community".[6] At least 56 of their 165 species (34 per cent) are large demersal carnivores whose relative abundances reflected the same community differences as their prey species did.

Changes in the ratio of relative abundance among the large predators in this study were compared with decreasing *P. leopardus* abundance in areas subjected to increasing fishing pressure (figure 2). It can be seen that areas with different keystone species population indices had widely divergent predator community structures. It is my contention that, although based on a series of separate areas, figure 2 reflects the dynamics of one part of a demersal reef fish community as a predatory keystone species is gradually removed through selective fishing. It is of interest that changes in the ratio of relative abundance were large enough to bring about changes at the family level under conditions of very heavy fishing pressure (for example, Serranidae).

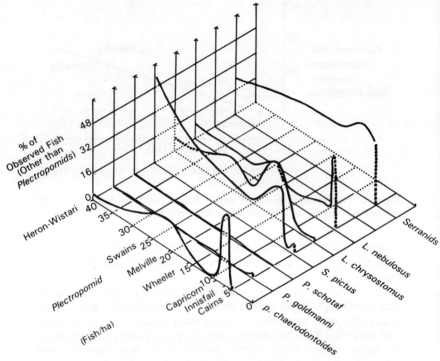

Figure 2 The relative proportions of large predator species related to decreasing Plectropomid abundance. Serranid species have been pooled due to visual identification problems among several similar species.

Discussion

It has been shown that *P. leopardus* populations have been significantly reduced in many parts of the Great Barrier Reef. Because this species is so dominant among the other large demersal predators, it can be thought of as a keystone species. This notion is supported by apparently unpredictable changes in the abundance of the remaining large predators including species which are only rarely taken by fishermen (for example, Plectorhynchids).

If an entire community undergoes a species compositional change as the result of some modification to keystone species abundance, then the community's stability will pass through a state of flux until it reaches a new stable species composition. The amount of community change or flux relative to keystone species abundance can be described by the expression:

$$F_c = \frac{\sum\limits_{i=1}^{N} \left| \frac{(d_{ij} - d_{ik})}{(D_j - D_k)} \right|}{N}$$

where F_c is community flux, d_{ij} and d_{ik} are the densities of the ith species ($i = 1,2...N$) of a collection of species at sample locations j and k. D_j and D_k are the densities of the keystone species at sample locations j and k where j and k can be either temporally or spatially separated and are adjacent in ranked densities.

Because only a sample of the community was examined in this study, F_S, the flux of the community sample must be substituted in the above expression for F_c. The values of F_S were computed and are plotted against decreasing keystone species abundance (*P. leopardus* per ha) in figure 3. The relationhip fits the equation $F_S = 16.10\,D^{-1.43}$ where F_S is the flux of the community sample and D is the population density index for the keystone species ($r_S = 0.92$, $p < .05$).

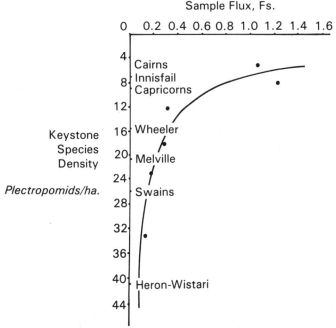

Figure 3 The relationship between decreasing Plectropomid abundance and flux of the community sample, F_s.

Although there is little change in F_S with *P. leopardus* density indices greater than about 40 fish per ha, the density at Heron-Wistari, the story is not so pleasant at the other end of the spectrum where the Cairns reefs have an average sample flux of 1.52. Specific reefs within this area, the ones used more often by the Cairns based amateur fishermen,[7] have extrapolated values of F_S ranging from 3.51 to 26.81 reflecting incredible changes in the structure of the predator community.

With a knowledge of the effects of fishing pressure on part of the predator community it may be possible to pick an "acceptable" level of exploitation from figure 3, where F_S is still close to an undisturbed state and where continued fishing will bring about minimal changes in the community structure. If demersal reef fish communities are essentially deterministic,[8] then Burdon may be correct when he states that "There are some Australian fisheries [demersal coral reef species] in which management measures are unnecessary ... [because] ... over-exploitation is reversible".[9]

If the demersal reef fish community is based on stochastic processes,[10] then it is possible that the role of the keystone species may be filled by previously less dominant populations. Should this be the case then the concept of renewable resources may not be broadly applicable to coral reef fish stocks.

Management Options

There are four basic management options which can be applied to the demersal fishery along the Great Barrier Reef. The first is to let the fishery manage itself on the basis that fishermen will move on when grounds reach a minimum level of productivity. This strategy relies on fishermen making firm decisions regarding a minimum catch per unit effort, a high degree of mobility along the coast, and a highly resilient target species population. The first two requirements are not met in areas where the fishing effort is dominated by amateurs and the population resilience of a protogynous hermaphrodite species,[11] where only older fish become males, could be expected to be relatively low. The reefs in the Cairns area are probably the best example of the failure of a liassez-faire management policy for reef fishes.

A second management option is the closure of certain reef areas. Although this scheme will increase adult survival in the closed areas it does so at the expense of the surrounding reefs to which fishing pressure is diverted. While the closure of certain reef areas within a larger group may have a considerable cosmetic value it is unlikely to be of any benefit to the stocks as a whole. This fact is highlighted for those species whose populations may depend on the successful recruitment of pelagic larvae from areas outside the man-made boundaries of a closed area.

Seasonal closures are a third option. The complete removal of exploitation for a part of the year has met with considerable success in many fisheries and hunting situations. Unfortunately its effect on demersal stocks along the Great Barrier Reef would be difficult to predict since both amateur and commercial fisheries are almost entirely weather dependent. A long period of calm seas outside the closed season could produce catches well above the most desirable average level while long periods of rough seas during this time could result in unnecessarily low levels of exploitation.

The fourth management option is the amateur bag limit together with a limited entry commercial fishery. This technique provides the greatest degree of freedom — people can fish when and where they want — but cannot take fish in excess of true requirements. Most amateurs will continue to catch their "evening meal" and the professional will operate under reduced competition. Only the "shamateur" will be unable to exist. An amateur bag limit would bring about a reduction in the overall catch by limiting the efforts of the most successful fishermen with little or no effect on the majority of noncommercial fishermen.

It is my contention that, of the four options proposed, the imposition of an amateur bag limit has the greatest potential for an immediate reduction in fishing pressure in those areas which now appear to be overexploited. The long-term maintenance of the amateur bag limit with regular reassessments of the allowable catch coupled with a limited entry commercial reef fishery would provide the best method of managing the demersal reef fishery along the Great Barrier Reef.

Notes

1. G.B. Goeden, "Managing Marine National Parks: Conflicts in Resource Exploitation", *Proceedings of the Ecological Society of Australia* 8 (1975). N.V. Ruello, and G.W. Henry, "Conflict between Commercial and Amateur Fisherman", *Australian Fisheries* 36, 3 (1977).
2. S. Siegel, *Nonparametric Statistics for the Behavioural Sciences*, (Sydney: McGraw-Hill, 1956).
3. P. Saenger, "An Analysis of Australian Recreational Spearfishing Data" (Proceedings Fourth World Congress of Underwater Activities Stockholm, 12-18 September 1975) (1978).
4. J.H. Choat, "Feeding Habits and Distribution of *Plectropomus maculatus* (Serranidae) at Heron Island", *Proceedings of the Royal Society of Queensland* 80 (1968); G.B. Goeden, "A Monograph of the Coral Trout", *Queensland Fisheries Service Research Bulletin* 1 (1978).
5. R.T. Paine, "A Note on Trophic Complexity and Community Stability", *American Naturalist* 103 (1969).

6. R.S. Jones and M.J. Thompson, "A Comparison of Fish Faunas in a Highly Stressed and Less Stressed Tropical Bay—Guayanilla and Jobos Bay, Puerto Rico" *Proceedings of the Southeast Ass of Game and Fish Committee* 27 (1978).
7. G.B. Goeden, "Green Island Management Plan—Submission on Marine Resources" *Queensland Fisheries Service Committee Report* (1979)
8. J.E. Randall, "The Endemic Shore Fishes of the Hawaiian Islands. Lord Howe Island and Easter Island", Colloque Commerson 1973. *O.R.S.T.O.M. Tranaux et Documents* 47 (1976); A.R. Emery, "The Basis of Fish Community Structure: Marine and Freshwater Comparisons", *Environmental Biology of Fishes* (1978); C.L. Smith, "Coral Reef Fish Communities: a Compromise View", *Environmental Biology of Fishes*, (1978).
9. T.W. Burdon, "Licence limitation" (National Fisheries Seminar, Proceedings Pt 2, ANU: Canberra, 1971).
10. B.C. Russell, F.H. Talbot, and S. Domm, "Patterns of Colonisation of Artificial Reefs by Coral Reef Fishes", Proceedings of the Second International Coral Reef Symposium, 1 (1974); R.S. Nolan, "The ecology of patch reef fishes" (Ph.D. Thesis, University of California, San Diego, 1975); P.F. Sale, "Maintenance of High Diversity in Coral Reef Fish Communities", *American Naturalist* (1977), 337-359; P.F. Sale, "Coexistence of Coral Reef Fishes—a Lottery for Living Space", *Environmental Biology of Fishes* 3, 1 (1978): 85-102.
11. G.B. Goeden, "A Monograph of the Coral Trout". *Queensland Fisheries Service Research Bulletin* No. 1 (1978): pp 42.

References

Burdon, T.W. "Licence limitation". National Fisheries Seminar, Proceedings Part 2, A.N.U., Canberra, 1971, pp. 44-49.
Choat, J.H. "Feeding Habits and Distribution of *Plectropomus maculatus* (Serranidae) at Heron Island, *Proceedings of the Royal Society of Queensland* 80 (1968): 13-17.
Emery, A.R. "The Basis of Fish Community Structure: Marine and Freshwater Comparisons". *Environmental Biology of Fishes* 3 (1978): 33-47.
Goeden, G.B. "Managing marine national parks: conflicts in resource exploitation". *Proceedings of the Ecological Society of Australia 8 (1975): 147-155.*
Goeden, G.B. "A Monograph of the coral trout". *Queensland Fisheries Service Research Bulletin* No. 1 (1978): pp 42.
Goeden, G.B. "Green Island Management Plan—Submission on Marine Resources". *Queensland Fisheries Service Committee Report* (1979), pp. 15.
Jones, R.S. and M.J. Thompson "A Comparison of Fish Faunas in a Highly Stressed and Less Stressed Tropical Bay—Guayanilla and Jobos Bay, Puerto Rico." *Proc. Southeast. Ass. of Game and Fish Comm.*, 27th (1978), pp 675-688.
Nolan, R.S. "The Ecology of Patch Reef Fishes." Ph.D.Thesis, University of California, San Diego, pp 230.
Paine, R.T. "A Note on Trophic Complexity and Community Stability", *American Naturalist* 103 (1969): 91-93.
Randall, J.E. "The Endemic Shore Fishes of the Hawaiian Islands, Lord Howe Island and Easter Island. Colloque Commerson 1973." ORSTOM *Tranaux et Documents* 47 (1976): 49-73.
Ruello, N.V. and G.W. Henry, "Conflict between Commercial and Amateur Fishermen". *Australian Fisheries* 36, 3 (1977): 4-10.
Russell, B.C., F.H. Talbot, and S. Domm. "Patterns of Colonisation of Artificial Reefs by Coral Reef Fishes". Proceedings of the Second International Coral Reef Symposium 1 (1974), 207-215.
Saenger, P. "An Analysis of Australian Recreational Spearfishing Data". Proceedings Fourth World Congress of Underwater Activities Stockholm, 12-18 September 1975. (1978).

Sale, P.F. "Maintenance of High Diversity in Coral Reef Fish Communities". *American Naturalist* 111 (1977): 337-359.

Sale, P.F. "Coexistence of Coral Reef Fishes—a Lottery for Living Space". *Environmental Biology of Fishes* 3, 1 (1978): 85-102.

Siegel, S. *Nonparametric Statistics for the Behavioural Sciences*. Sydney: McGraw-Hill, 1956, pp. 312.

Smith, C.L. "Coral Reef Fish Communities: a Compromise View". *Environmental Biology of Fishes* 3, 1 (1978): 109-128.

Smith, J.L.B. *The Sea Fishes of Southern Africa*. South Africa Central News Agency, Ltd, 1949.

17

The North Queensland Black Marlin Game Fishery: A Case Study on Its Economic Significance

K. E. Owen

With the proclamation of the 200 nautical mile Australian fishing zone on 1 November 1979 Australia assumed responsibility over all fishing operations within those new boundaries.

The fishery most affected, at least in terms of number of boats, by the introduction of AFZ legislation was the predominantly Japanese longline fishery which had attracted boats since the early 1950s. Prior to the AFZ coming into effect those foreign boats were entitled to fish anywhere beyond twelve nautical miles of Australia as they laid their lines for tuna to supply the lucrative Japanese sashimi market. But while tunas were the "target" species the inevitably indiscriminate longline method took several other species such as marlin and sailfish.

Concern was expressed that the longliners were taking too much incidental black marlin (*Makaira indica*), a fish for which Cairns had achieved worldwide fame as the "capital" since the first game boats operated out of Cairns in the 1960s. Since those first boats went to sea the fleet of charter boats has grown to about twenty-five, and the fishing brought employment, investment and income to the region. It was argued that Australia, now having the power to regulate foreign fishing within its waters, should address the question of whether the longliners did, in fact, threaten Cairns's appeal (and thus its profitability) as a game fishing resort.

It was for this reason that the Game Fish Working Committee (GFWC) was established. It was to examine the fairly scarce information available and make recommendations to government as it considered appropriate. The committee was comprised of representatives of the Commonwealth Department of Primary Industry, Queensland Fisheries Service, New South Wales State Fisheries and persons with expertise in and knowledge of the Cairns game fishing industry.

Data studied by the GFWC included an exercise by the economic analysis section of the Commonwealth Department of Primary Industry. This paper will discuss that study which attempted to assess the "value" of the game fishery to Australia and to the Cairns region in particular. It will also address itself to the problems inherent in trying to isolate the economic effects of an industry which has become part of the infrastructure of the whole Cairns economy.

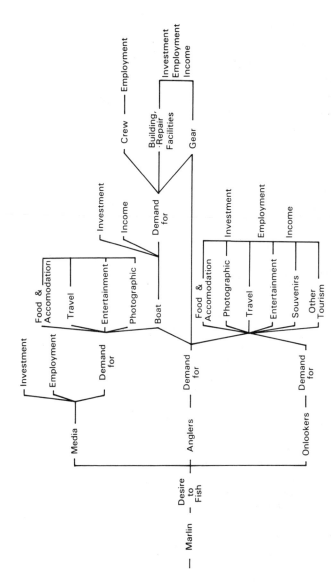

Figure 1 Flow chart identifying some of the benefits generated directly or partly because of the game fishery.

A simple flow chart can be used to identify some of the benefits which are generated directly and at least partly because of the game fishery. "Users" of the game fishery can be divided into three catergories, all of whom are attracted to the region by the black marlin. The angler, quite obviously, goes to Cairns to catch fish but the media and the "onlooker" would seem to be motivated by a vicarious desire to fish, to be involved, albeit peripherally, in an exciting and exclusive sport.

The flow chart, however, takes into account the fact that marlin is only one part of Cairns's overall appeal as a tourist resort so that although the fish can be seen as one of the reasons that, say, accommodation facilities are in demand it is incorrect to attribute all of that demand to the game fishery.

Indirect Benefits

At the outset it is imperative to recognize that the benefits which are derived by the Cairns economy extend well beyond those direct effects such as employment aboard charter boats and income received in the form of charter fees. The two major indirect benefits include:
1. The fact that Cairns has become known, worldwide, even to nonanglers because of its marlin and, just as importantly, the people who do visit Cairns to fish the marlin—people like Lee Marvin and Jack Nicklaus. Cairns is a tourist resort of long standing; the industry commenced before the second world war. The region could (and did) support a thriving tourist trade without marlin, but the recognition achieved overseas (and there have been numerous film and TV documentaries screened abroad) has been used as a banner by organizations like the Far North Queensland Promotion Bureau under which the area's other attractions can be listed. Black marlin, then, can be viewed as a factor in attracting nonanglers to the region. One of the difficulties in a study of this type is to make allowances for this indirect effect. No one would argue that people visit Cairns solely to watch marlin being weighed, but the fish does provide part of the reason for tourist visits, at least inasmuch as awareness of a particular tourist resort is the beginning of a decision to visit. Attempts to quantify the size of that "part", however, are most difficult if not impossible.
2. Much of the infrastructure of the Cairns tourist industry is geared as a high expenditure holiday resort. An American journalist, Stu Apte, described the Cairns marlin fishery as "the world's most expensive brand of fishing".[1] The ancillary industries such as restaurants and motels cater for those tourists by providing a high quality of facilities. Thus although the big game fishermen are

in the areas for only about three months, September to November, the facilities available may serve to encourage nonfishing tourists.

A major analytical problem was encountered in trying to estimate the relative importance of this indirect attraction. Just prior to the proclamation of the AFZ a good deal was written about the importance of the marlin fishery to the Cairns region; much of it appears to have been exaggerated. Attempts were made to attribute effectively all tourism to marlin fishing and to imply that the cessation of game fishing would cause Cairns to "close down". Quite obviously Cairns has other very important industries — prawns, beef and sugar. It is not strictly correct even to argue that the absence of black marlin would eliminate the charter fleet. The Great Barrier Reef abounds with many sought-after sport fish like Spanish mackerel and sailfish. Demand for charters would occur in Cairns as it does in Mackay and Townsville. By the same token, however, the fleet would probably not be as large nor would it boast the same level of sophistication as it does now.

Anglers and Owners

While it is possible to quantify (I believe fairly accurately) the direct benefits in terms of income, investment and employment derived from anglers, there remains the daunting task of attempting to allocate a value for the benefits not derived directly from the marlin fishery. To assess, even roughly, the total costs and benefits of the game fishery would require a far more detailed study than the one undertaken by DPI.

Attempts to conduct an economic study on recreational fishing are hampered by the fact that recreational fishermen are not motivated by strictly economic considerations. One can argue, of course, that if an angler is prepared to pay $15,000 for his fishing trip, the experience (and that is what he is paying for, not the actual fish, although the possibility of a big fish and ultimately the record fish is a definite motivation) is worth at least $15,000. There will come a point at which he is no longer prepared to pay the particular price so some kind of break-even analysis can be undertaken.

The angler, however, does not appear to be the only one who is not motivated by strictly economic factors. Indications from owners of charter boats are that not many of them are "good" investments in the economic sense, that is, outlay of resources in the expectation of generating profits. The majority of owners have other sources of income and are involved in the game fishing business mainly for enjoyment. Charter fees are useful in offsetting costs but are not a major determinant in deciding to retain or dispose of the asset. Those boats which do represent the main or sole source of income cannot do it on the basis of big game alone; their owners make them available for other charters, diving parties or to various government departments like the Bureau of Customs and Department of Primary Industry for surveillance patrols, etc.

This assertion that game boats are not profit makers may need some explanation when one reads the charter fees of $400 or $500 per day (1979). Gross revenue of $500 per day is certainly not insignificant but from that the owner must cover his running costs and a disproportionate amount of his overheads like depreciation and administrative expenses.

Running costs will include high season wages to skipper and two crew probably in excess of $150 per day. The two big motors of a boat will consume at least $60 worth of fuel per day depending on the fishing strategy adopted; and after that the owner must meet depreciation, repairs and maintenance and insurance on an asset worth well in excess of $200,000 as well as the cost of a range of fishing gear.

The "fact" that owning a charter boat does not represent a money-making proposition seems to be confirmed by the relatively small number of charter boats available. In 1979 there were twenty-five boats available for charter and during high season the demand for charters outweighs their supply. Under normal "market place" economics, given that there is no restriction on entry of boats to the industry, it could be expected that, were profits being generated, the fleet would expand. This has not occurred.

It could be argued, of course, that under normal "market place" economics one could expect a price increase. This also had not occurred. The reasons are not readily obvious, because I believe that the market would pay price increases. The explanation would appear to be in the fact that profit maximization is not the primary goal of boat owners.

It is unfortunate, for Cairns and for anglers, that this "primary sector" is of generally marginal profitability. The small number of boats probably deprives some prospective anglers of the opportunity to fish big marlin and, consequently, the small number of anglers deprives other industries — motels, car rental agencies — of further gains. The majority of those other industries run on nearly all fixed costs in that the cost of serving one more customer — the "marginal cost" — is fairly low while the revenue derived from that customer is relatively high. A motel's major costs will probably be depreciation, interest, adminstration, etc., and accommodating one more guest will add only slightly to costs — power and food. A large increase in occupancy rates may necessitate the hiring of some additional staff.

Thus, given a situation of nearly all fixed costs, profitability depends almost solely on occupancy so the ability to entice more anglers to the area will inevitably increase returns to those industries.

Although the further development of the Cairns game fishing industry appears to be inhibited by the small number of boats available there appears to be little likelihood of any significant increase in fleet size. Prospective boat owners must have both the desire to be involved in (at best) a marginal operation and the financial ability (that is, other sources of income).

An extension of the high season would give owners a longer time in which to earn that peak revenue. Although costs (wages, fuel) would be increased, as long as daily revenue exceeds variable costs (running costs), the longer season will give owners a greater opportunity to cover those fixed costs of depreciation, insurance, etc.

Having accepted that extension of the high season may, and probably would, make charter boats viable and encourage further investment in them, then comes the question of how. There is no way that the season for big black marlin can be extended. The fish is a highly migratory species which passes through waters adjacent to Cairns and there is no way to keep them there. It is possible, however, that a fishery for Pacific blue marlin (*Makaira nigricans*) could be developed. Cairns based boats have found blue marlin wide off the Great Barrier Reef. The existence of these fish has caused some excitement in the area; Gary Wright, editor of *Fish and Boat* considers that "this might be the beginning of a whole new fishing season that could place Cairns at the forefront of world angling attention for at least another three months every year."[2]

This optimism expressed by Wright, however, although shared by some boat owners and skippers, is not unanimous. Other people involved in the fishery are concerned that there are already well-established blue marlin fisheries off Hawaii and New Zealand and that anglers would express interest in an Australian fishery only if it could be demonstrated to be likely to produce records. A large part of Cairns's attractiveness to anglers is that they firmly believe the record (1,560 pounds) will be broken off Cairns.

Although opinion on the likelihood of establishing a blue marlin game fishery is divided, the fact remains that some boats continue to assess that possibility and only time will tell if the type of fish is available.

The second means of bringing the game boats closer to break-even would be to increase charter fees. Without study on the "willingness to pay" mentioned earlier it is not possible even to guess at how much higher rates could go before people stopped going to Cairns. The popular image of black marlin fishing as being a millionaire sport is not totally correct. While there is no doubt that the sport is expensive it attracts many (admittedly wealthy) people not of the "money-is-no-object" class, fee increases of the magnitude which seem to be necessary to equate costs and revenue could render some anglers unable or unwilling to fish off Cairns.

At present, however, people do still fish and returns are generated in the region. It was on this basis that the study was conducted.

Direct Benefits

Perhaps the most obvious, certainly most publicized, benefit accruing to Cairns is that of angler expenditure (which becomes income to other people). A good deal was written on the subject, much of it somewhat emotive, but there can be no doubt that the game fishery does inject substantial sums of money into the Cairns economy.

In attempting to assess the value, the DPI study had to make several assumptions regarding such factors as points of embarkation, duration of charters, other activities pursued in Australia and in north Queensland particularly, numbers in fishing parties, etc. These assumptions were decided upon after discussions with people involved with the industry. I believe the assumptions to be reasonable; if anything they are probably conservative.

The study estimated that the fishery attracts 300 foreign anglers and 200 Australian anglers every high season. It assumed further that overseas anglers were accompanied by, on average, three others and that Australian anglers were accompanied by one nonangler. In total then the game fishery was estimated to attract, directly, 1,600 members of angling parties per high season. In the "off season" a further 600 Australians visited Cairns primarily because of the game fishery; not necessarily to seek big marlin but to make use of the well-equipped boats for diving, shell collecting or whatever.

Further assumptions were necessary to estimate, for example, air fares paid to QANTAS (as only that airline earns money for Australia), accommodation expenses for stopovers in Sydney, entertainment, etc. (Other airlines' visits to Australia do, of course, earn money in landing fees, etc. but they are insignificant as regards the fishery.)

The findings of the DPI study presented to the GFWC included an estimate of expenditure by foreign anglers and their guests of some $6 million per annum of which about half is spent in the Cairns region. A similar sum was believed to be spent in the area by Australian anglers.

This estimate of $6 million in expenditure in the Cairns region (and thus income) represents only the first stage of income generation. To assume that it represents total income generation is to make the patently nonsensical assumption that none of that money is re-spent in the Cairns region. The sum paid by an angler for charter fees or motel accommodation represents income to the boat owner and motel proprietor, but he, in turn, has costs to be met out of that sum in wages or fuel or maintenance. Thus the charter boat owner's income of $1,000 becomes income of, say, $600 to skipper and crew. That $600, or more correctly part of it, is then spent in service stations or hotels. The process is continued with some being removed from circulation (for example, repairs to a motor may involve replacement of an imported component, in which case the sum is paid to the United States or West Germany and thus removed from the Cairns economy), but labour costs and local transport expenses will remain in the region.

Evaluation of this "multiplier" requires data on the "marginal propensity to consume", that is, the portion of each additional dollar which is re-spent. Such data are, at present, unavailable although the convenor of this seminar, Tor Hundloe of the Institute of Applied Social Research, undertook research to calculate multipliers of the Fitzroy–Wide Bay Burnett region.[3] Making the rough assumption that the income multiplier applying to the Cairns game fishery is the simple average of multipliers for the several industries studied by Griffith University, the total income generated by that initial $6 million will be around $12 million.

The real income generation of the fishery, however, will be well in excess of that sum but, at least at present, it is not possible to estimate how much in excess. A start could be made by carrying out further research into spending patterns of anglers and their companions, but that would not take into account that indirect income generation caused by the fishery enticing nonanglers. The fishery is so ingrained into the total tourism infrastructure of the region that isolation of the marlin fishery is virtually impossible. The DPI study had to try to imagine a scenario in which the black marlin fishery off Cairns "stopped", while nothing else was affected, for example, the Spanish mackerel and sailfish.

Unfortunately one cannot claim that income generation of the fishery is "X" million dollars. One would have to be quite heroic to even try to estimate a range of values; the data are just not available.

Another important gain to the region is in the area of employment. It is a relatively straightforward matter to estimate total employment aboard charter boats and mother boats. It works out at around the equivalent of ninety persons employed for a full year. But like the multiplication of income, the staff employed aboard those boats, and those boats themselves also demand goods and services so the employment as a result of the game fishery will be greater than that. There is also the problem of trying to calculate employment in the industries established to cater for anglers and those whose presence in Cairns can be attributed to an indeterminate extent on the fishery. An often quoted misconception during the public debate on marlin fishing was that all tourism in Cairns resulted from the fishery. This is not so as there would be (and there were) motels, and so on in Cairns in the absence of the game fishery. It would be incorrect to attempt to extrapolate on the basis that motel employment is proportional to the number of tourists and that anglers account for a particular percentage of tourism, because such a method takes no account of the indivisibility of labour, and so on. It is possible that the same number of motels would operate but at lower rates of return in the absence of the fishery.

Again one must counter the continuing problem of indirect employment; that is, jobs created by the visits of the nonanglers whose visits were prompted, in some way, by the marlin. Also, because of the fishery's absorption into the regional economy one must consider other types of employment (and income). Information on these avenues was obtained from discussions with people in Cairns. They include boatbuilders and repairers, gear suppliers, souvenir shops, photographers, and others. The fame of the Great Barrier Reef and Cairns in particular has caused demand for TV documentaries and has encouraged the shooting of several commercials. The short term benefits in the flow of technicians, cameramen, and so on all add to the value of the black marlin fishery.

Conclusions

It was hoped that the conclusions oi the DPI study would show that closure of the fishery, for whatever reason, would have certain quantifiable effects on income, investment and employment in Cairns, in north Queensland and in Australia in general. It became apparent quite quickly, however, that such an "answer" would not be found. It is not possible to identify the extent to which marlin have promoted tourism in Cairns overall, nor was it possible to follow all the links with the rest of the regional economy through first stage, second stage multipliers, and so on.

While it was not possible to define the values of the various parameters, however, it was obvious that the game fishery plays an important part in the regional economy. Without it the region would be deprived of millions of dollars every year and probably hundreds of jobs. The major drawcard available to tourism promoters would no longer exist.

The GFWC and government recognized the potential adverse effects on the Cairns economy in the event of the area not remaining a game fishing capital; the result was that all longlining in designated areas of the Great Barrier Reef is now prohibited. According to Mr Nixon, at the time Minister for Primary Industy, "this will ensure that the Cairns region will continue as one of the world's greatest big game fishing centres".[4]

Notes

1. *US Sports Afield,* April 1978.
2. *NQ Fish and Boat,* March 1979, 5.
3. T. Hundloe, "Employment and Income Effects of a Queensland Fishery", *Australian Fisheries* 40, 3 (March 1981): 6-9.
4. Primary Industry Media Release PI80/152, 15 October 1980.

18
Fisheries Economics in Queensland: Its Infancy, Its Future

S. M. Driml

Fisheries economics research is a latecomer to Queensland and for that research economists owe those directly involved in fishing an apology. While the few fisheries economists in this state were certainly aware of the important issues and problems, at least from a theoretical perspective, the necessary data had not been gathered to allow for problem-solving research. In the last two or three years things have changed.

A significant effort has been made to gather baseline data. Some interesting findings have already been made from the little analysis that has taken place to date. Other articles in this volume have presented findings based on those data.

The economic research undertaken in Queensland has been a joint effort, undertaken by government agencies and researchers at Griffith University who are interested in fisheries problems. This cooperative approach is obviously cost-effective. It also allows the researchers involved to use a common data base to undertake different types of analysis.

Why Study the Economics of Fishing?

The reasons why the economics of fishing warrant study are—or should be—obvious. These reasons will not be dealt with here in any detail. Professor Crutchfield and Frank Meany have drawn attention to many good reasons. Suffice it to say the commercial fishermen, all those industries which either buy from or sell to those fishermen, the financial intermediaries which lend money to the industry, the government agencies charged with the responsibility to manage fisheries, not to forget the amateur fishermen, all need the information economic studies provide. Fishing, in this respect, is no different from any other industry but, as emphasized in earlier articles, it is far more complex than most others because of its common property nature.

This article commenced with an apology to those directly involved in fishing for the simple reason that, had a sufficient effort been made by researchers in the past, it can be assumed that some of the very real problems faced today could have been circumvented. Of course, it is never too late to start.

The previous statement is not meant to imply that research by fisheries economists is going to provide the solution to all problems. There are obviously many more facets to fishing. What economic research can do is provide a basis for decision making, whether it be by the individual fisherman or the fisheries manager.

The Present Research Situation

The challenge is being met now. How is it being approached? As with most other research, baselines had to be established. The Queensland fisheries had to be described in terms of fishermen and vessels engaged, gear used, costs, earnings, and a host of other factors. While there is a degree of analysis involved in presenting useful descriptive data, usually further work drawing on that data is required before information needed for policy making is generated. As a general proposition, it can be said that we are still very much engaged in gathering descriptive data.

What Types of Data are being Gathered?

Both commercial and recreational fishing are important economic activities in Queensland. These two broad categories can be further divided into various fisheries according to species sought, fishing method, geographical location, etc. A complete data base would cover all Queensland fisheries.

With regard to Queensland east coast commercial fisheries, the situation is as follows. Through a cooperative effort between the then Queensland Fisheries Service, the Commonwealth Department of Primary Industry, the Great Barrier Reef Marine Park Authority and the Institute of Applied Social Research, Griffith University, a sample of the population of commercial fishermen from Cooktown to Tin Can Bay has been surveyed with regard to costs, earnings and other relevant data.[1] The questionnaire, which is administered by personal interviews, is a modified version of the standard Commonwealth Department of Primary Industry interview schedule. One important modification is the addition of questions relating to the location of expenditure and sales by fishermen. The reason for this modification is that it allows the Institute of Applied Social Research to estimate the economic importance of fishing on a regional basis.

The other important modification is the inclusion of questions on the costs of fuel to the fisherman and the effects price increases are having on fishing effort. This follows similar investigations undertaken by the Commonwealth Department of Primary Industry for other fisheries around Australia.[2]

The costs and earnings data are essential for determining the average and overall profitability of a fishery. Other important information is gathered on the costs of finance to fishermen (that is, the interest rate on borrowed funds) and the source of funds. Again, this complements recent Commonwealth Department of Primary Industry research investigations on these matters.[3] Information is also gathered on vessel insurance.

While every individual fisherman knows only too well his individual costs and problems, he should not assume that governments know the overall situation in necessary detail. Only by economic surveys do valid statistical data become available to government agencies responsible for fisheries management.

To complete the coverage of Queensland commercial east coast fisheries, further surveys will need to be carried out in the area south of Tin Can Bay to the New South Wales border. There is also the interrelationship of Gulf of Carpentaria fishing to east coast fishing to consider.

With regard to recreational fishing, the situation at present is that a sample of the owners of the 74,000 registered motor boats has been surveyed. For the area adjacent to the Great Barrier Reef, two survey methods have been used. Fishermen returning from a trip have been interviewed at boat ramps. This has been a cooperative effort between the Great Barrier Reef Marine Park Authority, the then Queensland Fisheries Service and the Institute of Applied Social Research. This technique has provided very good data, but to obtain an estimate of the proportion of those 74,000 boats which are used for fishing (and where they usually go), a mail survey was administered. For the remaining parts of Queensland (mainly from Fraser Island south to the New South Wales border) only the latter method has been used to date. That work was done by the Institute of Applied Social Research.

Fishing by boat owners is only one method of recreational fishing. Fishing on charter-boat trips and from the shore is also widely engaged in. Some research had been done on these various recreational fisheries. Keith Owen's paper on the Cairns marlin fishery is one example. Work is under way by the Institute of Applied Social Research on beach fishing from Fraser Island, which is the mecca of tailor fishermen in Queensland, if not Australia. Still more needs to be done before we have a reasonable description of recreational fishing in Queensland. A reliable estimate of the population of fishermen is required, as are estimates of the expenditure and effort involved.

The questionnaires used for mail surveys of recreational fishing have been standardized, after initial experimentation. Data are collected on catch, time spent fishing, number of trips per annum, areas fished, annual costs of such items as boats, gear, and so on, and last-trip costs of motor vehicle expenses, boat expenses, bait, ice, and so on. The city or town where expenditure is incurred is recorded, as is the occupation of the respondent.

The first step in researching recreational fishing is the collecting of comprehensive baseline data. Subsequent analyses of these data will be determined by the information needs of the agencies involved. Economic baseline data used in conjunction with biological information, as in the Great Barrier Reef research, is an example of this.

As for commercial fishing, the data being gathered is of such a nature that the regional economic impact of recreational fishing can be estimated. The data also will allow application of the travel-cost methodology as a means of estimating the economic value of particular fishing sites.

To have a full understanding of the importance of the fishing industry, or particular fisheries of which it is composed, it is necessary to look beyond basic statistics on production and employment and consider the impact of the industry on the general level of economic activity.

The Queensland fishing industry is highly decentralized along the entire Queensland coast. It is a major industry in many of Queensland's coastal towns. Through forward and backward linkages with related industries, it supports many businesses and jobs both within and outside local, regional economies. Forward linkages are established with processors, wholesalers, distributors and retailers who market the output of the industry. Backward linkages result from the demand the industry creates for goods and services such as boats, gear, repairs and maintenance, food supplies, etc.

This economic impact of the fishing industry can be estimated by the calculation of the "multiplier effect". If the multiplier effect is known, those involved in the fishing industry have a ready means of knowing, for example, what effect increases or decreases in the value of fish catches have on total employment (and output and income) in Queensland's fishing regions, or on the state-wide economy.

What is meant by the "multiplier effect"? Any economic activity will, in the first place, add to the value of output and employ labour. This is the direct or "first round" effect. This output will be accompanied by indirect effects as firms that have increased their output because of sales to the industry in turn purchase higher levels of goods and services from other firms. These "industrial support" requirements are felt throughout the economy in question. Next there are "induced" or consumption-generated effects. As the wages and distributed profits of an industry are spent, there is an increase in sales and therefore the output and employment of other firms through second and subsequent round effects.

Relative economic impacts are commonly expressed through multipliers which express the ultimate change in economic activity as a result of a unit change in an economic variable. Multipliers are calculated by using input-output tables describing the flow of purchases and sales from one industry to other industries in the economy.

Conclusion

Having dealt with the present situation in fisheries economics research, what of the future? To date researchers have done little more than make a sound start on gathering baseline data. That task has to be completed, with one component being a complete study of the aggregate economic impact of both commercial and recreational fishing.

A comprehensive list of subsequent research tasks would be rather long. I shall mention just a few of immediate concern, some of which will have been mentioned in other articles.

The economic efficiency of our various fisheries needs to be analysed. All who are concerned with Queensland fisheries need to know if, and to what extent, there is overutilization of resources. We need to evaluate the economic implications of various management tools, such as limited entry, seasonal closures, replenishment areas, gear restrictions, bag limits, and so on. As well as this, we need to research the social implications of management policies; for this, socioeconomic profiles of owners, skippers and crew are required. We need to monitor management plans. We should strive for the utopia where we can anticipate problems and implement management policies before disasters occur.

Research should continue into the aspects of fuel price increases. The effect of high interest rates for borrowed finance and the costs of boat insurance also require analysing. The extent of the black market and its effect on price needs further research. The degree to which imported fish is affecting prices for local products is another research priority. Market research is required to assess the possibility of expanding domestic and overseas markets.

The present shipbuilding subsidy needs evaluation, with particular emphasis on equity aspects and its effect on economic efficiency. There is also an important task to estimate equitable "rents" to be paid by foreign fishing operations in the Australian Fishing Zone; also the economic feasibility of developing Australian fisheries in the Australian Fishing Zone needs consideration.

It should be noted that most of this research requires a system of accurate record-keeping. This is one way in which fishermen and those associated with fishing can assist researchers.

Research into all these issues should be of a multiobjective nature, that is, paying due regard to: (i) economic efficiency (in use of all resources—capital, labour, fish stocks, etc.); (ii) equity (not discriminating against certain categories of fishermen); (iii) employment (at a regional and state-wide basis); (iv) conservation (defined as "wise use" of natural resources). Research of this nature is by necessity interdisciplinary. Economics, biology, geography, public administration, sociology and law, are just some of the disciplines that immediately come to mind. Because of the interdisciplinary nature of this research, coordination between researchers in the relevant agencies is highly desirable, in fact necessary. It is fortuitous that much of the research that has been undertaken in the last few years has been coordinated.

In conclusion, it should be emphasized that whatever research is done should be of immediate use to those most closely involved with fishing; that is, fishermen, processors, sellers, suppliers, finance houses, insurers and managers. This means that the results should be made available as soon as possible. In this way, we, the researchers, can assist those whose livelihoods and recreation are dependent on fishing. Of course, they, in turn, can help us help them by continuing to provide the data needed.

Notes

1. Prawn trawling in southeast Queensland was the subject of a similar study by the Commonwealth Department of Primary Industry in 1975.
2. S. Jarzynski, "Fuel Prices a Growing Burden for Australian Fishermen", *Australian Fisheries,* 39, 5 (May 1980).
3. C. Lightfoot, "Sources of Finance for the Fishing Industry", *Professional Fisherman,* 3, 6 (April 1981).

19

The Ecology and Management of Exotic and Endemic Freshwater Fishes in Queensland

A. H. Arthington
R. J. McKay
D. A. Milton

In 1977 a grant from the Australian National Parks and Wildlife Service, Canberra, enabled the Queensland Museum to survey the creeks of the Moreton Bay and Hervey Bay regions for introduced aquarium fishes. A further grant extended the survey northwards to Cairns.[1]

The mosquito fish, *Gambusia affinis*, was found in many of the streams and drains between Brisbane and Cairns. The guppy, *Poecilia reticulata* and the platy, *Xiphophorus maculatus*, were not as widespread but the swordtail, *Xiphophorus helleri*, was common in the Brisbane region. The swordtail was also found at Gladstone and the platy at Hervey Bay and Babinda. In sixty-three creeks throughout the Brisbane region, 90 per cent contained *Gambusia*, 37 per cent contained swordtails, 8 per cent had guppies and 5 per cent supported platies. The rosy barb *Puntius conchonius* was present only in Seven Hills Creek, Brisbane; the goldfish *Carassius auratus* was widely distributed in southern Queensland, but was not abundant in the creeks of the Brisbane region.[2]

Indications of the impact of these introduced species on native freshwater fishes were obtained from the surveys. Native fishes usually comprised less than 5 per cent of the total fish catch at sites supporting *Gambusia* and *Xiphophorus*, and in some creeks only introduced species were found. McKay concluded that "the native freshwater fishes most severely affected by introduced live bearing fishes are the surface-feeding or mosquito larvae eating genera such as *Melanotaenia*, *Pseudomugil*, *Craterocephalus* and *Retropinna*".[3]

In January 1981 a research consultancy was contracted between the Australian National Parks and Wildlife Service and the School of Australian Environmental Studies, in conjunction with the Queensland Museum. Its brief was to investigate the ecology of introduced and native freshwater fishes in southeastern Queensland streams and to determine the factors underlying the decline of native species in the presence of introduced species.

This article outlines the results of preliminary studies on habitat and food preferences of native and introduced species which are common in the Brisbane region. It comments on their reproductive biology and describes the results of experiments on temperature and dissolved oxygen tolerance. Aquarium studies on the predatory preferences of the cardinal fish, *Glossamia aprion,* are also summarized. On the basis of these preliminary studies and data from the literature, the impact that exotic species may have on native fishes, is discussed and the management problems arising from the importation of exotic fishes into Australia are then summarized.

The Study Area

The study was focused on several of the major creeks in the Brisbane region (figures 1 and 2). Six main study sites were selected on Enoggera Creek and Kedron Brook for long-term routine sampling of fish distribution and abundance. During this preliminary study these sites (A to F) were monitored twice. Main study sites were chosen on the basis of accessibility, the presence of a well-defined pool and an associated riffle and the particular fish species present. Pools were small enough to be sampled efficiently but large enough to support fish populations representative of the creek section. To

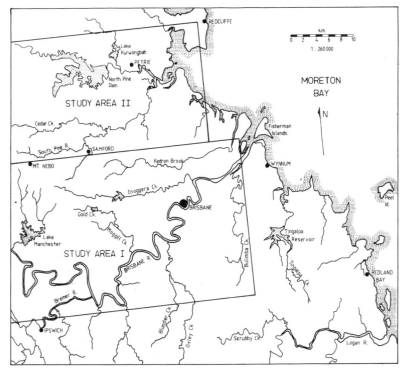

Figure 1 Locations and general features of Study Area I and Study Area II. (Source: Gregory's Street Directory 1980.)

Key to Sampling Sites: A – F Main study sites 1981 : G – Z Additional study sites 1981 : 1 – 50 Sites sampled by McKay 1977 : 20M, 21 L, 32V, 33V, 33U Sites sampled by McKay 1977 and in 1981 : * Sites sampled by Mr B Pearse or Mr R Ham in 1981 : *I – VI Sites where water quality was obtained but not fish data obtained 1981.

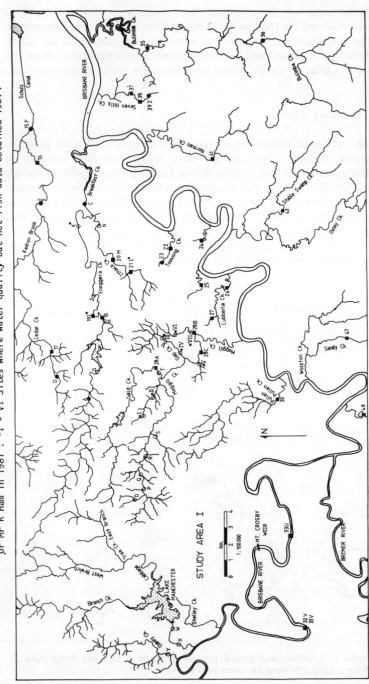

Figure 2 Details of Study Area I showing location of main and additional sampling sites. (Source: 1:100 000 Topographic for Ipswich and Beenleigh.)

avoid depletion of fish stocks, the main study sites were sampled twice with a two-month interval between sampling. Introduced species were present at all sites except site A. A number of additional sites were also surveyed during the study (figure 2).

Methods

Classification of Fish Habitats

During the initial phase of the project five days were spent observing field populations in undisturbed conditions, in an attempt to determine any recognizable habitat selection by fish species. By definition, a "habitat" only existed if it was occupied by fishes. There were three major fish habitats in the creek studied. These were:
1. open water—the area which comprised the body of most pools, regarded here as that section > 0.3m from the bank, without aquatic macrophytes;
2. water weed—rooted or suspended aquatic vegetation;
3. edge—the area of the pool which comprised the interface between the terrestrial and the aquatic environment; comprised mainly of shallow areas with overhanging terrestrial vegetation or semiterrestrial species growing in the water.

The habitats were visually well defined and most fish species spent about 80 per cent of their time within one of them, although there was some movement between habitats. Each habitat was further subdivided, depending on the characteristics of the particular site. Open water habitats were subdivided according to differences in substrates present, to check on preferences for feeding sites, etc. Water weed and edge habitats were subdivided according to plant species present, to check on preferences of fish for weedbeds and edge areas with particular characteristics.

Sampling Fish Populations

On arrival at any site fish were always collected from edge habitats first, because sampling of open water habitats tended to drive fish into the shelter of water weed and overhanging terrestrial vegetation. Electrofishing and rotenone poisoning were used to obtain quantitative data for intersite comparisons. When these methods were not available or practical various netting techniques were used.

Water Quality Measurements

At each study site, flow rate, temperature, dissolved oxygen, pH and conductivity were measured on every occasion of sampling fish populations. Flow rate was measured using an Ott Model C_2 Small

Current Meter (No. 3 propellor), temperature and dissolved oxygen with an automatic Delta Model 2110 Multirange Meter which was calibrated to oxygen saturation on each day of use, pH with a Townson pH meter and conductivity with a YSI Salinity/Conductivity Meter and electrode.

The measurements were made at the same reference point at each site on each occasion. Open water habitats were monitored below the surface and on the bottom at the deepest point; measurements in weedbeds and at the edge of sites focused on the middle of the habitat.

Sampling Fish Food

The range of food items available to fishes was estimated for each habitat type at the main study sites A-F in March 1981. Macrobenthos was estimated from three random samples for each habitat. The invertebrates of weedbed and edge habitats were sampled by dip netting along the length of the habitat for approximately 50 seconds, using 40 cm diameter dip nets.

Drifting invertebrates and terrestrial insects falling into the water were sampled with a drift net of standard design. The net had a $0.1m^2$ square mouth and steel frame; the mesh aperture was 0. 25 mm. Nets were placed in narrow, shallow riffle areas immediately downstream from each sampling site, and were emptied twice daily, after 12 hours and 24 hours.

Treatment of Fish

All fish specimens were identified to species, sexed (where practical) and their standard length (from the anterior extremity of the mouth to the hypural joint) was measured using dial calipers. The guts or entire viscera were removed and preserved in 5-10 per cent formalin for later analysis of gut contents.

Gut Content Analysis

Most of the fish species under investigation had small stomach volumes, making volumetric analysis of food items impractical. An appropriate method of analysis proved to be measurement of "area".[4] The stomach contents were squashed in a petri dish to uniform depth and the area of the squash measured in mm^2. The areas of digested material, plant material and recognizable invertebrate taxa were measured and individual food items enumerated. The source of error in the area method is estimated to be about 3.5 per cent[5].

The importance of each food category was calculated in several ways:

1. the number of individuals (N) in each food category was expressed as a percentage of total individuals in all food categories, for all stomachs in a sample. The mean number of individuals per stomach was also calculated when feasible;
2. frequency of occurence (F) was calculated and expressed as a percentage of all stomachs containing food;
3. total area (A) of each food category was expressed as a percentage of total area of all stomach contents in a sample. Stomachs of all "fullness" types were included in the total;
4. the "index of relative importance" (IRI),[6] was calculated from the percentage contribution of each food category by number (N), area (A) and frequency of occurrence (F):

$$IRI = (\%N + \%A) \times \%F.$$

In some instances, one or more of these measures of dietary importance could not be calculated, usually because the gut contents were partially digested, or plant fragments were present.

Determination of Critical Thermal Minimum

Fish were collected from two sites on Enoggera Creek and acclimatized at 15°C for at least four days prior to testing at a photoperiod of 12 hours light and 12 hours darkness. Individual fish were placed in a 250 ml beaker containing 75 ml of water at 15°C. The beaker was immersed in a 1,000 ml beaker which was maintained at 2-3°C with ice. The temperature in the test beaker dropped at a rate of approximately 0.8°C per minute. Continuous stirring and aeration prevented the development of thermal gradients and oxygen deficits. The temperature in the test beaker was measured continuously with a mercury in glass thermometer accurate to ± 0.1°C. All tests were conducted between 0930 and 1230 hours on consecutive days. Johnson[7] found no variation in the thermal tolerance of *Gambusia affinis* during this period of the day.

The species tested were *Gambusia affinis, Xiphophorus helleri, Melanotaenia fluviatilis, Hypseleotris galii, Craterocephalus marjoriae* and *Mogurnda striata*. Ten mature individuals of each species were tested.

Two behavioural responses to low temperatures were noted in all species; Johnson recorded similar responses.[8] These were: loss of orientation and inability to control lateral movement and remain upright; and spasmodic movements, accompanied by a complete lack of secondary movement (except of gills) followed immediately by death. Water temperatures at the onset of these behaviours were recorded and the fish allowed to recover in aquaria at 23°C.

Data were analysed for significant differences in behaviour between species using the statistical package AVIF (analysis of variance) and Duncan's Multiple Range test. Both behavioural responses were analysed, to determine the most appropriate indicator of the critical thermal minimum.

Determination of Critical Oxygen Requirements

Selected fish species were held in aquaria (1 m × 40 cm × 40 cm) for two weeks at 23°C before the experiments. Most were fed on commercial fish food; *Mogurnda* were given live *G. affinis* and *X. helleri*.

For each experiment, two individuals each of *Mogurnda striata, Hypseleotris galli, Melanotaenia fluviatilis* and *Xiphophorus helleri* were placed in 4-litre glass jars containing dechlorinated tap water. Three replicates were set up. Each jar was fitted with a dissolved oxygen probe and sealed. Dissolved oxygen levels in the jars were monitored continuously using a Delta Model 2110 Multriange Meter. There was no agitation of the water, which was maintained at 30°C to exhaust the oxygen present as rapidly as possible. Most experiments required two days for the dissolved oxygen level to fall to 0.5 mg/1.

The behaviour of each species was observed as the dissolved oxygen level decreased. Experiments were terminated before the dissolved oxygen level fell to zero because of the accumulation of toxic wastes.

Predation Experiments

The predacious cardinal fish, *Glossamia aprion,* was tested for preferences in prey species and prey size, using both native and introduced fish species.

Ten cardinals were maintained in an aquarium 1 m × 40 cm × 40 cm over a five-week period. Healthy prey fish were placed in the test aquarium at 0800 hrs on the day of each experiment and the numbers of prey species remaining were counted at intervals of 2½ hours during daylight. At the end of each day the prey stocks were replenished to initial numbers.

When only two prey species were offered, the size range of the individuals offered was comparable, given differences in build between species. Where three or more species were offered, it became extremely difficult to achieve comparable size ranges. Such experiments were therefore repeated with each prey species offered once as the smallest individuals in the test (Experiments 2, 3 and 4). From these experiments it was possible to test, in a preliminary way, the influence of prey size on food selection by *Glossamia aprion*.

Two prey species comparisons were analysed for differential predation using Mann-Whitney U tests on the proportions of each species eaten during each measurement interval. The multiple species comparisons were analysed by ANOVA and Duncan's Multiple Range test.

Discussion of Results from the Preliminary Study:
The Ecology of Introduced Species

The Distribution of Introduced Species

The mosquito fish was found to be the most widely distributed introduced species in the Brisbane region (table 1). Since 1977 it appears to have spread into systems which were previously *Gambusia* free, for example, the Brisbane River below Mt Crosby weir (at College's Crossing). In the upper tributary of Ithaca Creek *Gambusia* is now less abundant than in 1977, but futher downstream *Gambusia* is still present. Some of these apparent changes in the relative abundance of *Gambusia* may simply reflect differences in sampling techniques employed in the 1977 and 1981 surveys.

The swordtail, *X. helleri,* was found in 45 per cent of the eleven creeks surveyed in 1981, compared to 37 per cent of the creeks surveyed by McKay in 1977. In nearly half of the fifteen sites where *X. helleri* and *G. affinis* were present together in 1981, the swordtail dominated the total fish population (Cedar Creek, Kedron Brook, site J, on Enoggera Creek, Ithaca Creek and Seven Hills Creek, table 1).

Xiphorphorus maculatus has a much more restricted distribution in Queensland than the swordtail.[9] Around Brisbane it is known only from the upper Brisbane River at College's and Kholo Crossings and in the Redcliffe area (table 1). The Brisbane River populations have persisted at least five years and the Redcliffe populations at least twelve years.

Poecilia reticulata was found only in Seven Hills Creek during this study, where it has been present for at least eight years. McKay recorded the guppy in four separate creeks in the Brisbane region and in many areas further north.[10]

No other introduced species were recorded during the study. Rosy barbs (*Puntius conchonius*) were present in Seven Hills Creek in 1977, but were not found there in 1981.

Reproductive Biology

The reproductive biology of *Gambusia affinis* is well known from many studies conducted in other parts of the world.[11] The maturation rate varies according to temperature and productivity and early maturing females generally produce fewer and smaller broods, and die in the same summer in which they reach maturity. The females are hardier and longer lived than the males, and those females which mature late in the second summer produce more broods (up to 5 broods) and larger broods over a longer period (14 to 15 weeks).

In tropical areas, females may reproduce throughout the year, but

Table 1 Distribution of introduced and native species in the Moreton Bay region (* indicates that the species was present in 1981 surveys).

	A	B	C	D	E	F	G	H	I	J	K	L	M	N	O	P	Q	R	S	T	U	V$_{main}$	V$_{isolated}$	W	X	Y	Z
INTRODUCED																											
Gambusia affinis	*	*	*	*	*	*	*	*	*	*	*	*	*					*						*	*	*	*
Xiphophorus helleri	*	*	*	*	*	*	*	*	*	*	*	*		*										*	*	*	*
Xiphophorus maculatus														*													*
Poecilia reticulata																									*		
NATIVE																											
Mogurnda striata							*	*	*	*		*	*	*	*	*	*	*	*	*		*		*		*	
Mogurnda australis				*																							
Ambassis marianus						*																					
Ambassis nigripinnis					*		*	*	*	*	*	*	*	*	*	*		*		*	*				*		*
Pseudomugil signifer								*																			
Hypseleotris galii																	*					*					
Hypseleotris compressus																											
Crateocephalus marjoriae									*	*																	
Crateocephalus																											
stercusmuscarum							*																				
Philypnodon grandiceps							*						*					*	*	*							
Melanotaenia fluviatilis							*																				
Retropinna semoni							*	*	*				*			*				*							
Anguilla reinhardti					*	*	*									*											
Anguilla australis				*			*																				
Tandanus tandanus				*			*				*							*									
Mugil cephalus																									*		
Glossamia aprion						*																					
Pseudogobius Sp. 1						*																					
Pseudogobius Sp. 2						*																					
Notesthes robusta																											
Nematolosa erebi						*																					
Gerres ovatum																											

Species lists for sites A-F based on two sampling occasions. All other lists based on one sampling occasion.

in southern Queensland reproduction apparently slows down in April and ceases during winter months.

Although our data are limited they are in agreement with the literature. The populations sampled had 1:1 sex ratios in younger fish but there was a predominance of females amongst older individuals, as elsewhere.[12] Newly born young were as small as 5 mm long[13]; our data suggest that there were very few births in April and May, and only one pregnant female was found after February (in May catches). However, in an isolated pool on Griffith University campus, *Gambusia* were still breeding in May; subsequently, sampling on 10 June 1981 yielded a few juvenile *Gambusia*, indicating recent births. The water temperature on that date was 12.5°C and the ambient temperature was the lowest recorded for Brisbane in 1981. Large numbers of *X. helleri* juveniles were also present.

Regular monitoring of *Gambusia* populations has commenced to enable us to establish the length of the breeding season, the number of broods produced and brood size, the maturation rate under various environmental regimes and the brood interval.

Little is known about the reproductive biology of swordtails and platies under field conditions; there is a sizeable literature on aquarium observations but this is of little value except to aquarists.

Xiphophorus helleri has a gestation period of 4 to 6 weeks and up to 240 young are released.[14] In comparison, female *Gambusia* of 58 mm may produce up to 315 embryos in a brood.[15]

Pregnant *X. helleri* were found in Brisbane streams through to mid May and some populations were dominated by newly born and young swordtails. The oldest and largest fish were usually females. More work of the type outlined above will enable us to compare the reproductive biology of *Xiphophorus* and *Gambusia* in southern Queensland. From the present study there are indications that *X. helleri* and *g. affinis* have similar breeding seasons but that *X. helleri* maintains a higher rate of recruitment in May and June than *Gambusia*. This may be sufficient to give swordtails dominance in some systems.

Habitat Requirements

Both *G. affinis* and *X. helleri* showed a preference for edge habitats away from fast flowing water and appeared to avoid water weeds. In systems where introduced para grass (*Brachiaria mutica*) and reeds were well established and overhung or invaded the water, mosquito fishes and swordtails were abundant, sheltering along the banks and under the overhanging vegetation. They were captured in open areas only when there was no flow. McKay concluded that "the establishment of an aquatic floating plant, or a grass that invades the creek water, appears to favour the population growth and survival of introduced *Gambusia, Xiphophorus* and *Poecilia* species, [and] is usually deleterious to the free swimming native egglaying fishes (including the introduced rosy barb, *Puntius conchonius*)".[16] Our data bear out these observations.

McKay further suggested that para and other invading grasses provide cover for introduced species which may fall prey to water birds or to predatory fishes such as *Therapon unicolor* in open water.[17] The grasses also impede water flow, so favouring *Gambusia* and *Xipohorus,* especially during floods when the grass lies flat along the banks and bottom, shielding fish from the full force of the water.

Observations on Predation

Predacious native fishes recorded in study sites included *Mogurnda striata, M. australis, Therapon unicolor, Glossamia aprion* and *Hypseleotris* spp.

Predation experiments conducted in aquaria with *Glossamia aprion* and selected introduced and native fishes showed that the factors which influenced prey selection by *Glossamia* were the number of prey individuals available and their size. The smallest individuals were eaten first when the numbers available were equal, regardless of the species of prey (tables 2, 3, & 4).

Table 2 Results of Predation Experiment 1, conducted over a 36-hour period with 10 *Glossamia aprion* and replenishment of prey to initial numbers.

Prey species	Initial numbers	Size range (mm)	Proportion eaten after 18 hrs	Proportion eaten after a further 18 hrs	Significance of differences in proportions of species eaten
X. helleri	10	15-25	0.3	0.3	**
X. maculatus	10	15-25	0.6	0.33	**
G. affinis	5	> 25	0.0	0.6	**
M. fluviatilis	6	12-15	0.17	0.8	**
P. signifer	10	12-15	0.7	1.0	**

** Significant at the 0.01 level.

When *Gambusia affinis* and *Xiphophorus helleri* occur together in the field, predation by priscivorous species such as *Mogurnda striata* may result in selective reduction in *Gambusia* populations, because of their small size compared to *X. helleri.* Our data show that at several sites where *X. helleri* was the dominant introduced species, *Mogurnda striata* and/or *M. australis* were present. Selective predation may have eliminated *Gambusia* from site L on Ithaca Creek and permitted *X. helleri* to establish there. At four sites with sizeable populations of *Mogurnda striata*, neither introduced species was present.

Table 3 Results of Predation Experiments 2, 3 and 4, conducted over an 11-hour period with 8 *Glossamia aprion*.

	EXPERIMENT 2			EXPERIMENT 3			EXPERIMENT 4			Duncan's Multiple
	Initial numbers	Size range (mm)	Proportion eaten	Initial numbers	Size range (mm)	Proportion eaten	Initial numbers	Size range (mm)	Proportion eaten	Range comparison
Xiphophorus helleri	10	20-25	0.2	10	20.25	0.2	15	8-12	1.0	n.s.
Gambusia affinis	10	15-20	0.2	5	12-15	0.6	15	12-20	0.6	n.s.
Melanotaenia fluviatilis	10	20-25	0.2	10	12-20	1.0	15	20-30	0.73	n.s.

Table 4 Results of Predation Experiment 5 conducted over a 144-hr period with 8 *Glossamia aprion*, and replenishment of prey to initial numbers at the end of each day.

	Initial number	Initial size (mm)	Prop. eaten 32 hrs	Prop. eaten 40 hrs	Prop. eaten 24 hrs	Prop. eaten 16 hrs	Prop. eaten 3 hrs	Prop. eaten 21 hrs	Prop. eaten 8 hrs
Gambusia affinis	30	20-25	0.4	0.66	0.83	0.65	0.14	0.83	1.0
Xiphophorus helleri	30	20-25	0.26	0.86	0.66	0.6	0.0	0.37	0.8

236 A.H. Arthington, R.J. McKay and D.A. Milton

Further experimental work of a more refined nature is needed on the predatory behaviour of species which coexist with *Gambusia* and *Xiphophorus* in the field.

Temperature Tolerance

The ability of *Gambusia* to withstand extremes of temperature well outside those experienced in the natural environment is noteworthy. Cherry *et al.* observed *Gambusia affinis* in a drainage system where the water temperature exceeded 44°C,[18] and Otto found that although the fish tolerate temperatures of up to 42°C for brief periods, the critical thermal maximum of a hot adapted population was 35°C and the lower lethal temperature of the cold adapted population was 0.5°C.[19] Further laboratory tests by Otto on a hot adapted population showed that half the fish survived a temperature of 37.5°C when acclimated to 35°C.[20] In Utah, the first introduction survived their first winter of 1932–33 only in thermal springs; the mild winter of 1933–34 allowed some populations to survive in cold water pools and streams and since 1934 these fish have survived the winter in Utah under favourable conditions where the water temperature was fairly constant (0°C–22°C) and the surface free from ice.[21] This selection for increased tolerance of heat and cold is discussed by Otto, who demonstrated that environmental selection for cold tolerance in the Utah stock reduced the level of heat tolerance and increased cold tolerance, whereas in the hot adapted fish from Indian Hot Springs this shift resulted in increased heat tolerance at the cost of a comparable loss in cold tolerance, i.e., selection acted on temperature tolerance as a unit.[22]

Cold-adapted *Gambusia* populations occur in Australia but these have not been studied.

Laboratory determinations of the critical thermal minimum of *Gambusia affinis* taken from Brisbane streams showed that this species was capable of spasmodic movement at 1.79°C, whereas *Xiphophorus helleri* was stressed at 7.7°C, lost its righting ability and moved only spasmodically at 5.26°C (table 5). The statistical significance of these differences is shown in table 6.

McKay observed that swordtails were distressed at water temperatures of 9.0 and 9.5°C; some adults were comatose, others had died, but a number of adults and juveniles were apparently unaffected.[23]

The diurnal movements of *Gambusia* have been studied by Maglio and Rosen who found that the fish occupied shallow water during the day and retreated to the warmer deeper waters during the night.[24] "Water temperature appears, therefore, to be the overriding stimulus that regulates the gross diurnal movements of the population. If it is true in *Gambusia*, as it is for so many other poikilotherms, that

Table 5 Observed mean water temperature for the onset of loss of orientation and spasmodic movement in various species (standard deviation in brackets).

Species	Loss of orientation °C	Spasmodic movement °C
Gambusia affinis	3.14 (± 0.45)	2.33 (± 0.54)
Xiphophorus helleri	7.00 (± 0.71)	6.03 (± 0.77)
Melanotaenia fluviatilis	5.74 (± 0.42)	4.15 (± 0.28)
Hypseleotris galii	6.40 (± 0.29)	5.60 (± 0.24)
Craterocephalus marjoriae	5.40 (± 0.56)	4.41 (± 0.43)
Mogurnda striata	6.45 (± 0.64)	6.06 (± 0.68)

Table 6 Results of Duncan's Multiple Range test (a line linking species indicates no significant difference at the 0.05 level). Species are ranked from highest to lowest temperature at which response occurred.

Response	Species
1.	Loss of orientation *Xiphophorus Mogurnda Hypseleotris Melanotaenia Craterocephalus Gambusia*
2.	Spasmodic movement *Mogurnda Xiphophorus Hypseleotris Crateocephalus Melanotaenia Gambusia*

sexual maturation and reproduction rates are greatest at the highest temperatures, it may be inferred that colonisation of a habitat by this species might be enhanced by its characteristic of maintaining a position at the higher temperatures."

Diurnal movements of *Gambusia* into deep stream pools at night and in winter and its tolerance of very low temperatures may give this species an adaptive advantage over *Xiphophorus*. Further work is needed on the behavioural responses of both species to temperature extremes.

Dissolved Oxygen Requirements

Gambusia are exceptionally hardy fishes and can tolerate very low oxygen tensions.[25] In a study of an anaerobic spring in Florida, Odum and Caldwell found that *Gambusia affinis holbrooki* and mollies, *Poecilia latipinna,* survived oxygen tensions less than 0.3 mg/l by gulping air at the surface; although they died when held below in cages, all survived in cages below the surface at 1.3 mg/l oxygen.[26] Lewis has observed that *Gambusia affinis* and *Poecilia latipinna* survive in oxygen-depleted waters by virtue of their upturned mouth and their habit of skimming below the surface; these fishes are morphologically well suited for using well-oxygenated water at the surface, and due to their small size may use surface oxygen for prolonged or indefinite periods regardless of age.[27] Their presence in oxygen-deficient waters in some southern Queensland drains attests to their ability to survive under anaerobic conditions for prolonged periods.

Laboratory tests showed that *Xiphophorus helleri* survived in water with 0.5 mg/l of dissolved oxygen. Like *Gambusia*, the swordtail gulps at the air-water interface at low oxygen tensions.

Field populations of *Gambusia and X. helleri* were found thriving in water with daylight dissolved oxygen levels of 3.4 to 3.9 mg/l; although lower levels would be expected to occur at night (as observed in Bulimba Creek and Norman Creek by Arthington *et al.* and Morton *et al.*),[28] these levels would not unduly stress either species.

Salinity Tolerance

Gambusia affinis can survive in salinities more than twice seawater concentration, given time to adapt.[29] However, according to Rosen, "Species of *Xiphophorus* apparently have little or no tolerance for salt or brackish water environments. This is indicated by their conspicuous absence from brackish water deltas and by the notable distinctiveness of the many geographical races inhabiting adjacent rivers. Some of the races and subspecies of *Xiphophorus* live in rivers whose mouths are separated by less than 20 miles of coastline."[30]

He further states that, "The results of a few casual tests in the laboratory in which several groups of platyfish and swordtails were subjected to a series of decreasing concentrations of seawater (pure seawater to slightly brackish) reaffirm the above conclusion; no group survived longer than one hour even in the lowest concentrations of seawater. This is in marked contrast to the ability of other poeciliid groups, such as the *poeciliins* and *gambussiins*, to occupy successfully a wide variety of brackish and marine environments."

Most of the sites sampled in the Brisbane region had conductivities within the normal range for southern Queensland freshwater streams. Two sites with unusually high conductivity (1480 and 2670 μS/cm) supported *Gambusia, Xiphophorus helleri; Poecilia reticulata* was also present at the latter site.

McKay has argued that any translocation of freshwater fishes from one creek to another during the 1974 Brisbane flood was highly unlikely considering the rate of creek and river discharge at that time.[31] However, if tolerant of saline estuarine conditions, *X. helleri* might survive being swept downstream from creeks discharging into the Brisbane River and be carried upriver on high tides. Pearse has found that large tongues of fresh water penetrated the estuarine sections of the Brisbane River during and after the 1974 floods; these tongues moved upstream with the tide.[32] He has further determined that *X. helleri* from Brisbane creeks can survive salinities as high as half sea water if given time to acclimatize. Thus, the spread of swordtails via the Brisbane River during floods may be a possibility.

However, the patchy distribution of the swordtail in the Brisbane region does not indicate extensive spread via the Brisbane River. It is possible that the platy, now established in the upper Brisbane River, may spread from these localities via the river.

Food Preferences

Although *Gambusia affinis* and *Xiphophorus helleri* lived predominantly in the still-water areas along the edges of stream pools, they had different food preferences in this preliminary study. Nearly 80 per cent of the food items in mosquito fish guts were terrestrial insects, mainly ants (73 per cent of all food items). *X. helleri* preferred algae and plant material and took only a few aquatic invertebrates.

According to Maglio and Rosen (1969), *Gambusia* are secondary consumers which feed primarily on zooplankton and aquatic insect larvae.[33] The eggs and larvae of native freshwater fishes are also consumed, and larger fishes may have their fins nipped, or in some instances, entirely removed (aquarium and field observations). The presence of *Gambusia* may alter the ecosystem by reducing zooplankton populations,[34] and due to their aggressive behaviour they may contribute to the decline of other freshwater fishes.

Tolerance of Pollutants

Dense populations of introduced species may be found in polluted drains; in many cases, *Gambusia affinis* is the only species present. This tolerance to pesticides and pollutants is well documented.[35] This adaptability, coupled with a tolerance to low oxygen or anaerobic conditions, high temperatures, varying salinities and their habit of feeding at the surface, allows mosquito fish to remain in highly polluted waters for prolonged periods.

During this study, *Gambusia* was collected from localities known to be severely contaminated with organic wastes, hydrocarbons, insecticides and metals (site F on Kedron Brook). Mosquito fish are also present in Bulimba Creek, which is contaminated with organic wastes and metals and has anaerobic pool areas.[37]

X. helleri, although less abundant at site F, nevertheless maintained reasonable populations there and may be as tolerant as *Gambusia* of some pollutants. This aspect of the study requires detailed

examination under controlled laboratory conditions. If the native
species are not as tolerant as introduced species, this may be the main
factor responsible for the decline in native species in some highly
urbanized areas.

Effects of Introduced Species on Native Species

Hypseleotris galii and H. compressus

Hypseleotris galii maintained large populations at sites B, G, H and
I below Enoggera Reservoir, but further downstream abundance
declined; above the reservoir this gudgeon was present but not very
abundant. Seine netting in weedbeds around the shoreline of the
reservoir yielded large catches of *H. galii,* and we suggest that the
dam maintains a reservoir population of this species. Immediately
downstream, overflow populations persist in the creek, but further
downstream *H. galii* may be affected by interactions with introduced
species and/or by pollutants.

Interactions between introduced species and *H. galii* may take
several forms. The *H. galii* feeds on a fairly wide range of aquatic
invertebrates in the zooplankton and benthos; overlap of *Gambusia*
and *H. galii* diets may be important in periods of food scarcity.
Gambusia, with its high reproductive rate and extended breeding
season, may swamp suitable habitats with juveniles and deplete food
supplies before *H. galii* populations can build up. Aggressive
behaviour, fin nipping and predation by *Gambusia* on the eggs and
juveniles of *H. galii* may also contribute to the decline of this
gudgeon. We have shown that *H. galii* is much more sensitive to
low temperatures and low dissolved oxygen tensions than *Gambusia*.
However, it has a greater tolerance of low temperatures than *X.
helleri* (tables 4 and 5). *H. galii* does not often gulp at the air-water
interface, as do the two introduced species.

Hypseleotris compressus was reasonably abundant in the presence
of introduced species at some sites, but is not a widespread species
in the Brisbane region. It is much less widespread now than in 1977.

Melanotaenia fluviatilis

The rainbow fish is an open water species known from a range of
natural freshwater systems, including lakes, stream pools and riffles.
It is a surface feeder, taking a range of aquatic invertebrates and,
to a lesser extent, terrestrial insects. In open still-water areas there
may be direct competition for food with *Gambusia* in particular,
although *M. fluviatilis* may turn to algae when other foods are scarce.

Large populations of *M. fluviatilis* were found most often where

Gambusia was not abundant, or was absent. Conversely, when *Gambusia* was very abundant, *M. fluviatilis* tended to be rare or absent from stream pools. However, the rainbow fish appears able to persist in the presence of *X. helleri.*

M. fluviatilis has some capacity to survive at low oxygen tensions and can readily gulp well-oxygenated surface water because of the position of the mouth. However, the individuals tested at very low dissolved oxygen concentrations did not display gulping behaviour at the water surface. This species is more tolerant of low temperatures than *X. helleri,* but less tolerant than *Gambusia.* Responses to pollutants are unknown and require investigation.

Craterocephalus spp.

The hardyheads are open-water surface feeding fishes which may be affected by introduced species in the same ways as *M. fluviatilis.* Hardyheads were rarely present together with *Gambusia* in any numbers in our study areas.

Pseudomugil signifer

The blue-eye is also an open-water zooplankton feeding species. It was seldom abundant in the creeks studied. In areas where para grass has established the surface feeding species *M. fluviatilis, Craterocephalus* spp. and *P. signifer* are usually uncommon,[38] whereas swordtails and mosquito fish thrive in creeks invaded by introduced grasses.

Other Native Species

The remaining native species were much less common in most of the sites studied, altough *Mogurnda striata* and *Ambassis nigripinnis* were sometimes abundant. At this stage of the study we are unable to say with any certainty how these species interact with exotic fishes. However, in general terms, it appears that all native fishes in the study area are able to coexist with exotic species, provided their preferred habitats are available and water quality has not been severely impaired. Where habitats have been altered or destroyed and water is of poor quality, native fishes are much less abundant than exotic species, particularly *G. affinis.* Further work on most of the topics outlined in this article is under way and will be published in due course.

The Management of Imported Fishes

Australia imports about 13 million live fish annually. About 25 per cent are goldfish, a few are of marine origin and the remainder comprise some 200 regularly imported species. Since 1963 close to 700 species of freshwater aquarium fishes have been legally permitted imports.

Over a hundred exotic fish species have been declared prohibited imports, and the task of inspecting each consignment for nonprescribed fishes, invertebrates and plants, without adequate facilities at the airport, is beyond the capacity of most Animal Quarantine Officers. At some airports, only a cursory inspection is made and some illegal fish species are imported.

Despite Australia's admirable quarantine service, it is alarming that millions of live fish enter the country without undergoing a period of quarantine and no inspection is made for disease organisms or parasites on fishes or in the water used for transportation. Most fish consignments come via Singapore but some are sent from Japan, Hong Kong and Indonesia. Singapore imports vast quantities of live aquarium fish from Southeast Asia, South America and other countries for transshipment. Research into the diseases and parasites associated with imported aquarium fishes is now under way, but the magnitude of the risk of such imported pathogenic organisms to Australian fresh waters, livestock or human populations, has not been assessed.

The Australian Department of Health is currently reviewing the present situation and it is hoped that an adequate system of inspection and quarantine with increased research on the diseases associated with imported fishes will soon be in force and thus safeguard the future of aquaculture in a very vulnerable country that has had a long history of freedom from the main fish diseases of the world.

Notes

1. R. J. McKay, "The Exotic Freshwater Fishes of Queensland" (Report to Australian National Parks and Wildlife Service, Canberra, 1978).
2. Ibid.
3. Ibid.
4. cf. E. J. Hyslop, "Stomach Contents Analysis – A Review of Methods and Their Application", *Journal of Fish Biology* 17 (198): 411-429.
5. Ibid.
6. Ibid.
7. C. R. Johnson, "Diel Variation in the Thermal Tolerance of *Gambusia affinis* (Pisces: Poeciliidae)", *Comparative Biochemistry and Physiology* 18 (1948).
8. Ibid.
9. McKay, "The Exotic Freshwater Fishes of Queensland".
10. Ibid.

11. S. F. Hildebrand, "Notes on the Life History of the Minnows *Gambusia affinis* and *Cyprinodon variegatus*", Report to the U.S. Commissioner of Fisheries for 1917, Appendix 6 (1918), Bureau of Fisheries Document No. 857.
L. A. Krumholz, "Reproduction in the Western Mosquitofish, *Gambusia affinis* (Baird and Girard) and its Use in Mosquito Control", *Ecological Monographs* 18 (1948):
V. J. Maglio and D. E. Rosen, "Changing Preferences for Substrate Color by Reproductively Active Mosquitofish, *Gambusia affinis* (Baird and Girard) (Poeciliidae, Atheriniformes)", *American Museum Novitates* 2397 (1969).
C. P. Goodyear, C. E. Boyd and R. J. Beyers, "Relationships between Primary Productivity and Mosquitofish (*Gambusia affinis*). Production in Large Microcosms", *Limnology and Oceanography* 17 (1972).

12. L. A. Krumholz, "Reproduction in the Western Mosquitofish, *Gambusia affinis* (Baird and Girard) and its Use in Mosquito Control".

13. Ibid. cf. 8-9 mm.

14. W. A. Whitern, *Livebearers*, (T.F.H. Publ. Inc. Neptune, N.J., 1969).

15. L. A. Krumholz, "Reproduction in the Western Mosquitofish, *Gambusia affinis* (Baird and Girard) and its Use in Mosquito Control".

16. McKay, "The Exotic Freshwater Fishes of Queensland."

17. Ibid.

18. D. S. Cherry, R. K. Guthrie, J. H. Rodger Jr., J. Cairns Jr. and K. L. Dickson, "Responses of Mosquitofish (*Gambusia affinis*) to Ash Effluent and Thermal Stress", *Transactions of the American Fisheries Society*, 105 (1976).

19. R. G. Otto, "Temperature Tolerance of the Mosquitofish, *Gambusia affinis* (Baird and Girard)", *Journal of Fish Biology* 5 (1973).

20. R. G. Otto, "The Effects of Acclimation to Cyclic Thermal Regimes on Heat Tolerance of the Western Mosquitofish", *Transactions of the American Fisheries Society*, 103 (1974).

21. D. M. Rees, "Supplemental Notes on Mosquito Fish in Utah, *Gambusia affinis* (Baird and Girard)", *Copeia* (1945).

22. Otto, "Temperature Tolerance of the Mosquitofish, *Gambusia affinis* (Baird and Girard)".

23. McKay, "The Exotic Freshwater Fishes of Queensland".

24. Maglio and Rosen, "Changing Preference for Substrate Color by Reproductively Active Mosquitofish".

25. Hildebrand, "Notes on the Life History of the Minnows *Gambusia affinis* and *Cyprinodon variegatus*".

26. H. T. Odum and D. K. Caldwell, "Fish Respiration in the Natural Oxygen Gradient of an Anaerobic Spring in Florida", *Copeia* (1955).

27. W. M. Lewis Jr., "Morphological Adaptations of *Cyprinodontoids* for inhabiting Oxygen Deficient Waters", *Copeia* (1970).

28. A. H. Arthington, D. L. Conrick, D. W. Connell and P. M. Outridge, *The Ecology of a Polluted Urban Creek* (AWRC Technical paper No. 68. Department of National Development and Energy. Australian Government Publishing Service, Canberra, 1982).
H. Morton, D. W. Connell and F. Bycroft, "Oxygen Budget for Norman Creek, Brisbane" (Internal Report, Griffith University, Brisbane, 1979).

29. S. K. Ahuja, "Salinity Tolerance of *Gambusia affinis*", *Indian Journal of Experimental Biology* 2 (1964).

30. D. E. Rosen, "Middle-American poeciliid fishes of the Genus *Xiphophorus*", *Bulletin of the Florida State Museum, Biological Sciences*, 5, (1960).

31. McKay, "The Exotic Freshwater Fishes of Queensland".

32. Pearse, pers. com.

33. Maglio and Rosen, "Changing Preferences for Substrate Color by Reproductively Active Mosquitofish".

34. S. H. Hurlbert, J. Zedler and D. Fairbanks, "Ecosystem Alteration by Mosquitofish (*Gambusia affinis*)", *Science* 75 (1972).
35. S. B. Vinson, C. E. Boyd and D.E. Ferguson, "Resistance to DDT in the mosquitofish (*Gambusia affinis*)", *Science*, 139 (1963);
   D. E. Boyd and D. E. Ferguson, "Susceptibility and resistance of mosquitofish to several insecticides", *Journal of Economic Entomology*, 57 (1964);
   D. E. Ferguson, J. L. Ludke and G. G. Murphy, "Dynamics of Endrin Uptake and Release by Resistant and Susceptible Strains of Mosquitofish", *Transactions of the American Fisheries Society*, 95 (1966);
   D. E. Ferguson, J. L. Ludke, M. T. Finley and G. G. Murphy, "Insecticide-resistant Fishes: A Potential Hazard to Consumers", *Journal of the Mississippi Academy of Science*, 13 (1967);
   P. Rosato and D. E. Ferguson, "The Toxicity of the Endrin Resistant Mosquitofish to Eleven Species of Vertebrates", *Biological Science*, 18 (1968);
   D. D. Culley and D. E. Ferguson, "Patterns of Insecticide Resistance in the Mosquitofish *Gambusia affinis*", *Journal of the Fisheries Research Board of Canada*, 26 (1969);
   B. Kynard, "Avoidance Behaviour of Insecticide Susceptible and Resistant Populations of Mosquitofish to Four Insecticides", *Transactions of the American Fisheries Society*, 103 (1974);
   Cherry, Guthrie, Rodger Jr., Cairns Jr., and Dickson, "Responses of Mosquitofish (*Gambusia affinis)* to Ash Effluent and Thermal Stress".
36. Ibid.
37. Arthington, Conrick, Connell and Outridge, *The Ecology of a Polluted Urban Creek*.
38. McKay, "The Exotic Freshwater Fishes of Queensland".

References

Ahuja, S. K., "Salinity Tolerance of *Gambusia affinis*". *Indian Journal of Experimental Biology* 2 (1964): 9-11.
Arthington, A. H., D. L. Conrick, D. W. Connell and P. M. Outridge. *The Ecology of a Polluted Urban Creek*. AWRC Technical Paper No. 68. Department of National Development and Energy. Australian Government Publishing Service, 1982.
Arthington, A. H., R. J. McKay and D. A. Milton. "Ecology and Interactions of Exotic and Endemic Freshwater Fishes in South Eastern Queensland Streams". Report I to the Australian National Parks and Wildlife Service, Canberra, June 1981. p. 96.
Boyd, D. E., and D. E. Ferguson. "Susceptibility and Resistance of Mosquitofish to Several Insecticides". *Journal of Economic Entomology* 57 (1964): 430-431.
Cherry, D. S., R. K. Guthrie, J. H. Rodger Jr., J. Cairns Jr. and K. L. Dickson. "Responses of Mosquitofish (*Gambusia affinis*) to Ash Effluent and Thermal Stress". *Transactions of the American Fisheries Society* 105 (1976): 686-694.
Culley, D. D. and D. E. Ferguson. "Patterns of Insecticide Resistance in the Mosquitofish *Gambusia affinis*". *Journal of the Fisheries Research Board of Canada* 26 (1969): 2395-2401.
Ferguson, D. E., J. L. Ludke and G. G. Murphy. "Dynamics of Endrin Uptake and Release by Resistant and Susceptible Strains of Mosquitofish. *Transactions of the American Fisheries Society* 95 (1966): 335-344.
Ferguson, D. E., J. L. Ludke, M. T. Finley and G. G. Murphy. "Insecticide-resistant fishes: a potential hazard to consumers". *Journal of the Mississippi Academy of Science* 13 (1967): 138-140.
Goodyear, C. P., C. E. Boyd and R. J. Beyers. "Relationships between Primary Productivity and Mosquitofish (*Gambusia affinis*) Production in Large Microcosms". *Limnology and Oceanography* 17 (1972): 445-450.

Hildebrand, S. F. "Notes on the Life History of the Minnows *Gambusia affinis* and *Cyprinodon variegatus*". Report to the U.S. Commissioner of Fisheries for 1917, Appendix 6 (1918), Bureau of Fisheries Document 857.

Hurlbert, S. H., J. Zedler and D. Fairbanks. "Ecosystem Alteration by Mosquitofish *(Gambusia affinis)*. *Science* 75 (1972): 639-41.

Hyslop, E. J. "Stomach Contents Analysis—A Review of Methods and their Application". *Journal of Fish Biology* 17 (1980): 411-429.

Johnson, C. R. "Diel Variation in the Thermal Tolerance of *Gambusia affinis* (Pisces: Poeciliidae)". *Comparative Biochemistry and Physiology* 55a (1976): 337-400.

Krumholz, L. A. "Reproduction in the Western Mosquitofish, *Gambusia affinis* (Baird and Girard) and its Use in Mosquito Control". *Ecological Monographs* 18 (1948): 1-43.

Kynard, B. "Avoidance Behaviour of Insecticide Susceptible and Resistant Populations of Mosquitofish to Four Insecticides". *Transactions of the American Fisheries Society* 103 (1974): 557-561.

Lewis, W. M. Jr. "Morphological Adaptations of Cyprinodontoids for inhabiting Oxygen Deficient Waters". *Copeia* (1970): 319-326.

Maglio, V. J. and D. E. Rosen. "Changing Preferences for Substrate Color by Reproductively Active Mosquitofish, *Gambusia affinis* (Baird and Girard) (Poeciliidae, Atheriniformes)". *American Museum Novitates* 2397 (1969): 1-39.

McKay, R. J. "The Exotic Freshwater Fishes of Queensland". Report to Australian National Parks and Wildlife Service, Canberra, 1978.

Morton, H., D. W. Connell and B. Bycroft. "Oxygen Budget for Norman Creek, Brisbane". Internal Report, Griffith University, 1979.

Odum, H. T. and D. K. Caldwell. "Fish Respiration in the Natural Oxygen Gradient of an Anaerobic Spring in Florida". *Copeia* (1955): 104-106.

Otto, R. G. "Temperature Tolerance of the Mosquitofish, *Gambusia affinis* (Baird and Girard)". *Journal of Fish Biology* 5 (1973): 575-585.

Otto, R. G. "The Effects of Acclimation of Cyclic Thermal Regimes on Heat Tolerance of the Western Mosquitofish". *Transactions of the American Fisheries Society* 103 (1974): 331-335.

Rees, D. M. "Supplemental Notes on Mosquito Fish in Utah, *Gambusia affinis* (Baird and Girard)". *Copeia* (1945): 236.

Rosato, P. and D. E. Ferguson. "The Toxicity of the Endrin Resistant Mosquitofish to Eleven Species of Verebrates". *Biological Science* 18 (1968): 783-784.

Rosen, D. E. "Middle-American Poeciliid Fishes and the Genus *Xiphophorus*". *Bulletin of the Florida State Museum, Biological Sciences* 5 (1960): 57-242.

Vinson, S. B., C. E. Boyd, and D. E. Ferguson. "Resistance to DDT in the Mosquitofish *(Gambusia affinis)*". *Science* 139 (1963): 217-218.

Whitern, W. A. *Livebearers*. T.F.H. Publ. Inc. Neptune, N.J., 1969, p. 93.